THE VOICES OF RESOLVE

The Voices of Resolve

The Patriots of Liberty Point
The Story of the Cumberland Association and Its Signers

Published by
the Cumberland County Public Library's
Local & State History Department

DISTRIBUTED BY THE UNIVERSITY OF NORTH CAROLINA PRESS

Suggested citation: Cumberland County Public Library Local & State History Department. *The Voices of Resolve: The Patriots of Liberty Point*. Fayetteville, NC: Cumberland County Public Library Local & State History Department, 2026.

DOI: https://doi.org/10.5149/9781469698816_CumberlandCountyPublicLibraryLocalandStateHistoryDepartment

ISBN 978-1-4696-9880-9 (cloth: alk. paper)
ISBN 978-1-4696-9881-6 (open access EPUB)
ISBN 978-1-4696-9882-3 (open access UPDF)

Cover design by Patrick Holt

CONTENTS

ACKNOWLEDGMENTS

This project was produced with assistance from the America 250 North Carolina initiative, administered by the North Carolina Department of Natural and Cultural Resources. Any opinions, findings, conclusions, or recommendations expressed in this material are those of the author(s) and do not necessarily reflect the views of the State of North Carolina.

This project was aided by the help of the *Le Marquis de Lafayette Chapter* of the North Carlina Society of the Sons of the American Revolution, which provided helpful research tips and information on both the topic broadly and a number of individual signers. The department wishes to thank the North Carolina State Archives and University of North Carolina's Wilson Library for their assistance and helpfulness in accessing primary sources. The department also wishes to thank the following individuals for their assistance in making the manuscript better: Professor Kelli Cardenas-Walsh of Fayetteville State University, Professor Christopher Thrasher of Fayetteville Technical Community College, Bruce Daws, former historic properties manager and historian for the City of Fayetteville, and Charles Broadwell, former editor and publisher of the *Fayetteville Observer*. Their comments and insights were particularly helpful.

Finally, the department wishes to thank Lee Davis and Nya Smythe for their proofreading of the manuscript. Though they were only here for a short while, their assistance was appreciated.

INTRODUCTION

Why Is This Study Needed?

NOTE ON TERMINOLOGY: The Liberty Point Resolves was originally called the Cumberland Association. For the sake of consistency, and to adjust for the present-day usage, the document will be referred to as the Liberty Point Resolves in this book. Names are also tricky due to historical variations in spelling. We standardize the spellings of names according to our best knowledge of the way each man signed his name on the document itself, and how the names appear in deeds, wills, census records, etc. In the biography section, signers who were left off the original monument will be noted as forgotten in parentheses.

After the Coercive Acts, the Liberty Point Resolves emerged as one of the earliest documents in North Carolina that called for autonomy and self-defense of colonialists. It is one of the oldest mutual defense pacts against the royal government in the colonies, following the more well-known Mecklenburg Resolves.[1] However, while the (contested) Mecklenburg Declaration is on North Carolina's state flag, with the date May 20, 1775, the Liberty Point Resolves are all but ignored in North Carolina histories of the Revolutionary Era.

For instance, some of the most well-known histories of North Carolina do not mention the Resolves. Martin Lefler's four-volume history of North Carolina, written in 1956, fails to mention the Resolves. Currently, Milton Ready's *The Tar Heel State: A New History of North Carolina* also leaves out the Resolves. Even the *Encyclopedia of North Carolina* by noted state historian William S. Powell has only one sentence on the Resolves, saying: "In Cumberland County, 54 men signed a similar document at Liberty Point on 30 June 1775, using wording much like that of the New Hanover Association."[2]

Historian H. G. Jones's 1995 *North Carolina History: An Annotated Bibliography* mentions only a pamphlet from 1831, and that pamphlet deals more with the Mecklenburg Declaration of Independence than the Resolves.[3] Throughout early America, Fayetteville remembered the Resolves, and the local newspaper, the *Fayetteville Observer,* would regularly list the signers on the anniversary of the Resolves. However, this practice died away by the outbreak of the Civil War. In 1875, with America's centennial birthday approaching and the presses of the *Observer* not yet restored from their destruction in 1865, the short-lived Fayetteville newspaper the *North Carolina Gazette* took up the tradition to once again publish the Resolves with a list of signers.[4] Unfortunately, they followed the list as published in John H. Wheeler's 1851 *History of North Carolina* and only included thirty-nine names, leaving off sixteen of the fifty-five signers.[5] When Fayetteville put up a historical marker in 1933 to commemorate the Resolves, the city also left off the same sixteen signers, seeming to have forgotten about them.[6] Additionally, the original copy of the Liberty Point Resolves was not discovered until 1975, and at Wilson Library at UNC Chapel Hill, not in Fayetteville's possession.[7]

Even among those who know about the actual document, there has been confusion over who signed it and how many signers there were. In *Cumberland County: A Brief History*, local journalist Roy Parker Jr. mentions that sixty-nine people signed the Resolves, but other sources put the number of signers at fifty-four or fifty-five.[8] How many individuals really signed it? Both Parker and John Oates wrote two of the most well-known histories of the area, but neither have more than two pages on the Liberty Point Resolves. Even today, both the county and the city's websites fail to mention the Resolves. The *Fayetteville Observer* noted in 1975 that "nobody is sure just what happened prior to and on June 20, 1775."[9]

Why was this document forgotten? And why has it been overlooked on a state level? This book will answer these questions to shed light on the regional significance of the Liberty Point Resolves as America celebrates its 250th, and is a comprehensive study of the events, facts, and legends of the Liberty Point Resolves.

Notes

1. Morgan, "Cross Creek."
2. Powell, *The Encyclopedia of North Carolina*, 966.

3. *The Declaration of Independence by the Citizens of Mecklenburg County*, 622.

4. "The 20th of June 1775." For more information on the destruction of the *Fayetteville Observer* see Jacobs, "5 Days of Destruction in Fayetteville."

5. Wheeler, *History of North Carolina*, 2:125; "The 20th of June 1775."

6. Anderson, "Will Commemorate Early Independence Declaration"; Johnson, "Sixteen Names Added to Liberty Point Boulder."

7. Clark, "Notes on the Post Revolutionary War History of the Liberty Point Resolves."

8. Parker Jr., *Cumberland County*, 19. John Oates, in *The Story of Fayetteville and the Upper Cape Fear*, mentions thirty-nine signers (130–31), but his book was written before they rediscovered there were more signers. Peter Force, compiler and editor of the American Archives series, lists fifty-four signers, leaving off Lewis Bowell ("Committees of Wilmington District, North-Carolina"). The *State and Colonial Records of North Carolina* also list fifty-four, leaving off William Carver. The actual document shows fifty-five names.

9. Ely, "Dramatic Resolves Reenactment Raises Question: 'What's the Point?.'"

CHAPTER 1

Liberty Point Resolves: The Story

On June 20, 1775, fifty-five patriots of the Cumberland Association met at the triangular point between Bow and Person streets in Cross Creek. Cross Creek was a merchant community located on the Cape Fear River, approximately ninety miles from Wilmington. Cumberland County, which at the time included the present-day counties of Moore, Hoke, and Harnett, was inhabited by a large concentration of Scottish Highlanders, many of whom were loyal to the Crown. Yet on this date, Cumberland Patriots, led by Robert Rowan, took a stand for independence by signing the Liberty Point Resolves, a document declaring their determination to defend their rights against abuses of the British government.

A 1975 newspaper article described the scene stating: "a table was brought from Barge's Tavern, and Robert Rowan, a former sheriff of the county and a militia officer, signed first, followed by the others."[1] The move toward independence in Cumberland County had begun.

The document said the following:

> At a general meeting of the several committees of the district of Wilmington, held at the court-house in Wilmington, Tuesday, the 20th June, 1775;
>
> Resolved, that the following association stand as the association of this committee, and that it be recommended to the inhabitants of this District to sign the same as speedily as possible.
>
> The Association
>
> The actual commencement of hostilities against this continent by the British troops in the bloody scene on the 19th of April last near Boston—The increase of arbitrary impositions, from a wicked and

> despotic ministry, and the dread of instigated insurrections in the colonies, are causes sufficient to drive an oppressed people to the use of arms:
>
> We therefore the subscribers of Cumberland County, holding ourselves bound by that most sacred of all obligations, the duty of good citizens towards an injured country, and thoroughly convinced that under our distressed circumstances we shall be justified before God & man in resisting force by force; Do unite ourselves under every tie of religion and honour, and associate as a band in her defence against every foe, hereby solemnly engaging that whenever our continental or Provincial Councils shall decree it necessary, we will go forth and be ready to sacrifice our lives and fortunes to secure her freedom and safety: This obligation to continue in full force until a reconciliation shall take place between Great Britain and America, upon constitutional principles: an event we most ardently desire; and we will hold all those persons inimical to the liberty of the colonies, who shall refuse to subscribe this association; and we will in all things follow the advice of our General Committee, respecting the purposes aforesaid, the preservation of peace and good order, and the safety of individual and private property.[2]

It was very similar to the Wilmington-New Hanover Association's document, which had been signed on June 19 in Wilmington. The next day, on June 20, the Wilmington-New Hanover committee recommended that the inhabitants of their district follow suit: "to sign the same, as speedily as possible."[3] As Jack Crane notes above, tradition held that Robert Rowan rode up from Wilmington with New Hanover's Association, which Cumberland residents signed on the 20th.[4] North Carolina researcher Jim Morgan claims this was the highest number of signatures on a rebel petition from North Carolina during the Revolution.[5]

The associations were a test, forcing residents to publicly "declare their sentiments" to the Patriot cause.[6] Cumberland's committee had members who had visited the Wilmington committee, and they were part of Wilmington's district, making their Association a way of signing on to the Wilmington-New Hanover Association. By August, other committees made statements advocating for defense of their liberties, such as the Tryon County Committee's Resolves, which resolved to obey the King, but only if he "secures to us those Rights and Liberties which the principles of Our Constitution require."[7] The

Cumberland Association fit neatly into the growing independence movement in America.

Cumberland's Association document was similar to the other published associations in North Carolina.[8] In terms of language, it is almost identical to the first paragraph of the Wilmington-New Hanover Association, with only "Cumberland" in place of "New Hanover" and "General Committee" instead of "our Committee." However, the Wilmington Association then goes on for another couple of pages, listing separate resolves regarding Governor Martin's June 16 proclamation, while Cumberland's stops after the one paragraph.[9] The language of the document is also similar to the Tryon Resolves of August, with both commenting on the actions of the British troops at Lexington and Concord and declaring the right to defend themselves and their rights against British violations.[10]

A month later, the Wilmington Committee of Safety had two Cumberland County Committee of Safety members visit, Farquhard Campbell and Robert Cochran, and told their Committee of Intelligence to "write to the Committee of Cumberland & congratulate them on the favorable disposition of their Committee & County to support the Common cause of America."[11]

Notes

1. Crane, "The Signing of the Liberty Point Resolves." Some say that the table was brought from Aaron Vardey's Tavern. See Rose III, "The Signing of the Liberty Point Resolves," 209–27. Another story says that Col. Robert Rowan erected a Liberty Pole in front of his store, "and on the pole was inscribed, '*often for my king, but always for my* country'—'LIBERTY OR DEATH;' under this standard was placed a table with pen and ink, and the 'Association.' Col. R. addressed the people, and urged them to sign, and as a proof of his sincerity, was the first man who affixed his signature. At that time only 54 more came forward and placed their names to the 'Death Warrant,' as it was then termed" ("American Independence").

2. Cumberland Association Papers, SHC Z box 106, folder 1: 1775, 1830, scan 8.

3. NC General Assembly, *CSR*, 10:25–26.

4. The tradition is almost certainly not true— Rowan may have signed on the 20th, but with signers spread out throughout the county, and with the distance from Wilmington to Fayetteville, it probably took a couple of days for all the signers to sign the document.

5. Morgan, "North Carolina Loyalists." This author says that "every Patriot association I came across in my research is on the website, and Liberty Point's had the highest known number of signatures," which appears to be true regarding purely 'rebel' petitions, though the Pitt County Resolves, which tried to play both sides, did have more signers.

6. Watson, "Committees of Safety," 143; *CSR*, 10:161–64.

7. *CSR*, 10:163.

8. There were similar Association-type documents published across the colonies around this time; for instance, see South Carolina's document, which is almost exactly the same as Wilmington's, from June 3, 1775: Force, *American Archives*, 2:897.

9. Compare *CSR*, 10:16–29 for New Hanover's to 10:29–30 for Cumberland.

10. *CSR*, 10:162; Parker, "The Tryon County Patriots of 1775."

11. McEachern and Williams, *Safety Committee Minutes*, 45–46.

CHAPTER 2

Why Did the Association Exist?

IN THE FALL OF 1774, following the closure of the Port of Boston by the British after the Boston Tea Party, the First Continental Congress met in Philadelphia. At the meeting, Congress created the Articles of Association, a non-importation, nonconsumption, and nonexportation agreement in October.[1] This Association sought to compel the British to recognize American rights, and called for the creation of committees of safety throughout the colonies to enforce the Continental Congress's mandates.[2] By the end of 1774, North Carolina had eighteen counties and four towns with safety committees, and New Hanover's was perhaps the most active, led by Cornelius Harnett, the "Samuel Adams of North Carolina."[3] These committees would enforce the resolves passed by the Continental and Provincial Congresses.

Cumberland was part of the New Hanover region.[4] Cumberland already had a close connection to New Hanover, being only around ninety miles away up the Cape Fear River. Since 1750, the development of Cross Creek had extended the Lower Cape Fear trade to the Upper Cape Fear.[5] Cross Creek's location allowed it to link Salem and Hillsboro and even Charlotte to Lower Cape Fear markets. Cross Creek became so important to Wilmington that it "owed its prosperity to Cross Creek."[6] Many merchants in Wilmington had business ties to, and even stores in, Cross Creek.[7] Trade was strong enough between the two towns that nearly half of the prominent Wilmington merchant Robert Hogg's invoices between 1768–73 document trade between Cross Creek and Wilmington.[8] Cross Creek would send butter, tobacco, pork, corn, beeswax, flour, and other items on to Wilmington.[9] The close connection helps explain why fifty-five Cumberland residents were willing to sign on and join Wilmington-New Hanover with their own Association.[10]

Cumberland County had its own committee of safety, as the *Cumberland County Court Minute Abstracts* acknowledge a committee of safety in their 1779 minutes, and Cumberland had members who served as visiting members for Wilmington's committee, though original committee minute records have not yet been found.[11]

The growing Patriot movement through the committees put pressure on Royal Governor Josiah Martin. In April 1775, Governor Martin summoned the General Assembly to meet, but at the same time the Patriots organized the Second Provincial Congress, which endorsed the Continental Association.[12] In response, Martin dissolved the General Assembly, saying it was "incompatible with the Honour of the Crown and the safety of the people."[13] It never met again.[14]

Shortly afterward, news of the Battle of Lexington and Concord reached North Carolina.[15] This added to the unrest, and local safety committees started to take action. On May 20, the Wilmington-New Hanover committee called for a joint meeting of all the committees in their district on June 20 to discuss "the General Cause of America."[16] That same day, Mecklenburg County signed their (disputed) Mecklenburg Declaration of Independence, and days later, the Mecklenburg Safety Committee published their Mecklenburg Resolves on May 31, 1775.[17] Shortly after that, the Safety Committee of Rowan County resolved "that by the Constitution of our Government we are a free People, not subject to be taxed by any power but that of that happy Constitution."[18]

By June, Governor Martin was threatening to use force to resist all "Promoters of Sedition, and Disturbers of the Peace," so this "pushed the combined safety committees from the town of Wilmington, as well as New Hanover, Brunswick, Bladen, Duplin, and Onslow Counties, to issue a new 'Association' on June 21, 1775, that had to be signed by all inhabitants of the Lower Cape Fear. This association committed its signatories to resist 'force with force' and sacrifice their lives for the Continental or Provincial Congresses."[19] Other counties 'signed onto' the second half of the Wilmington-New Hanover Association itself: Brunswick, Bladen, Duplin, and Onslow counties, which all had members at the June 20 meeting in Wilmington.[20] Cumberland did not have members at the meeting, and they only used the first two paragraphs of the Wilmington Association (ignoring the later lengthy section), but their Association mirrored Wilmington's and seems to have been in response to Wilmington's call for other counties to join them.

Royal Governor Martin had written General Gage, the commander of British forces in America, for more men because of these Safety Committees, but the letter had been intercepted.[21] By July, he was no longer on North Carolina soil.[22] Governor Martin later denounced the committees, especially the one at Wilmington, in a proclamation on August 8, 1775, saying they spread "the basest and most scandalous Seditious and inflammatory falsehoods" and were "evil, pernicious and traiterous Councils."[23] Around this same period in 1774–75, the Third Provincial Assembly had organized minutemen in several counties, and in Cumberland, those appointed as officers were Thomas Rutherford (who shortly after turned Tory), Alexander McAlister, and Duncan McNeil, among others.[24]

By February 1776, North Carolina was heading toward war. On February 27, 1776, Loyalist Scots of the Upper Cape Fear fought against Patriot rebels at Moores Creek.[25] The Loyalist forces were planning on meeting up with British regulars as well as Governor Martin, who was off the coast of North Carolina near Wilmington, but Patriot forces blocked their path.[26] In less than ten minutes, the Loyalists and their forces were repulsed.[27] Bobby Gilmer Moss notes "that encounter was one of the first clear cut victories for the American rebels since the beginning of the war."[28] The battle resulted in the capture of numerous Loyalists, including two who had previously signed the Liberty Point Resolves (Aaron Vardey and Maurice Nowlan), along with numerous other Cumberland County Loyalists.[29] The Patriot victory showed the British that the war would be more difficult than they had first suspected.[30] The battle has been known as the "Lexington and Concord of the South," saved North Carolina from conquest, and was the moment the colony became independent.[31] Almost half of the Liberty Point Resolves' signers participated in the battle.[32]

While Cumberland was not the only county to produce an association, Cumberland's is unique because of their active Loyalist population. Out of all the counties that produced associations in North Carolina, Cumberland had the most active Loyalist population, with more Loyalist claims made after the war than any other county in the state.[33] Cumberland was also the *only* county in the state where Loyalists captured at Moores Creek had also previously been members of the Provincial Congress: Farquhard Campbell, Thomas Rutherford, Alexander McKay, and James Hepburn.[34] These four individuals had been the only representatives from Cumberland during the four Provincial Congresses, except for Alexander McAllister, at the third Provincial Congress, and David Smith, who was a member of the fourth

Provincial Congress.[35] Cumberland, along with Anson and Bladen counties, "led all the others in the number who fought in both the loyalist militia and the regularly enrolled Loyalist regiments."[36] Historian Robert DeMond even estimated that as much as two-thirds of Cumberland County's residents were Loyalists, drawing on a letter from Col. David Smith to Governor Caswell in July 1777, where he said that it was "evident that two-thirds of Cumberland county intend leaving this State and are already become insolvent," as they had refused to take oaths to the Revolutionary government.[37]

The Loyalist sympathies were especially strong in Cross Creek, where the merchants were "almost unanimous in their support of the King."[38] The Loyalist movement in Cumberland was strong enough that even after the Resolves had been signed, in late 1775, reports circulated that Cross Creek merchants "refused to buy surplus produce or sell iron, sugar, and salt unless the vendor or purchaser agreed to take an oath of allegiance to the King."[39] The Scottish Highlanders were even said to have resisted the independence movement as fervently as any group in North America."[40] The strength of the Loyalists in Cumberland makes the signers of the Liberty Point Resolves stand out for their boldness. In light of the environment, it is even more notable that a group of fifty-five men banded together and created the Cumberland Association.

Notes

1. "Continental Association, 20 October 1774."

2. Watson, "Committees of Safety," 132.

3. Lefler, *History of North Carolina*, 1:212; Ready, *The Tar Heel State*, 79.

4. *CSR*, 10:24–25. The minutes of other committees make references to the "Committee of Cross Creek," with Cornelius Harnett writing to them to secure gunpowder at times.

5. The Lower Cape Fear region covers what is now Brunswick, New Hanover, Pender, Bladen, Columbus, Duplin, Onslow, and Sampson counties, while Cumberland, Harnett, Hoke, Lee, Robeson, and Moore counties are the Upper Cape Fear (Spencer, "There Is No Cape Fear, NC"). However, at the time, Bladen was considered part of the Upper Cape Fear.

6. Wood, *This Remote Part of the World*, 232.

7. Wood, *This Remote Part of the World*, 232.

8. Wood, *This Remote Part of the World*, 236.

9. Wood, *This Remote Part of the World*, 236.

10. There were similar Association documents outside of North Carolina as well. South Carolina's Provincial Congress had signed an Association almost identical to Wilmington-New Hanover's at the start of June 1775, and New York had done one on May 4, 1775. Both were in response to Lexington and Concord (Force, *American Archives*, 2:897, 471.

11. Fields, *Abstracts of Minutes*, 1:265; McEachern and Williams, *Safety Committee Minutes*, 45; Meyer, *Highland Scots*, 144–45.

12. *CSR*, 9:1205, 1202.

13. *CSR*, 9:1211.

14. McEachern and Williams, *Safety Committee Minutes*, 48–49. See also pages 27, 35, and 43–44 for the lead up to the call for a Provincial Convention.

15. McEachern and Williams, *Safety Committee Minutes*, 31.

16. McEachern and Williams, *Safety Committee Minutes*, 26.

17. There is still a debate today about whether the Mecklenburg Declaration happened or not. For more, see Syfert, *The First American Declaration of Independence?*.

18. Lefler, *History of North Carolina*, 1:214.

19. Rayburn, "Infallible Power," 411–12.

20. *CSR*, 10:27.

21. McEachern and Williams, *Safety Committee Minutes*, 42–44.

22. Lefler, *History of North Carolina*, 1:214.

23. Lefler, *History of North Carolina*, 1:216.

24. Meyer, *Highland Scots*, 145–46. However, Thomas Rutherford then promptly came out as a Loyalist in early 1776, urging Loyalists to join the King's standard in Cross Creek in February 1776 (*CSR*, 10:452).

25. Rankin, *The Moores Creek Bridge Campaign*.

26. Rankin, *The Moores Creek Bridge Campaign*, 31–32.

27. Moss, *Roster of the Patriots*, vii.

28. Moss, *Roster of the Patriots*, vii.

29. The following Loyalists from Cumberland County were taken captive at the Battle of Moores Creek: Thomas Rutherford, Angus Campbell, Donald Campbell, Neil Colbreath, Donald Gray, Malcolm Love, Neil McArthur, Alexander McDonald, James McDonald, John McDonald, Neill McGeachy, Alexander McKay, John Mackenzie, Lauchlin McKinnon, Daniel McLean, John McLeod, William McLeod, William McLeod (different William), and John Murchison (Coldham, *American Migrations*, 609–53).

30. Moss, *Roster of Patriots*, vii.

31. Lefler, *History of North Carolina*, 1:223.

32. Robert Rowan and Arthur Council each led a company in the Battle of Moores Creek Bridge, and Council's company included twenty-four additional Cumberland Association signers: Simon Banday; William Blocker; Robert, Samuel, and William Carver; John Clendenin; John Elwell; James Emmet; David and Theophilus Evans; George Fletcher; Joseph and Robert Greer; Joshua Hadley; Samuel Hollingsworth; John Jones; Martin Leonard; Peter Messer; John Parker; James Pearl; David Shepherd; Charles Stevens; Micajah Terrell; and Thomas White (Haun, *NC Revolutionary Army Accounts*, 1:6–7, 30; Lewis, "Capt. Arthur Council").

33. This information was compiled from Coldham, *American Migrations*, 609–53, by adding up the number of claims made from each county. Cumberland had fifty, the most in the state.

34. *CSR*, 10:594–95; DeMond, *Loyalists*, 80–81.

35. *CSR*, 9:1042, 1178; *CSR*, 10:165, 500, 914. Alexander McAllister himself later showed Loyalist sympathies and was ordered to leave the state because he refused to take the oath of allegiance in 1778 (Fields, *Abstracts of Minutes*, 1:307; see also Willcox, *A History of the House in the Horseshoe*, 79–80). Yet McAllister also served as a colonel in the local militia and is well regarded as a local Revolutionary hero ("Colonel Alexander McAllister").

36. DeMond, *Loyalists*, 59.

37. DeMond, *Loyalists*, 57, drawing on *CSR*, 11:xviii; *CSR*, 24:10–11.

38. DeMond, *Loyalists*, 54.

39. Rankin, *The Moores Creek Bridge Campaign*, 16.

40. Wood, *This Remote Part of the World*, 242.

CHAPTER 3

Signers

THE FOLLOWING WILL BE brief biographies of the fifty-five North Carolina settlers who put their names on the Liberty Point Resolves in June 1775.

Simon Banday

There are not a lot of historical records directly tied to Simon Banday. He was one of the twenty-four signers who served in signer Arthur Council's company of militia during the Battle of Moores Creek Bridge in February 1776.[1] He was also said to have enlisted "under Capt. Robert Rowan, of the Continental Service, in an independent unit."[2] This is very possible as militia units in the area were not known for their record keeping.[3] He next appears in a land entry dated October 9, 1779, (filed February 1780) for 50 acres of land in what was then Washington County, North Carolina, but is now Carter County, Tennessee.[4]

He has the distinction of being the first settler on Gap Creek, just south of what would become the City of Elizabethton, and he built his house by Big Spring, the current location of one of the three ground sources providing water to the city.[5] In May 1780, he made a trip to Jonesborough, Tennessee, to serve as a member of the Grand Jury for the May session.[6] Unfortunately, by the time his land was officially patented in October 1782, he had already died.[7] The Washington County Court Minutes for May 29, 1781, discuss "George Bundy & Reuben Bundy, Orphans of Simeon Bundy deceased," providing the final record for this signer.[8]

Lewis Barge

Lewis Barge was born in Philadelphia in 1741, and he moved to the Cross Creek area of Cumberland County around 1763.[9] Barge was a hatter by trade but would also become a tavern-owner and planter.[10] In July 1763, he took on an apprentice named Thomas Wilkinson for Wilkinson "to learn his art, trade or mystery of making hats."[11] In November 1764, he was first granted a license to keep an "ordinary" (a tavern) at his house.[12] His tavern business became so successful that by the time of the American Revolution, running Barge's Tavern was Barge's primary occupation.[13] In fact, Barge may have been the wealthiest of the fifty-five signers. In May 1780, he successfully petitioned the General Assembly to waive a portion of his tax burden, stating that he "lost all his Buildings in the Town of Campbelton [*sic*]" to a fire in November 1779, the value of said buildings having been assessed at £12,000.[14] In his May 1808 will, which was executed upon his death in 1809, Barge devised or bequeathed 1,346 acres of land, three houses, two stores, one shop, one brickyard (with dwelling), his "large tavern in Fayetteville lately occupied by James Baker," two additional lots in Fayetteville, at least three lots in Campbellton, $400 dollars in silver dollars, and an unspecified number of enslaved persons, farming utensils, horses, cattle, sheep, hogs, and cash on hand to his wife and various children.[15]

Throughout his lifetime in Fayetteville, Lewis Barge took an active role in the affairs of the community. He served as a constable, was one of the seven commissioners appointed in 1778 to "lay out and regulate" the newly combined town of Upper and Lower Campbellton, and was one of the seven men chosen as directors for Fayetteville in 1783 after it was renamed.[16] He also appeared regularly in the *Minutes of the Court of Pleas & Quarter Sessions* for witnessing and proving deeds, serving on a jury, etc.[17] His life prior to coming to Cumberland County is not well-documented, unfortunately. In *Hometown Heritage*, author Lucile Miller Johnson speculated that Lewis Barge was a descendant of French Huguenots but did not provide any evidence to support this.[18] However, since the late 1990s, this supposition appears to have been quite solidly refuted.

In 1998, Oliver C. Weaver Jr. of Birmingham, Alabama, published a book that had been more than twenty-five years in the making.[19] He focused on the Barge families of Philadelphia, Pennsylvania, and Cumberland County, North Carolina, and specifically Lewis Barge.[20] Weaver's in-depth research and analysis of primary source documents have led him to theorize that Lewis

Barge's great-grandfather was one "Ludwig Barch, Sen'r" of Upper Dublin Township on the outskirts of Philadelphia.[21] Quite simply "Lewis Barge" is the English version of the German name "Ludwig Barch," but in addition to that he is one of only two men in the Philadelphia area who could have been "the progenitor of the Barge families" in that area of Philadelphia County, and the other being a "Jacob Barge" ("Jacob Bertsch" in some records) who is shown to not be a direct ancestor of Lewis Barge.[22] Weaver points out, based on the circumstantial evidence available, that it is most likely that Lewis Barge was the son of William Barge, the grandson of Ludwig Barch.[23]

Additionally, Weaver provides information on the close association between the Barge and Robeson families in Philadelphia County, Pennsylvania, that was continued and renewed in Cumberland County, North Carolina.[24] He also is able to give some plausible options regarding the maiden names of Lewis Barge's two wives, Mary and Christiana, something others have not been able to provide any information about.[25] All in all, *Barge Families of Philadelphia, Pennsylvania, Cumberland County, North Carolina, and Butler and Wilcox Counties, Alabama* does an excellent job of providing a fuller picture of Lewis Barge's life than any previous work.

George Barnes (Forgotten Signer)

In New Hanover County, there is a recorded George Barnes during the 1760–1770s. In June 1767, Barnes was the defendant in a court case against plaintiff Henry Nagles.[26] During the October term of 1768, he participated in two more court cases, a plaintiff in one case and a defendant in another. For instance, he was the plaintiff in the case against Archibald Ross but was the defendant in the case against Hog & Cross.[27] In July of 1769, his name was listed as one of the men to whom a certain David Wallace must show "his good behavior for 12 months" or else he would lose his bond of forty pounds.[28]

In 1772, Barnes applied for a license to keep an ordinary.[29] The next year, he put an advertisement into *The Cape Fear Mercury*:

> Run away from the subscriber September 8th 1773, an Indented [indentured] Servant Girl named Mary Kelly lately from Ireland.... Whoever takes up the said run-away servant, and secures her in any of his Majesty's Goals [*sic*] so that she may be had again, shall be entitled to the above reward, and if brought home all reasonable charges paid by me.[30]

In April 1774, he renewed his ordinary license.[31] Yet, by October 1774, this Barnes died, and his will was exhibited and proved by Robert Bennerman. Judith Howell was designated the executrix of the deceased's will.[32]

William Bathgate (Forgotten Signer)

William Bathgate most likely first lived in Falkirk, Scotland, in the county of "Sterling," which is currently known as Stirlingshire. He had one brother by the name of Archibald Bathgate, who was a merchant in Falkirk.[33] When considering his Scottish heritage, he may have traveled with other Scots to Cumberland County, North Carolina.

In an earlier period, he lived with another individual named John Jones as a young watchmaker in Virginia.[34] William Bathgate dwelled in Petersburg, Virginia, until 1774, in which he released an advertisement in the *Virginia Gazette* on August 11:

> The subscriber intends to leave Petersburg about the 11th of September, and as he has several WATCHES belonging to different people in his custody, will be much obliged to the proprietors to call for them as soon as possible, otherwise I propose taking them away with me.[35]

It is currently unknown how Bathgate is related to the Cumberland Association, besides the signing of the Liberty Point Resolves; however, he was in Cumberland County long enough to be listed under a taxable list for the area. He is listed as having £640 in taxable wealth for the year 1777.[36] Around this time between 1777–1778, he and Daniel Sutherland also paid bail for a court case between James Jones [Senior] and Thomas Reid in Cumberland County.[37]

On November 7, 1789, Bathgate and Henry Bragg witnessed a land exchange between a resident of Bertie County, North Carolina, named Robert Freeman, and a Norfolk, Virginia, resident named William Farrer.[38] By this time of 1789, he had moved to Norfolk, Virginia, although he had mostly paid for rentals, seen within the Norfolk Deed Books.[39] On June 30, 1791, William Bathgate leased property from Nathaniel Boush, with payments of twenty-two pounds annually.[40] That same year in December, Bathgate signed a petition for a national bank to be settled in Norfolk, Virginia.[41]

The next year in 1792, he rented a storehouse on Main Street for six years, paying sixty pounds annually.[42] Bathgate appeared in records again with Henry Bragg on May 1, 1796, in which there was a tripartite agreement between Henry Bragg, William Bathgate, and the widow Brigett Bragg. Bathgate paid Bragg in full and received nine enslaved persons altogether, including children: "by these presents doth sell unto the said William Bathgate one negro man named Norfolk[,] one named York & a boy named Davy[,] one negroe woman [named] Beck and her child Sam[,] Mytilla and children named Polly and Ben and a negro girl Patience."[43]

Two years later, on August 26, 1798, Bathgate passed away.[44] In November, his brother Archibald wrote a letter to the British consul in "Northfolk" to give the power of attorney over William's estate to John Hamilton.[45] Bathgate's estate was auctioned off, with his inventory including: "a box of watch springs, 43 ounces of old silver plate, 1 8-day clock…, 4 male and 2 female slaves."[46] The enslaved persons were named in the record of his estate: an older Will, a younger Will, Mathew, Simon, Affa, and Dina (also spelled as Dianna).[47] Bathgate was buried with Masonic honors in Norfolk, Virginia.[48]

William Blocker

Not much is known about William Blocker. He had inherited 100 acres of land on the northeast side of the Cape Fear River from his father, later selling it to James Dyer.[49] A land deed from April 1, 1771, records, "William (X) Blocker, son of late George Blocker, to James Dyer, both of Cumberland, for £25 N.C., 100 a. on NE/S of Cape Fear River, 3 mi. above Rockfish…"[50]

A list of claims from James Gammel & Co. from January 1776 records William Blocker as, "Now living in the Town of Fayetteville… Quite able to pay," his debt of £7 3s. 11d.[51] William had land in what is now downtown Fayetteville, with a land deed between Robert Cochran and Stephen Gilmore recording property "beginning at William Blocker's corner on Maiden Lane."[52] William Blocker is listed in the Sampson County Census in 1790 as living with a wife, two daughters, six sons, and one enslaved person, and not much is known about him after that.[53]

Lewis Bowell

Lewis Bowell was a well-known baker in Cumberland County, who was also described as "a little Dutchman."[54] On March 13, 1772, Lewis Bowell signed his name under a petition for a new town charter for Campbellton, in response to the increasing number of transient voters in the region. The new charter would limit civic votes to landowners that most often lived within miles of the courthouse, which included Bowell himself.[55]

During the time that the British military stayed in Cumberland in 1781, the story goes that Bowell had his own incident with the soldiers. The British soldiers checked his bakery and searched the premises. Since Bowell stored his flour in barrels, he had spare empty ones in the loft; he and his wife stuffed him into one of these empty barrels. One of the soldiers grabbed the barrel he was in and kicked it downstairs without realizing a man was inside. "It struck against the side of the house with such force that it burst open, when, lo, and behold, the little Dutchman sprung to his feet, and stood up in his full dimensions, ...and exclaiming at the top of his voice, "Lewis Bowell! Py Got, true Whig from de start. I'd as lief die as live.'"[56] The British soldiers left the bakery, since they did not know if other men were in the rest of the barrels.[57]

Aside from his participation in rebellious and civic matters, Bowell had a significant appearance in debt-related records. In 1752, Lewis, under the name of "Lewis Powell," was registered on a list for debtors in the Cape Fear River Basin.[58] During a September 1774 record, British merchants wrote a list of names for their claims; James Gammel & Co. wrote a claim identifying "John Bowell" as the debtor within the Cumberland County area. A note was added beside the name, stating: "No such man ever lived here...there was a Lewis Bowell who died in 1793 insolvent."[59]

By 1786, Bowell became active in the community by serving and watching over prisoners.[60] General Rutherford brought Bowell's monetary request to the North Carolina General Assembly:

> Resolved. That Lewis Bowell, of the Town of Fayetteville, be allowed the sum of eighty-nine pounds one shilling current money in full for provisions, &c., by him furnished sundry persons confined agreeable to a resolution of the General Assembly, that the Treasurer pay him the same and be allowed.[61]

Two more excerpts at later dates discuss Bowell watching over the prisoners:

> Resolved, That Lewis Bowell be allowed the sum of fifty-five pounds four Shillings for provisions, rum, &c., furnished the prisoners lately confined at this place in full. That the Treasurer pay him the same and be allowed.[62]

> Received from the Senate a resolve of this House allowing Lewis Bowell a certain sum therein mentioned. Endorsed, "read and concurred with."[63]

Based on the year and location, Bowell was most likely watching the state prisoners charged with money fraud and counterfeit. The men, including Memucan Hunt, had received payments from the North Carolina Treasury and mishandled and embezzled their funds. The General Assembly had these prisoners held in Fayetteville in preparation for their hearings.[64]

On March 13, 1782, in the District of Wilmington, Lewis Bowell submitted a claim and received a pay voucher for twelve pounds.[65] The next year on August 20 in the same district, Bowell received £20 5s. 0d. for his service in the militia, as well as two additional vouchers of £43 2s. 0d. and £8 1s. 8d. for approved claims.[66] In the 1790 Census, Lewis Bowell was registered to cohabitate with six other older, white males, three young, white males, and three white women.[67] Bowell appeared in North Carolina newsletters in November 1792. He put in advertisements to search for his missing horse.

> STRAYED or STOLEN/ From the subscriber on the 6th inst, a bay Horse, about 14 hands high, one glass eye. I believe he had shoes on before- has been used as a saddle horse, and is in tolerable order. The person who will give information, so that I get said horse again, shall receive five pounds reward, if strayed, and if stolen, ten pounds for detecting the thief, if convicted.[68]

Lewis Bowell passed away in Cumberland County in April 1795. His inventory of movables supports the previous census's evidence of a large family. Items within the inventory included: ten featherbeds and bedsteads, sixteen chairs, and eight tables. Other inventory items were categorized under garden and kitchen materials, "...baking and garden tools and kitchen furniture."[69] The inventory's reference to baking tools aligned with his position as the "Baker of the Province and County" under the written name of Lewis "Bowel."[70] Rebecca Bowell, his wife, was the named administrator after Lewis Bowell's death.[71]

Thomas Cabeen (Forgotten Signer)

Thomas Cabeen was born in Scotland in 1752, and after coming to the colonies, was a tanner in Cumberland County, living at Cross Creek since 1774.[72] In 1777, his tax worth in Cumberland is listed as £118.[73] In July 1778, he was appointed as one of the patroller's of the Campbellton district, along with George Fletcher and John Dobbins.[74] That same year, he signed the petition to the state legislature in 1778 to move the courthouse to Cross Creek.[75] He is listed as getting a land grant for 100 acres on the waters of Rockfish near the mouth of Beaver Creek on October 13, 1783, in Cumberland County.[76] He served in the militia for the Wilmington District in North Carolina during the Revolution, and contributed money to the war effort.[77] In 1778, he married Effey (Euphemia) Graham, daughter of Donald and Catherine Graham of Cumberland County.[78] By 1780, he is listed as owning "300 ac piney land £270, lot £162, 12 cattle £120, money £52, total £604" in the tax lists for the Campbellton district.[79]

During the Revolution, when the British passed through Campbelltown on the way to Wilmington on March 30, 1781, Cabeen was taken prisoner but managed to get parole.[80] Cabeen then accompanied Colonel Rowan to Wilmington to help recover Rowan's enslaved persons who had escaped and then had purchased "a Negroe Wench" from Joseph Waller near enemy lines.[81] When he returned, he found that Cumberland Commissioner Patrick Travers and his brother-in-law Joseph Hadley, son of the sheriff, had "entered his house and taken his slave woman because he was consorting with the enemy. Since then, he has been afraid to return home because of Andrew Beard, who has taken to shooting people supposed to be enemies of the government. Beard had since threatened his life," Cabeen said in a June 19, 1781, legislative petition.[82] The Hadley family was known for using the war as an excuse to seize property of others, so mostly likely they used Cabeen's absence as an excuse to take some of his property.[83] There was also a close connection between Travers and Andrew Beard.[84] Beard had earlier been shot by Duncan Ferguson, a Loyalist suspected of taking part in the Piney Bottom Creek Massacre, which might explain Beard's behavior.[85] Nevertheless, the General Assembly did not pity Cabeen's plight, and they rejected his petition.[86]

In late December 1784, Cabeen entered into a deed with Alexander McIver and the carpenter James Dick as trustees where he had arranged for his children to get land if something happened to him.[87] Around this same time, Mary Brown made a deed of land to Thomas Cabeen.[88] Later that year, James Dick and four others publicly whipped Cabeen along with tavernkeeper Mary Brown. [89]

The men had tried to drive Thomas Cabeen and Mary Brown out of town with their whipping, due to their "many immoralities repeatedly committed and continued by them, and by their lewd life and Conversation" and had been charged with an incitement to riot in the Wilmington Superior Court Docket in June 1785 and had been fined.[90]

Yet in November 1786, sixty-one residents of Fayetteville protested the fines, saying it imposed a hardship upon the men.[91] Seven of the signers of the petition were Liberty Point Resolves signers: Rowan, who signed first, Lewis Barge, John Wilson, James Gee, Lewis Bowell, David Shepherd, and William Gillespie.[92] Two of the signers of the petition were also children of the signers: William Barry Grove (Rowan's stepson) and James Leonard, Martin Leonard's son.[93] In the petition to the General Assembly, they vouched for the character of James Dick and the other men:

> Knowing our neighbors who are immediately prosecuted for the offenses aforesaid to be peaceable, and orderly, and of good character and report, and that the payment of the fines imposed as above would greatly injure them, their properties and families if collected, and as we look upon their conduct to be the desired act of the citizenry of Fayetteville at large, no other means being left to disencumber them from so dangerous a nuisance.[94]

The committee that examined the petition agreed, and "in consequence of this report releasing the persons therein mentioned was delivered."[95] The fines were waived. The state assembly did this even after the Wilmington District Superior Court had said that the legislature had no right to suspend fines without consent of the people.[96]

Shortly after that, Thomas and his wife moved to South Carolina, where Thomas later died.[97] In the 1790 Census, Thomas is listed as living in Chester, South Carolina, in a household with twelve total members: four enslaved individuals, three males under sixteen and four females.[98] By 1800, he lived in the same place and had a household of eleven people.[99]

He had nine children with his wife Effey, and died in 1801 in Chester, South Carolina.[100] At his death, he gave his "beloved wife Effy" an enslaved woman named Lucy, half of his household and kitchen furniture, his sorrel mare, a new bridle and saddle, and three cows and calves of her choosing, as well as the use of his plantation so long as she remained a widow.[101] He gave to his daughter Mary, (when she married), an enslaved woman named Jane, a feather bed, a saddle and bridle, his two year old filly, and three cows and calves.[102] To his daughter, Eleanor (at her marriage), he gave an enslaved person named Doll, one horse or mare worth twenty-five dollars, a new saddle and bridle, three cows and calves, and a bed.[103] His daughter Isabella, upon her marriage, would receive one enslaved person named Charlotte, a horse worth seventy-five dollars, a new saddle and bridle, a bed, and three cows and calves.[104] He gave his daughter Betsy a "mulatto girl named Nan" and any children Nan had, along with the enslaved woman Jane's second child, if any.[105] He further specified that Mary was to take care of Betsy, and when Betsy died, then Nan, Nan's children, and Jane's second child would go to Mary.[106]

To his daughter, Nancy Hill, he gave items already "in her possession," namely an enslaved girl named Minda, one bay horse, a saddle and bridle, and a bed and furniture, but he also gave her the first child (if any) of the enslaved woman Jane.[107] He also dictated what was to happen with the first two children of the enslaved girl Doll (if she were to have any): the first would go to his son John, and the second to his son Daniel, with the stipulation that both of these children, and Jane's first child, who would go to Nancy, "must be taken away at two years old."[108] Lastly, he gave his plantation, his tan yard and assorted instruments, his enslaved person Sam, his farm implements, and his lot in Fayetteville, North Carolina, along with his outstanding debts and the remaining part of his estate to his four sons Alexander, William, John, and Daniel, stating his youngest son Daniel should "have necessary English schooling" and that the children should stick together to take care of the farm and tan yard as usual and learn the trade, and he named his wife, his son-in-law Solomon Hill, and his friend David Tomb as executors of the estate.[109] Solomon and Nancy Hill later became the parents of Daniel Harvey Hill, who grew up to become a general in the Confederate Army under Robert E. Lee in the Civil War.[110] A.C. Avery notes that Thomas, Nancy's father, was a native Scotchman, and that Nancy was a Scotch Presbyterian who "enacted of her sons the most rigid observance of the Sabbath."[111]

John Carraway (Forgotten Signer)

John Carraway was a large planter and a cooper (a trade person who made wooden barrels and tubs) in Cumberland County and owned land by the Black River.[112] He lived in what is today Harnett County.[113] He had lived in the county since the 1750s and owned a good deal of property in the area, receiving numerous land grants.[114] He was the guardian of Elizabeth Stewart, orphan daughter of Thomas Stewart, in 1762.[115] He was part of Capt. Alexander Avera's company as an assessor relating to the county districts in 1777.[116] He was paid fourteen pounds for his service as an assessor for his two years (1777–1779) and later was a constable for District 4.[117] He probably served in the militia for the Wilmington District during the American Revolution.[118] In the 1790 Census, he was listed as owning fourteen enslaved persons.[119]

Carraway had numerous sons: Charles Stewart, James, Thomas, William, and John.[120] His son James is listed as part of the militia paroled by Lord Cornwallis in 1781.[121] He died in October 1793, and in his will, he left his plantation of 360 acres and cattle to his wife, and gave land to his sons Thomas, William, James, and Charles, and his grandson John (William's son). Both Thomas and William inherited land along the Black River, with William's plot being next to John Rea's land on one side and Virginia Ellie Avera's on the other. Carraway also distributed many enslaved people in his will: to his wife, Margaret (maiden name Stewart), he left Balaam and Jude and their two children, Grace and Joshua, along with two other enslaved persons named Ben and Phoba; his son Thomas received the enslaved individuals Peter and Rhody; his son John received an enslaved person named Frank; James received a person named Sam, a woman named Satna [Satina], and a boy named Isaac; and his son Charles received a man named Simon and a woman named Sylva.[122]

Robert Carver

Robert Carver was the son of William Carver and had many siblings, including fellow signers William and Samuel Carver, and was born around 1754.[123] In 1772, fellow signer Samuel Hollingsworth and Joseph Dunn were appointed as guardians of the Carver children after William Carver's death, as they were all under twenty-one.[124]

Robert Carver married a woman by the name of Elizabeth Newberry.[125] They had a son named Marshall and five daughters: Elizabeth, Mary, Sarah, Susy, and Nancy.[126] Robert served in the militia in the Wilmington district.[127] The 1780 Cumberland County tax list shows Robert Carver as having, "200 ac land improved £630, 5 Negroes £2,150, 3 horses & 12 cattle £300, cash £12.10, total £3,092."[128]

Robert Carver is seen in the 1790 Census as living with seven free white females and seventeen enslaved persons.[129] In Robert Carver's will, he divides his numerous enslaved persons, property, and plantation between his wife and kids.[130] One of the enslaved persons, Tommy, is given three acres of land on the plantation.[131] Robert Carver also stipulates that Tommy and Venus, another of his enslaved persons, be freed two years later by the discretion of the executors of the will.[132] He died in 1796.[133]

Samuel Carver

During the 1730s–1800s, documentation reports at least three Samuel Carvers within both Bladen and Cumberland County. One Samuel Carver had immense ownership over 640 acres as part of his land patent in 1735 for Cumberland and Bladen.[134] On October 11, 1751, this Carver gained 500 acres "on the Eastside of the white marsh joining the upper side of Joseph Soul's Land & opposite to Roger Hannes Land."[135] The deed for the 500 acres took place in Bladen County.[136] In 1753, Samuel Carver Sr. then wrote a will, because he was experiencing sickness and weakness in his body.[137] He gave his four children, his wife, and his brother different properties after his death.[138] For example, he gave his wife the plantation he owned, with 150 acres running parallel to Samuel Pike's property.[139] Once the wife passed away, the will said that the plantation and the related acres would then be transferred over to his son, Samuel Carver.[140]

Aside from the two previously referenced Samuel Carvers, the signer of the Liberty Point Resolves was from a different Carver family. This Samuel Carver was one of the sons of William Bracewell Carver and brother to the signers William and Robert Carver.[141] At a young age, Carver became an orphan in 1772, and he and his siblings had their guardianship transferred over to Samuel Hollingsworth and Joseph Dunn after their father's death.[142] During 1772–1779, Samuel was still under Hollingsworth's guardianship. In one census record in 1779, Samuel Carver, along with four other siblings, had a note, stating, "Samuel Hollingsworth[/] Guardian."[143] This same census also recorded that Samuel Carver owned 600 acres of land in Bladen County and had five horses.[144]

In Wilmington, North Carolina, on March 27, 1782, Samuel Carver applied and received a pay voucher for military claims in the amount of forty-two pounds.[145] On October 23, 1787, Carver acted as a security to the agreement that Rachel Wilson would be the guardian of her children, Rachel and James Wilson.[146] The next year, in the August Term, Sarah Willis gifted

Samuel Carver "two negroes named John and Jim to have and to hold..."[147] Her husband, Benjamin Willis, owed Samuel Carver £127 10s. over timber and sawing.[148] Since the couple could not pay the debt off, they transferred the men over to Carver to solve the debt instead.[149] This deal was proved by John Elwell and Jeremiah Willis.[150]

In 1791, Samuel Hollingsworth went to court against the administrator of Samuel Carver. The docket mentions that the court case was a general issue over payments, and a jury was picked out in judgement. The defendant, the administrator, claimed that they did "not assume."[151] Similarly, the docket referenced the statute of limitations, which may mean that the issue between the parties occurred outside the seven-year limitation period of that time.[152] Then, in 1796, Robert Carver, Samuel's brother, released a will that mentioned giving his daughters land "formerly the property of My Brother Samuel Carver..."[153] With both the court case and Robert's will, Samuel Carver's death can be estimated to be within the years of 1790–1791, with no wife and children.

William Carver[154]

William Carver was born in 1753 and was the son of William Bracewell Carver and Mary Wilson. He was the second-oldest sibling, with brothers Sampson, Robert, Samuel, Jesse, James, and John, and a sister, Mary, who married signer David Evans.[155] He married Elizabeth (maiden name unknown) in 1771, and had the following children with her: Elizabeth, David, Brazel, Clary, Lisy, Peggy, John, James, and Nelly.[156]

William lived on the west side of the Cape Fear near the mouth of Rockfish Creek, on Stage Road.[157] The US Census in 1790, 1800, 1810 and 1830 indicates that he owned enslaved persons.[158] During the Revolution he was drafted as a private in 1777, serving under cavalry Capt. William G. McDaniel and later Col. Thomas Robeson, serving on and off as a cavalryman.[159] Previously he had served at the Battle of Moores Creek Bridge with his two brothers, Samuel and Robert, along with their cousin Isom Carver under Capt. Arthur Council.[160] While serving near Wilmington they had to return to Cumberland because of "the Tories becoming troublesome in the neighborhood of [Campbellton] now Fayetteville."[161] Starting in May 1779, he served as a minuteman until the end of the war under Capt. Peter Robeson, where his call ups were so frequent yet boring that by his pension application, he had forgotten most of it.[162] In 1833, fellow Patriot Zachariah Reeves testified that William was a "staunch and active Whig during the whole war."[163] Reeves further says that "Carver was one of the Old Cumberland Association of Whigs formed in the year 1775 for defense of the Liberties of the Country."[164] According to the Phoenix Lodge of Fayetteville (formerly known as the Union Lodge), William Carver is also a founding member of the lodge, established in November 1788.[165] He may have been a miller, as he had received permission to erect a mill on Plummer Creek.[166]

William Carver was the last of the fifty-five signers to die. He died on March 29, 1836, at age eighty-two.[167] The *Fayetteville Observer* said in his obituary that he was the "last of that gallant band, who, in the face of all the discouragements of a numerous and implacable Tory foe, united in the Association known as 'the Cumberland Association,' in April [sic] 1775; by which they renounced all allegiance to Great Britain."[168] At his death, his estate was quite small. His estate's administrator, Jonathan Evans, listed William as having only one cloak, one bed with clothing and bed stand, one trunk, an old hat, and three old chairs.[169]

John Clendenin (Forgotten Signer)

Under the name John Clendinning, he served as ensign in the Continental Army under Capt. Arthur Council.[170] During his time as ensign, he was recommended to be transferred to another company to fill vacancies.[171] In October of 1777, Col. Jethro Sumner recommended Clendenin for a promotion to lieutenant.[172]

During 1779, Clendenin was appointed as the regional quartermaster.[173] On May 12, 1780, he was taken prisoner during the Fall of Charleston in South Carolina.[174] He was exchanged on June 14, 1781, and paroled.[175] He broke parole when he returned to Orange County in North Carolina, where he raised a militia group and joined Lt. Thomas Farmer to fight in the Battle of Eutaw Springs, South Carolina. He was taken once more as a prisoner of war while at Hillsborough on September 12, 1781, and was exchanged a year later on November 26, 1782.[176] He served until the end of the war.[177] In a record for Buckner Smith and Joshua Thompson, they established that they served under a "Capt. John Clendennin" from Orange County.[178] They served together at the Battle of Cane Creek, before Smith was discharged at

"Hawfield near Hillsboro N.C."[179] Clendenin died between 1788–1789, with his property taken over by Elizabeth Clendenin.[180]

Arthur Council

The Council families of Cumberland and Bladen Counties originally came from Isle of Wight County, Virginia.[181] Arthur's branch of the Council family spent some time in South Carolina before finally settling in Cumberland County, North Carolina. The first available record for Arthur Council, who was born in 1739, is from 1745 when he was listed in a parish register in an area that included modern-day Horry County, South Carolina.[182] His brother, James, and sister, Sarah, are also listed, along with his parents "Hardy Councill & Beatrix his Wife," and the birth dates of each of the children is recorded.[183] Arthur Council's first land purchase was in 1762 in Bladen County, though the land was soon added to Cumberland County.[184] A 1773 deed book from Charleston County, South Carolina, provides confirmation that the Arthur Council (son of Hardy) who was listed in the South Carolina parish register in 1745 is the same Arthur Council who was the signer from Cumberland County, North Carolina. The deed sold 200 acres of land that had been granted to Hardy Council in 1748 and stated it was "between Arthur Council Of Cumberland County in the Province of North Carolina[,] Gentl.[,] Eldest Son and heir at Law of Hardy Council[,] Late of Cumberland County aforesaid[,] Intestate[,] Deceased[,] of the one part and Wm. Henry Mills of Long bluff in Cheraws District in the Province of South Carolina[,] Esqr."[185]

Arthur Council was active in the community in many ways but in particular with the militia.[186] In a list of "Officers of the Cumberland Regiment of Militia," dated November 1770, he is shown as being an ensign in the Sixth Company (Cross Creek District Company).[187] By the Battle of Moores Creek Bridge, he had raised his own company which included twenty-four of his fellow signers.[188] In April 1776, he served as a member of the General Assembly as the representative from Campbellton.[189] During this session he was appointed to a committee to determine how much ammunition was available in the Province, appointed to another committee tasked with inquiring into "the conduct of the insurgents and other suspected persons," and was commissioned as a captain in the NC Continental Line and assigned to the 6th NC Regiment under Col. Alexander Lillington.[190] One young soldier assigned to Arthur Council's company named Hugh McDonald later wrote an account of his time as a Soldier in the Revolutionary War based on his journals.[191] The Hugh McDonald papers describe the movements of his unit from their formation in Cross Creek in June 1776 to their activities in South Carolina later that year and then the death of Arthur Council in the spring of 1777.[192] Arthur Council was buried in the William C. Gause Cemetery, Horry County, South Carolina, nearby to where the 6th NC Regiment had been bivouacking.[193]

Robert Council

Robert Council and fellow signer Arthur Council were second cousins; Robert's grandfather, John, and Arthur's grandfather, Hardy Sr., were brothers, meaning Robert and Arthur shared a set of great-grandparents.[194] Like his cousin, Robert Council also took up arms in defense of North Carolina, serving as an ensign in the 1st NC Regiment.[195] On May 6, 1799, his heirs purchased land from Peter Mallett.[196] Their names were Hardy, Mary, Arthur, Thomas, and Elizabeth Council.[197]

Joseph De Lespine

Joseph De Lespine's life in Cumberland County is mostly a mystery, as he spent most of his time in the colonies in Charleston, South Carolina. Walter Hartmann in "Munro's Doctrines: A Forgotten Pioneer in Holism and Hypnosis" claimed that Joseph De Lespine came to America with the Comte d'Estaing's fleet in 1778 and served as a surgeon in Charleston, South Carolina.[198] The information regarding Joseph De Lespine's arrival with said fleet is inaccurate, as his life in Charleston is recorded well before the arrival of d'Estaing's fleet, at least as early as 1770.[199] An ad in the *South-Carolina Gazette* published through October and November of 1770 reads, "Joseph De L'espine Lately settled in this Place, and who formerly practiced physick surgery and midwifery in this Province..."[200] De Lespine worked in Charleston alongside another physician by the name of William Loocock.[201]

In 1772, a court record orders that Joseph De Lespines' then-wife, Elizabeth, be allowed to separate from him legally. They had been living separately for some time as the court document states, "Whereas diverse animosities disputes & unhappy Differences have lately arisen & are still unhappily subsisting between the said Joseph Delespine & Eliz. his Wife... the said Joseph De Lespine shall & will allow Permit & Suffer the said Elizabeth his said Wife to live separate & apart from him & shall not nor will sue or compel her to cohabit with him nor sue trouble molest or disturb any Person or Persons that shall receive her into their habitations."[202] The document goes on to state that Joseph De Lespine will have no rights to any of the property accrued by Elizabeth and transfers those rights over to William Loocock and George Gabriel Powell.[203]

However, besides his signature, further circumstantial evidence that De Lespine was in Cumberland County is found in Maurice Nowlan's Loyalist claim after the war, where he said that around 1775 he delivered a huge quantity of medicines that he had received from a French Doctor in payment for a debt.[204] De Lespine was a French doctor, and he was believed to live in Cumberland, so he is most likely the doctor that Nowlan is referencing.

Joseph De Lespine later married again to a Sarah Russell Irwin on December 23, 1780.[205] Joseph and Sarah had a daughter, Harriet De Lespine Munro, born in Charleston, South Carolina, in 1784 and a son, also named Joseph, born August 28, 1789, on the island of St. Salvador.[206] The younger Joseph went on to become a successful merchant and "one of the largest landholders in the state of Florida" via the purchase of Spanish land grants which claimed almost 150,000 acres of East Florida.[207] The signer Joseph De Lespine died in San Salvador, the Bahamas, around 1791.[208]

The obituary of Harriet De Lespine Munro, published in Southern Christian Advocate in Georgia, includes an account of her father, Joseph De Lespine:

> Her father was Joseph Delespine, a French surgeon ... He remained in Charleston three years after the birth of my mother, and moved to Norfolk, Virginia. From thence to New York city, where he remained several years and then made a visit to his parents who lived previous to the insurrection at Cape Francois, on the Island of St. Domingo. During his absence her mother accompanied her brother, John Russel, to Nassau, New Province, and was met by her husband on his return from St. Domingo. The family remained at Nassau till 1790, and moved to St. Salvador, where her father died.[209]

James Dick (Forgotten Signer)

James Dick was a carpenter by trade and very active in his community.[210] In the July 1777 session of the Cumberland County Court of Pleas and Quarter Sessions, James Dick and fellow signer William White were two of the four appointed patrollers for the district of Campbellton.[211] He was elected one of the seven town commissioners in January 1791 and again in March 1793.[212] In September 1797, he was elected to represent the town of Fayetteville in the next North Carolina General Assembly.[213]

His involvement with the local militia is not very well documented, but there are two North Carolina Revolutionary War pay vouchers made out to him that are available: one from August 1783 for £14 10s. and the other from September 1783 for £1 18s.[214] His signature is clearly legible on the back of the August voucher and it matches his signature on the Liberty Point Resolves.[215] In later years, he was referred to as Capt. James Dick, so it is likely that he continued to be involved in the militia outside of the war. When Thomas Jefferson was elected president of the United States, forty-seven Republicans in the Fayetteville area got together for a celebratory dinner in March 1803, and "Capt. James Dick" was appointed as president of the event.[216] Following the *Chesapeake–Leopard* affair in 1807, the men of Fayetteville held a meeting in the Town House on July 15 and chose Captain Dick and six others "as a committee to retire and bring in Resolutions to express their sentiments of this portion of the community on the subject."[217]

The records make it clear that James Dick cared very much for his community.[218] Although he was one of the sixteen "forgotten signers" his name has made a lasting mark on Fayetteville because he is the namesake of Dick Street. In April 1783 when the North Carolina General Assembly passed the act to change the name of Campbellton to Fayetteville, the same act appointed a group of men "commissioners for laying out the streets of the said town" and specified "the principal streets be one hundred feet wide."[219] The commissioners were also ordered to conduct a survey of the portion of town that had once been Cross Creek and to bring before the General Assembly the following year their plan for the streets.[220] Their plan was presented and accepted in October 1784 with six principal streets and two squares.[221]

When the large landholder Mark Russell sold an acre of land to James Dick in September 1784, the deed of sale describes the boundary of the lot as starting at a stake "on the fifty foot street" and then to a stake "on the Corner of the hundred feet street leading to the lower Town known by the name of Russells street."[222] Then, in April 1791, Mark Russell sold another acre to James Dick and its boundary began at the "corner of his other acre Lott [*sic*] on Russell Street" and going the other direction on Russell Street until the third segment ended at "a Stake on the fifty foot Street" before returning to the beginning, thus making James Dick the owner of the land on both sides of the "fifty foot" street.[223] By February 1796, however, deeds were being recorded with verbiage specifying "a fifty feet street known by the name of Dick Street," and the name stuck.[224]

After the summer of 1807, James Dick does not appear very often in the records. His wife died in early November 1807 "after a long and painful illness," and the 1810 US Census shows him as living alone, his kids having all moved out as well.[225] The last record for him was in February 1811 when he sold the lower portion of both of his one-acre lots to a David Mitchell.[226] He appears to have died sometime in the mid-1810s. The 1816 article on the Liberty Point Resolves by the *Carolina Observer* (picked up by the *National Intelligencer*) does not list him as one of the seven signers still living at the time, but more concrete evidence is a deed dated October 1817 which refers to him as "James Dick (now decd.)."[227]

Daniel Douse (Forgotten Signer)

This signer is listed on the historical marker at Liberty Point, 1800s newspapers, and present-day contemporary papers as being "Daniel Douse"; nonetheless, that is *not* the correct name. The original manuscript was said to show "Daniel Douse," and the *Cheraw Intelligencer* article of 1825 and the State Pamphlet of 1831 both say, "Danl. Douse."[228] There is no record of a "Daniel Douse" living in Cumberland County at the time, and his name does not show up on deeds, in court minutes, or in the county taxables. Across the colony, there is no mention of a Daniel Douse.

Furthermore, when one examines the original document, on the second page of signers, the third name down from the top on the left side does not appear to be "Douse" at all. The signature looks like "Daniel Doyle" instead.[229] A search of local records then found a Daniel Doyle in the Cumberland County 1767 tax list and on a list of debts owed to John Burnside & Company in October 1771.[230] While nothing else about him is known, what most likely happened is that someone misread the individual document as "Douse," and that error stuck and got transmitted down as the correct name.

David Dunn

A David Dunn from Fayetteville is listed as having owed a debt to the John Hays Company in the 1798 debtors list, which lists his residency in South Carolina.[231] While this shows a David Dunn did live in the Fayetteville area, the only the only other records we have for a David Dunn is one in South Carolina, showing one who enlisted to join the revolutionary war under the 5th SC Regiment on July 8, 1776, and served in the milita in 1781 and 1782.[232] However, it is unlikely that this David Dunn and the signer are the same person as the David Dunn living in South Carolina signed a receipt of payment with his mark which is written in a distinctly different style than the signature of David Dunn seen on the resolves.[233]

James Edmunds (Forgotten Signer)

Not much is known about James Edmunds (also seen as 'Edmundson' or Edmonds). He served under Capt. Arthur Council, so he may have participated in the Battle of Moores Creek Bridge.[234] There is also a James Edmund said to have lived in Cumberland County in 1767 and is listed in the Cumberland County taxables for that year.[235] In Captain Livingston's Fayetteville district 1783 tax list, James Edmonds is listed at twenty-five pounds.[236] What is known is that he did not own much property, as John Hay, one of the British merchants who made claims after the war (he had a store at Campbellton), said for the 1801–1802 report that James owed him 19s. 6d. and that "This man was always insolvent until he moved himself away, which was about fifteen years ago," meaning that Edmunds left the area around 1785.[237]

Benjamin Elwell

One of the earliest records of Benjamin Elwell occurs in Cumberland County in 1768. Both Benjamin Elwell Sr. and Benjamin Jr. witness and prove the transfer of deeds between George Cooper and William Farmer, but Benjamin Sr. could only make his mark meaning that Benjmain Jr. is the Resolves signer.[238] In 1773, Benjamin Elwell and his father-in-law Joseph Lock received a grant for land on "both sides of Singletary Lake" in Bladen County.[239] This portion of land included 300 acres.[240]

In the 1780 Campbellton District taxables, Benjamin Elwell is listed as having £780 13s. in taxable property. As part of the total amount, £450 came from one house, £250 came from his two horses and seven cattle, and £80 13s. came from his personal cash.[241] In 1783, another tax record for Cumberland County documented the residents in "Livingston's or Fayetteville district."[242] Benjamin Elwell's taxable property made up £130 in the record.[243] In February 1784, Elwell gained more land in Bladen County, "on the northeast side of the northwest river on Frenches Creek," and received the patent for it on May 18, 1789.[244]

By 1800, the US Census identifies Elwell's location in Bladen County as being in Captain Lock's District; in his household, members included: one white male child under sixteen years old, two white males under twenty-six years, two white males under forty-five years, and one white male older than forty-five years of age. For the women in the family, there was one white female child under ten years, another under the age of sixteen, one white female under the age of twenty-six, another female under the age of forty-five years, and a white female over the age of forty-five years. There were two free persons in the household and three enslaved persons.[245] The household dynamic slightly changed in 1820, as the eldest women had most likely passed away, and there was an increased number of older men in the household.[246]

Benjamin Elwell appeared in the newsletter for Raleigh under "Sheriff Sales" in 1808. These sales helped individuals pay off their taxes by selling "following Lands" that similarly were priced. During this occasion, the sheriff sale took place at the courthouse in Bladen County on December 19th—his name is listed as "Benj. Elwell."[247] The name appeared again in an 1815 document, "Records of Men Enlisted in the U.S. Army," although this is a different individual.[248]

The Elwell family was known to have lived in Bladen County for years after the Revolution. In 1905, Walter Hayes Russ and John Roland Russ created and operated a ferry to cross people and vehicles over the Cape Fear River. They named their operation the 'Elwell Ferry.'[249] In 1952, a bridge was built to connect the land—before then, the Elwell Ferry was the only crossing over the Cape Fear River between Wilmington and Elizabethtown. The ferry still operates today on state marker I-84 and Highway NC 53, "among the last of inland river ferries once common in eastern N.C."[250] The North Carolina Department of Transportation owns and runs the ferry currently.[251]

John Elwell

John Elwell was a well-recognized member of Cumberland County. He served multiple times as a member of the jury for Cumberland County-related court cases and deed transfers. For example, he witnessed the deed transfers between Andrew Killet to Daniel Muse and Barnabas Stevens to John Crump.[252] On March 9, 1765, John Dukemineer gave John Elwell 66 ½ acres on the northeast and southeast side of the Cape Fear River, "above Nobles Camps..." Elwell paid about twenty pounds at the time for the land.[253] In 1776, Elwell served as a private under Capt. Arthur Council and Col. Thomas Robeson Jr.[254] In a later account his family members claimed he also served within General Greene's army during the Revolutionary War.[255]

Between October 1778 and April 1782, John Elwell, along with Benjamin Elwell and Samuel Carver, was appointed to work on the road between Rockfish and the "lower end of Upper Campbellton" under the watchful eye of David Evans.[256] Within a 1780 Campbellton District taxable, John Elwell was recorded as having about £4,825 in taxable property. Breaking the amount down, £1,800 came from "213 1/4 River Land," £225 came from "66 ½ Acre Back Land," £2,500 came from "6 Negroes," £250 came from two horses and seven cattle, and £50 10s. came from his personal currency.[257] In 1783, another tax record for Cumberland County released, documenting the residents in "Livingston's or Fayetteville district."[258] John Elwell had £2,125 in taxables.[259]

In the First Census of 1790 for Cumberland County, John Elwell's household included: one free white male over the age of sixteen, one younger white male under the age of sixteen, five free white females, and six enslaved persons.[260] The census record documents the exit of many household members in 1820, as John Elwell is accounted for, along with three white females of multiple ages, one enslaved male, and one enslaved female. The newer census also names the location in Cumberland County as Captain Newberry's District.[261]

Just as John Elwell served in the Revolutionary War, a newsletter documented the story of his wife's active participation in the conflict. Ann Carver Elwell rode on a horse across the Cape Fear River and led another horse through so that the "enemy" could not touch them.[262] In 1789, John "Ellwell" was the defendant in the court case against M. Hill; the verdict went to the plaintiff, so Elwell had to pay the costs. The jury at the time included

Lewis Bowell and James Leonard.[263] Later, in July, Elwell was the defendant of another suit, this time against the executors of Syvs. Willson; the jury found no cause of action.[264] In 1792, Elwell deeded a gift to his daughter, Ann Elwell, who married John Kelly.[265]

John Elwell passed away on January 7, 1835, in Cumberland County, at the age of ninety. He was buried at Kelly's Steps, a local cemetery.[266] He was at his residence on Aspies Creek during his death. The *Fayetteville Weekly Observer* reporting on the event remarked him as "a useful and respectable member of society—an active and patriotic Whig—a Revolutionary soldier."[267] On October 10, 2015, his grave was marked with the SAR and DAR markers: the Sons of the American Revolution and the Daughters of the American Revolution.[268]

James Emmet

James Emmet served as a captain of the 3rd NC Regiment beginning April 16, 1776.[269] He was promoted to major of the 1st NC Regiment on December 22, 1777, and retired from service June 1, 1778.[270] During that time, he participated in the battles of Ft. Moultrie, Brandywine and Germantown.[271] Also during that time, in 1777, James Emmet purchased ⅓ an acre lot and house on Cross Creek from Peter Mallet.[272] By 1781, he had become a colonel in the NC militia.[273] He later served as superintendent for the District of Wilmington during the war.[274]

In July 1781, Captain Edward Winston wrote to Governor Burke about Tory activity in the region, saying there were six to seven hundred in the region led by Duncan Ray, and that Colonel Emmet along with Colonel Robeson and Colonel Murphy were raising up horsemen to oppose them.[275] Shortly after, on August 14, 1781, Tories led by Colonel McNeil took possession of Cross Creek and captured James Emmet. In a letter to Governor Thomas Burke on August 19th, Emmett wrote the story of his capture by McNeil:

> Sir:—I am under the disagreeable necessity of acquainting your Excellency that on Tuesday last, the 14th inst., between 9 and 10 o'clock in the morning, this Town was in the most sudden Manner imaginable surprised by a party of the Enemy under the command of Colns. Kingsby, Ray, and McNeil. They entered the Town in so secret and sudden a

> Manner that it was out of the Power of any man, who was in it, to make his escape. I was at a Plantation I have about a Mile off, when I was alarmed by a Party of about 20 Horse. The noise of their Horses' Feet gave me just Time to slip into a Swamp, where I lay until the Party left the Plantation, which they did as soon as they deprived me of my Horse. I then got over the River, where I learned the Number to be about 300. I was likewise informed that same Evening that McNeil, with 100 men, had gone up the river on the West side and not being able to judge where they might intend to cross the river, thought it my best way to keep where I was. Had I done so I would have kept clear of them; but at such times so many reports are flying that there is no such Thing as distinguishing the true one. At Midnight between the 16th and 17th, word was brought to me that a Col. Fanning came down the Country with 100 Men, made a short stay at Cross Creek, had crossed the River at Lower Campbelton late in the evening and at that time was encamped with an Intention in the morning to pursue his March up the River and so join McNeil on the East side. On this Information, I unfortunately crossed the River early in the morning, and about 9 o'clock was made a Prisoner by McNeil, on his return to Town. It was not my intention to trouble Your Excellency with this tedious relation by way of Intelligence. I am sure you do not expect it from me in my situation, but as I have many private enemies in this County who would be glad to lay hold on any Circumstances to vilify my conduct and blacken my name, I have taken the liberty to trouble you with this by way of vindication. With all deference, I remain, Sir, your Excellency's obedient Servant.[276]

Another letter sent to Governor Burke two days later by John Ramsey provides further details on the raid and also mentions the capture of several other prisoners including another signer, Robert Rowan: "Their number was said to be between Six and Seven Hundred, and they took Fifty Prisoners, amongst which are Cols. Emmet[,] Rowan[,] Messrs. Cochran[,] Winslow, & I understand by different Accounts that they have left Cross Creek, and that Fanning crossed Cape Fear and is gone down to Wilmington on the North side to get his men armed, and that those under the Command of Mr. Niel and others, moved down the other side, but whether they are distanced for Wilmington or not is uncertain."[277]

Following the war, James Emmet was given a military land warrant for 1,600 acres in Davidson County for his service.[278] He was appointed as the sheriff of the newly named Fayette County in 1784 and also served in the General Assembly for that year.[279] In November of 1784, Fayette County was renamed back to Cumberland County and Emmet remained as sheriff of Cumberland County through 1786.[280]

Sometime around 1786–87, James Emmet, a Master of the Masonic Union Lodge, organized a meeting in Fayetteville for the formation of a Grand Lodge in the state.[281] However, it was not well attended, so it took until December 1787 for a Grand Lodge to form.[282] In 1788, Union Lodge was renamed Phoenix Lodge, and this lodge is still active in Fayetteville today.[283]

James was like other signers in that he had money, but not enough after the war to pay off all his debts. He was able to pay off a claim made by John Hay, but unable to pay off a debt to John Cruden, and claimed "insolvency" for that debt.[284] Emmet's ability to pay one but not the other is explained by how creditors would have to compete to receive payment before the debtor's assets had run out, and creditors who acted earlier took precedence over those who acted later.[285]

James Emmet died on February 22, 1787.[286] In his will, James Emmet mentions his wife Margaret, as well as his mother, who he stated lived in London "in very low circumstances."[287] He left everything to his wife and declared Peter Mallet to be the Executor.[288] After the death of Margaret, James Emmet desired his estate to go to Mary Mallett, Peter Mallet's eldest daughter.[289] James Emmet also mentions one of his enslaved persons in the will, "One negro boy named Harry, son of Sue, now about two years old..."[290]

David Evans

David Evans was born in North Carolina on December 23, 1753, to Jonathan and Mary Evans (maiden name Savage) and was the youngest of ten siblings, with five brothers and four sisters.[291] David Evans married Mary Carver, the sister of fellow signers William, Robert, and Samuel.[292] David and Mary had one child, Jonathan Evans.[293] David also received a grant of land from King George III "about seven miles Southeast of Fayetteville."[294]

David and his brother Theophilus fought under Arthur Council at the Battle of Moores Creek Bridge and served in the Revolution.[295] Legend holds that he also participated in the Battle of Elizabethtown in August 1781, where it is said that he "was one of a band of heroes, who, to the number of 90 only, waded Cape-Fear river at midnight, with the water up to their necks, and carrying their guns above their heads."[296] Then, under the command of "Browne, Owen, and Robeson, [they] attacked by surprize an army of tories, amounting to 500, commanded by Cols. Slingsley, McNeill and Ray, and completely routed and defeated them."[297] The battle resulted in what is now known as Tory Hole, and the victory rescued some Patriots who had been captured when the Tories had raided Cross Creek earlier in the month.[298]

David and Theophilus both lived on Rockfish Creek, and the Cumberland County Tax list for 1780 shows the Evans brothers with the following assets: "1,688 ac back land £1,000, 1,443 ac river land £3,600, 8 Negroes £3,350, 3 horses & 20 cattle £425, cash £352, total £8,727."[299] David later sold one of his enslaved persons, selling Oliver to John Ingram for £115 in March 1794.[300] Their brother, George Evans, listed both David and Theophilus Evans as heirs in his will.[301] David and Theophilus Evans both signed Robert Rowan's will as witnesses in 1799.[302] David Evans died on October 2, 1812.[303] An article from the Cumberland Centennial celebration in 1875, which celebrated the signers, records that the family still had relatives in the area, saying that "David Evans was the father of the late Jonathan Evans, whose children are of this assembly."[304]

Theophilus Evans

Theophilus Evans was the seventh-born child of Jonathan Evans and Mary Savage. The Evans Family Bible records that Theophilus Evans was born on November 10, 1746, at about 5 o'clock in the afternoon.[305] The DeLancy Evans Papers at UNC Library describe Theophilus as "a fun loving individual and given to jokes and frolic," and his mother at times served as a Quaker minister.[306]

Theophilus Evans married Susannah Carver, the cousin of fellow signers William, Samuel, and Robert Carver.[307] They had three children: George Washington Evans, born September 26, 1776, who married Betty Carver; Eliza, born January 18, 1790, who married Josiah Turner; and Henry Evans, born in 1791, who married Mary Thames.[308]

In January 1779, Theophilus Evans signed a petition for dividing Anson County into two distinct counties, as citizens in the lower part of the county complained about difficulty in accessing the courthouse for county meetings due to needing to cross several dangerous waterways.[309]

Theophilus Evans later served in the Wilmington District Militia.[310] During the war, he was one of the more energetic patriots, and was captured by the Loyalists with Rowan and barely escaped hanging.[311] Theophilus was quite prosperous, and was involved in multiple land transactions in Cumberland County, purchasing thousands of acres during the 1770s.[312]

An article from the Cumberland Centennial celebration in 1875 records another incident where Theophilus had to be rescued from Loyalist captivity. This story, told by Mary Gee's grandson, states that she "ransomed Theophilus Evans from the hands of his captors by giving them a bottle of whiskey, and this may account for the partiality of some of that old man's descendants for that exhilarating beverage. His captors we are told tied him under his horse's belly with ropes and chains, and it may be that Mary Gee, his deliverer, found him in this unpleasant attitude and novel way of securing a prisoner of war."[313] In this instance, Theophilus is believed to have been captured by Farquhard Campbell, who had previously been banished from the state for being a Loyalist, and who was going to hang Theophilus.[314]

Theophilus Evans owned land at Rockfish Creek and built a bridge across the creek.[315] In 1784, the general assembly granted Theophilus the right to charge a toll for the use of this bridge that was "convenient for the great road leading from Fayetteville to Wilmington."[316] Theophilus died around 1822, and in his will divides his land and enslaved persons between his children and grandchildren.[317] The enslaved persons mentioned include Ota, Adam, Hannah, Sarah, Matt, John, Old Lucy, Venus, Beckey, Mors, Julius, Adam, Joe, Mariah, Bob, and Mary.[318]

There is a good bit of family lore around either a sister or a daughter of Theophilus Evans as well. One story states that the seventeen year old daughter (another version claims sister) of Theophilus Evans swam across the Cape Fear River during a freshet with hers and her brother's horses to safely deliver them to Nathaniel Greene's camp on the west side of the river and reported the nearby Tory presence to Greene.[319] Another story states that the daughter of Theophilus Evans once challenged a British officer to a horse race and claimed that she could beat him racing backwards. The story goes that she rode with her face to her horse's tail and still won the race.[320] It should be noted that Theophilus' only known daughter, Eliza, was born in

1790, making her birth too late for these stories to be accurately attributed to her.[321]

George Fletcher

George Fletcher was a commissioner for the town of Upper and Lower Campbellton, who lived on Rowan Street, and was one of the Patriots who advocated moving the courthouse to Cross Creek in 1778.[322] He received a license to keep a tavern at his house in January 1776 and again in 1778.[323] According to Lucile Johnson, he lived on the west side of the Cape Fear River in the Rockfish Creek area, along with fellow signers the Evans, Carvers, Elwells, and Greers.[324]

He served as a captain during the Revolutionary War and was married to Rebecca, the sister of David and Theophilus Evans.[325] He also served as a Cumberland County purchasing commissary for the state in 1780, replacing Daniel Mallett in September.[326] Fletcher was instructed to be aggressive in purchasing supplies, "You will try to purchase from the Farmers, but if they will not sell you must then seize both Provisions for the men and Forage for the Horse."[327] He would acquire provisions for the Continental Army ranging from cattle to salt and flour.[328]

While he did not have any biological children with Rebecca, he raised Rebecca's daughter, Mary Brownlow.[329] Rebecca's first husband John Brownlow had previously been married to Sarah, the sister of Arthur Council.[330] Fletcher owned two enslaved persons in the 1780 tax assessment (as well as a horse and six cattle, for a total value of £1,500) and was holding six enslaved persons for Mary Brownlow (also sometimes referred to as "Polly") in the Campbellton district for 1780.[331]

In May 1781, a band of Highlanders ran into Capt. George Fletcher and his twenty-five men at Davis' Bridge, just above the confluence of Big and Little Rockfish Creeks.[332] Historian Malcolm Fowler says that Fletcher "could lay no claim to being a military man," and ordered his men to fire once then retreat.[333] After the action, Col. Thomas Armstrong said that Fletcher had "fled the scene of the fight too quickly."[334] Captain Fletcher "deemed it an insult to his honor and demanded satisfaction. Colonel Armstrong denied he meant any reflection on Captain Fletcher's courage but Fletcher was insistent on a duel."[335] 'Satisfaction' was a legal term meaning compensation for loss or damage to property, so "receiving satisfaction" referred to how an individual could receive compensation for a loss to their reputation through a duel.[336] Fletcher received his satisfaction, as Armstrong finally accepted his offer for the duel.[337]

At the duel, Armstrong withheld his fire, but Fletcher demanded another go. Armstrong supposedly responded, "I've done my best to avoid this. Now I an [*sic*] going to kill you!"[338] Armstrong's next shot killed Fletcher. Fletcher's wife was "dressing for a ball when her husband entered the house about sundown and said he would return in a half hour. He returned within the time but was a lifeless corpse."[339]

In spite of his owning enslaved persons in 1780, by the time he died in 1781, George was said to be insolvent.[340] He had been a partner with Thomas Sewell, forming Sewell & Fletcher, and they had lent Robert Rowan forty bushels of alum salt and ten bushels of fine salt for General Greene in September 1780.[341]

James Gee

James Gee was born on November 12, 1741, in Prince George County, Virginia.[342] As an inhabitant of Cumberland County by 1780, he was a signer for a petition to have the commissioners build better roads for Cross Creek.[343] Additionally, the petition requested the separation of town and village (to be called Upper and Lower Campbellton) and a new courthouse and jail, among other requests.[344]

On March 2, 1770, James Gee gave 100 acres to Hezekiah Hust, a planter in Cumberland County.[345] This portion came from the original 500 acres that were patented to James Gee.[346] The transfer was witnessed and proved by John Gee and witnessed by John Hust.[347] In 1771, John Newberry gave James Gee a parcel of land, which was proven by John Stevens in 1772.[348] The parcel sat on the east side of Cross Creek and lined against different neighbors in the area, including James McDonald and Archibald McKay.[349] On August 20, 1774, Gee reserved John Stevens' sawmill timber and 130 acres for nineteen years through a bill of sale.[350] On April 30, 1774, he was the security for Martin Leonard to get his license for tavern-keeping.[351]

The next year, Susannah Smith complained to a justice of the court that her son was being held under a false indenture.[352] William Armstrong was the initial purchaser of Nicholas Smith's servitude, but the purchase was then transferred to James Gee, who appeared for court. He produced the purchase, but the court then agreed that the indenture was illegal.[353] On July 23, 1777, James Gee was granted a license for tavern-keeping at his "dwelling house."[354] His securities included Phil. Alston and John Matthews, Esqrs.[355] Gee attended multiple court sessions as part of the jury.[356] By 1782, James Gee passed 130 acres to Charles Gee for £1,000. The witnesses included John Walsh and William Gillespie.[357] In July 1784, James Gee was appointed to the position of constable in place of Lewis Barge.[358] Six years later, in 1790, James Gee became the road overseer from Haymount to Beaver Creek instead of William McFerson.[359] Gee gained 200 more acres of land, bordering Daniel Munroe, on the southern side of Yadkin Road.[360]

During his life, James Gee and his family lived on the outskirts of Fayetteville, where Terry Sanford High School currently sits. He built the family house "and also a town house where the Prince Charles Hotel now stands."[361] Later, after the Civil War, the site of the Gee family home became the North Carolina Confederate Women's Home.[362] The Gee family cemetery is located one hundred yards away from where the house originally sat.[363]

Mary (Walker) Gee, his wife, told stories about her husband and herself to their grandchildren, such as G. W. Lawrence.[364] For instance, she told her grandson about the time James was shot in South Carolina.

> At the battle of Eutaw, when General Marion's men were displaying in face of the enemy, Captain Gee, who commanded the front platoon, was shot down, and supposed to be mortally wounded. The ball passed through the cock of a handsome hat that he had recently procured, tearing the crown very much, and in its progress, the head also. He lay for a considerable time insensible; the greater part of the day had passed without a favorable symptom; when, suddenly reviving, his first inquiry was after his beaver, which being brought him, a friend, at the same time, lamenting the mangled state of the head, he exclaimed—"O, never think of the head; time and the Doctor will put that to rights; but it grieves me to think, that the rascals have ruined my hat forever!"[365]

He is documented to have been in the army of General Greene and fought at the Battle of Guilford Courthouse. He may have served under Nathaniel Macon, primarily in battles that took place in South Carolina, such as Eutaw Springs, but this Captain Gee could also have been Charles Gee.[366] James Gee did have pay vouchers for his time in the war and as a militia member, which were picked up in the District of Wilmington.[367] Outside of his military service, he was a bricklayer in Cumberland County.[368] James Gee passed away on June 6, 1804.[369]

One of his sons was prominent in town as well, James R. Gee (also known as "Uncle Jimmy Gee"). His political stance was widely recognized, as he labeled himself a "true Democrat."[370] His descendants and family members repeated the story of James R. Gee spouting that if a Democrat governor was elected in North Carolina, he would give the state a plot of land for a public burying ground. In 1851, a Democrat named David S. Reid was the thirty-second governor of North Carolina to be elected, and to abide his own oath, Gee gave the state government his lot of land in the back of his property.[371] Later, as Gee lay on his deathbed, the story goes that he said:

> William, I am about at the end of my row, and for what lies beyond I must trust to God's mercy. But throughout my life I have kept one faith clean and unbroken. I have never been anything but a Democrat, and I have never voted anything but a Democratic ticket. When this poor body becomes clay, I want none but a good Democrat to lay me out for the grave. I would like my old friend W. T. Frizzell to do this service for me if he will.[372]

Overall, "Uncle Jimmy Gee" was remembered as a "short, stout built, one-armed man, with a comical face and a choleric temper," who did not have a bad word against him. His family and friends remarked that he was hospitable, faithful, and a positive character.[373]

James Giles (Forgotten Signer)

During the Revolutionary War, several men named James Giles participated in the conflict as Patriots. In New York, an individual named James Giles served as a second lieutenant in the Artillery during 1777 and later resigned on August 21, 1782.[374] Another notable Giles during the war was a soldier in South Carolina, who served as a captain.[375] Although it is doubtful that we have found records for the Cumberland County signer, some researchers have suspected that the signer was part of the Highland Scots community in Cumberland County, alongside other signers, such as Walter Murray, William Gillespie, and James Gee.[376]

William Gillespie (Forgotten Signer)

Although a signer of the Liberty Point Resolves, Gillespie was later arrested for expressing treasonous words against the cause of independence: "William Galespie brought into court and committed into custody of sheriff for speaking seditious and contemptuous words against the State..."[377] Both he and John Culbreath were sent to trial for treasonous words in Wilmington, North Carolina.[378]

Family members and friends wrote letters to the North Carolina governor at the time, Richard Caswell, to advocate for Gillespie's release.[379] Another Cumberland County resident, James Gillespie, wrote to Caswell on July 31, 1777, stating, "The bearer hereof, Mrs. Gillespie, Informs me that her Husband is in Confinement at Cross Creek. I have known Wm. Gillespie these several years and has no reason to believe him an Enemy to the American Cause."[380]

James Gillespie acknowledged that William Gillespie volunteered to fight in the Continental Army but blatantly argued against the captured man's request because of William Gillespie's age.[381]

Another staunch advocate for William Gillespie was his stepson, Dugald Campbell. Only a few days after James Gillespie's letter, Campbell sent another one to Caswell to make him aware of Gillespie's wife personally arriving to petition for her husband's release: "This is to acquaint you that my Mother Came from Cross Creek in Expectation of seeing your Excellency here Concerning her husband in Goal there, on Account of Curseing one of the Magistrates when he was in Liquor and keepes him still in Confinement and refuses Security for him—Now she and I request the favour of Your Excellency to Write to some particular person at Cross Creek that will release him from his Confinement or shew him Justice...my step father's Name is William Gillespie."[382]

During 1779, Gillespie sold land to Mark Cole and his wife, which was registered in 1785.[383] The deed states that Gillespie was a cooper in Cumberland County.[384] In 1787, he received £1 4s. as payment for collecting the tax list of Fayetteville district residents.[385] He died in 1794 from illness.[386] He was able to record his will, bequeathing both John Simpson Campbell and Levan Mitchell acres of land.[387] His wife, Margret, received his leftover property, and he passed his cattle to his wife and his granddaughter, Elizabeth.[388] Finally, he requested that his cooper tools would be given to his son, David "Galespie," and his son's heirs.[389]

Joseph Greer

Joseph and Robert Greer were brothers, the children of Thomas and Susanna Greer, along with their eldest brother, Thomas, and their sister, Susanna.[390] While their mother's maiden name has not been verified, family lore by the 1850s stated that it was Whitesides.[391] Their father, Thomas, was a native of Ireland and came to the United States around 1740 through Wilmington, North Carolina, and settled near Cross Creek.[392] The earliest available record showing the Greer family in Cumberland County is a 1755 deed in which Thomas Greer Sr. purchased 100 acres of land from a John James.[393] By 1770, Thomas Greer Jr. had moved to South Carolina and started his own family.[394] Then he too had a son named Thomas and, somewhat confusingly, began going by Thomas Greer Sr. in the records, even in records that also refer to his father.[395] By 1770, their sister Susanna had been married to Richard Grove and had a son, William Barry Grove, and then married Robert Rowan after Richard Grove died in 1766.[396] So in June 1775, when their brother-in-law Robert Rowan drew up the document that their nephew William Barry Grove would later label "Cumberland Association," it is not surprising to find Joseph Greer and Robert Greer signed the document as well.[397]

In the spring of 1783, Thomas Greer, the father of the Greer brothers, died.[398] In his March 1783 will, he left half of his estate to his wife Susanna and the other half to his son Joseph along with the stipulation that Joseph was to have his mother's half after she died.[399] Unfortunately, Joseph Greer died in late 1789 or the beginning days of 1790, because the minutes for the Cumberland County Court of Pleas and Quarter Sessions for January 30, 1790, record the following: "Susanna Greer mother of Joseph Greer deceased resigns her right of adminst. to Robert Rowan Esqr. who now prayed admns. which was granted Requiring bond with Wm. Grove security in the sum of £400." [400] Because of this record, we also know that Joseph Greer was unmarried when he died. When a person died intestate, or leaving no will, the right to serve as administrator for the estate would go to the surviving spouse and would only go to a surviving parent if there were no spouse and no children.[401]

Robert Greer

Robert Greer, brother of Joseph Greer, made his first appearance in the record of Cumberland County on a deed from 1764, in which he and his brother-in-law Richard Grove purchased ¼ of an acre lot in Cross Creek from

John and Grace Stevens and John Walsh.[402] In 1772, Robert Greer conveyed to John Brownlow:

> One half of a Tract of Land Lying & being on both sides of Cross Creek, [which the deed goes on to specify as] one half of a one hundred acre portion (to include one half of the sawmill on it), one half of a four hundred acre portion, and one half of a five hundred acre portion] together with one half of all the Buildings[,] improvements[,] hay[,] woods[,] waters[,] water courses[,] mines[,] Hereditaments[,] [tene]ments[,] & appurtenance to the Said Land belonging or appertaining [(]one half of all gold and Silver mines Excepted[)].[403]

This deed to John Brownlow also happened to be witnessed and then proved in court by fellow signer Philip Herin.[404] The last item bearing Robert Greer's signature prior to the Liberty Point Resolves document itself is a March 1775 deed. In this deed, Robert Greer sold to his new brother-in-law and fellow signer Robert Rowan a tract of land connected to Rowan's own land, which just so happened to be the ¼ of an acre lot Greer had purchased from John Walsh and John Stevens.[405]

Soon Robert Greer's name began to appear in records in conjunction with John Walsh. In response to a declared need to raise more battalions to serve on the Continental Line, both John Walsh and Robert Greer were nominated along with others from the Wilmington District to serve as officers in their battalion. Walsh was commissioned a captain and Greer a second lieutenant on November 28, 1776.[406] The next appearance of Robert Greer's name in the records was almost a year later in August 1777, while the Continental Army was encamped for thirteen days on Neshaminy Creek in Bucks County, Pennsylvania. The Army halted here while Gen. George Washington tried to determine where British Gen. William Howe had gone and what the next move of the Continental Army should be.[407] For a reason (or reasons) that did not survive as a part of the historical record, during this time 2nd Lt. Robert Greer was placed under arrest and tried before a General Court Martial.[408] What we know from the record is the court "found him Guilty of the Charge & Sentenced him to be Cashiered."[409] Being "cashiered" was equivalent to being kicked out of service with a Dishonorable Discharge today. According to Section IV, Article 5, of the Articles of War passed by the Continental Congress on September 20, 1776, an officer who had been cashiered "shall be thereby utterly disabled to have or hold any office or employment in the service of the United States," and Section XIV, Article 13, makes the term more clear by stating "shall be cashiered or dismissed from the service."[410] While each situation of being cashiered seems pretty serious, if an officer were cashiered due to fraud or cowardice then "the crime, name, place of abode, and punishment of the delinquent" was to be published in newspapers in and around the place the officer had been serving when dismissed as well as the "particular state from which the offender came, or usually resides."[411]

In the case of 2nd Lt. Robert Greer, the outcome was rather unusual. After the sentence was given he was "recommended by a Number of officers Among whom are the Greatest Part of the Members of the Court by which he was tryed [*sic*]," which led Brig. Gen. Francis Nash, commander of the North Carolina Brigade, to determine 2nd Lt. Robert Greer would be restored to his position, being "hopeful that this will serve as a Caution to him in future."[412] As a result, Robert Greer was released from arrest and sent off to join his regiment.[413] Making this episode even more peculiar is the fact that slightly more than three months later, 2nd Lt. Robert Greer was recommended for promotion to first lieutenant, "as Eldest 2d. Lt.," to fill a vacancy created by the resignation of First Lieutenant Richard Rispiss from Beaufort County.[414] First Lieutenant Greer's time in the Continental Army ended June 1, 1778, when the North Carolina Brigade was consolidated and reorganized at Valley Forge, Pennsylvania. The result was his regiment, the 8th, was disbanded, along with the 7th, 9th, and 10th NC Regiments, and the excess officers were sent back to North Carolina.[415] Just two weeks prior to this event, however, the NC Continental Line was placed under Lafayette, meaning that for a brief period Robert Greer served under the man who would become the namesake of his hometown.[416]

After the war, Robert Greer made a few more appearances in the records. In 1785, there are three separate pay vouchers where he was finally paid for his time in the NC Continental Line from 1776 to 1778.[417] In 1790, he appeared in the Cumberland County Census with his family, including four enslaved persons.[418] In 1792, Robert Greer signed an agreement with his older brother Thomas Greer of South Carolina, dividing between them the land that had belonged to their late brother Joseph Greer.[419] In October 1799, Robert Greer appeared in one more deed in which he sold to Stephen Beck the land that his father Thomas Greer had purchased in 1755.[420] After that the last appearance of Robert Greer the signer is the July 1800 probate records after he passed away.[421]

Joshua Hadley

Joshua Hadley, the son of Thomas Hadley and Mary Thompson, was born on July 13, 1753.[422] Joshua was the oldest son of seven siblings.[423] Joshua, his father Thomas, and his brother Simon, were all active in the Patriots' war efforts, as can be seen in an account from one of Thomas's servants, a woman named Dinah.[424] She recounted how Joshua Hadley was appointed captain of a company to hunt down the Tories.[425] He later enlisted under General Nash and fought with him at Brandywine and Germantown.[426] After the death of General Nash, Joshua Hadley returned to North Carolina and led a company at the Battle of Cane Creek.[427] Joshua's other brother, John Hadley, is said to have been, "regarded by the Scotch Tories as a gentleman, as he never took any part in the Revolutionary War."[428]

Military records show Joshua Hadley served as a lieutenant in the 6th NC Regiment starting on April 1, 1776, transferring to the 1 NC Regiment in June 1778.[429] He was promoted to captain in June 1779 and wounded at Eutaw Springs on September 8, 1781.[430] After the war, one source says that Hadley had been "a brave and excellent officer."[431] During the Jackson presidency, Capt. Joshua Hadley, along with several other veterans over the age of fifty, wrote to President Andrew Jackson offering service in support of their country despite old age, stating, "Under these impressions, we agree to embody ourselves—aged and infirm as we may be, offer our services and our fortunes to our country, in support of its laws and constituted authorities."[432] This group of veterans was referred to as the "Corps of Invincibles."[433] President Jackson wrote back, thanking them for the offer.[434]

The Hadleys were a Quaker family but the Cane Creek Friends meeting minutes from 1779 denounce Joshua's wartime activities: "'The preparative meeting enters a complaint against Simon and Joshua Hadley, sons of Thomas Hadley, in that they have joined in the present commotion, so far as to appear in a warlike manner [Chalmers Hadley note: "Military Uniform."], which is contrary to Friends' principles. This meeting agrees to show their disunity with them in their disorderly proceedings and here-by minutes them no members of our Society until they reform and suitably condemn the same, which is our desire they may. The Clerk is appointed to send them a copy of this minute and sign it on behalf of this meeting.'"[435] It was said of the Hadley family that during the war "if they could only hear of a Scotchman having anything valuable, from a good negro down to a cooking pot, that, according to their moral code, constituted a right to it."[436]

According to author and historian Louise Gillespie Lynch, "Joshua Hadley first married a Miss Livingston and then he later married Hannah Holmes in 1786."[437] However, according to Chalmers Hadley it was Joshua's younger brother John who married Margaret Livingston, half-sister to the same Hannah Holmes that Joshua married, and he gives the date of Joshua and Hannah's marriage as 1788.[438] Joshua and Hannah had seven children: William, Denny Porterfield, Amelia, James Holmes, John L., Evaline, and Emeline.[439] In 1787, Joshua was sent to Davidson County in what is now Tennessee to serve in the Cherokee-American War and Hadley's men were some of the first soldiers in Evan's battalion.[440] Joshua was granted 7,500 acres of land after the war and split this between Williamson and Sumner counties. He continued to accrue land in the area, and Lyle Hadley is quoted in *A Hadley Genealogy* as saying, "Mr. Robert T. Quarles, Director of Archives, State of Tennessee, told me (Lyle Hadley) in 1958 that at one time Joshua owned about one-half of Williamson, Sumner and Davidson counties. An exaggeration, no doubt, but he did show me card files of some ninety parcels of land ranging from a few acres to well over 1,000 acres, which Joshua had owned."[441] By 1807, Joshua Hadley was a merchant alongside Benjamin Rawlings, running "Hadley & Rawlings."[442]

Joshua and Hannah later separated. Hannah sued Joshua for half of the property on his plantation. Joshua gave this property in a trust to John L. Hadley, who would administer the property for Hannah.[443] Joshua died in Sumner County Tennessee on February 8, 1830.[444] His grave can be found in Williamson County, Tennessee.[445]

Philip Herin

Philip Herin, brother of William Herin, was a landowner and planter, though not necessarily a successful one.[446] He was in Cumberland County by the mid-to-late-1760s, because he is listed on a patent dated April 29, 1768, for 79 ½ acres of land along with a Nathaniel Holton.[447] A year-and-a-half later, though, he sold his half of the land to the said Holton.[448] In April 1771, he again purchased land, this time 640 acres from Robert Cochran but then had to sell half of it six months later to Miran Clark.[449] The following month, November 1771, he received a warrant for 200 acres in Cumberland County.[450] Unfortunately, it appears that he was never able to patent this land.

He returned the warrant and two plans of survey to court in January 1773, right outside the required twelve-month window.[451] This time limit was directed by the British Crown and placed on the warrant by the royal governor which read: "Observing His Majesty's Instructions for running out Lands; Two just and fair Plans whereof, with a proper Certificate annexed to each, you are to return into the Secretary's Office, within twelve months from the Date hereof: And if the Warrantee shall not within eighteen months from the Date hereof, take out a Patent for the said Lands, this Warrant, and all Proceedings thereon, shall be void and of no Force; and the said Land shall be deemed vacant, and free to be taken up by any Person."[452] Even if this timeframe requirement was not enforced, the surveys he returned were for a 35-acre tract of land and not the full 200 acres his warrant covered.[453] This would seem to indicate that he continued to struggle with keeping his finances 'in the black.' Additionally, there is no indication that a patent was issued in his name for any amount of acreage on the land indicated on his warrant, neither 35 acres nor 200 acres or any other amount. It could be that missing the twelve-month timeframe to turn in two surveys on the land in question disqualified him from continuing to pursue getting it. Or, possibly, he just could not come up with the funds to cover the patent for the land within eighteen months, which would void the warrant and revert the land to being available to anyone else.

Throughout his time in the county, Philip Herin had also been participating in many court sessions as a witness to the sale of deeds. Beginning in the summer of 1772, he was given more responsibility in the community. In July 1772, he and fellow signer Arthur Council were appointed as patrollers (Council specifically to replace a third signer, Peter Messer) and their district was to extend "no farther up the River than to Buchanan Ferry."[454] Likewise, in January 1775, Philip Herin was again appointed as a patroller in Cumberland County, this time with a Gabriel Harden, and their assigned area was "from James McDonalds [*sic*] on Deep River to James Muse's."[455]

At this point, however, Philip Herin was no longer tied to Cumberland County. In November 1774, he sold the remainder of his land, the other 320 acres he had purchased in April 1771, to George Mylne and Robert Hogg. One of the last recorded things Philip Herin did in Cumberland County, apart from signing the Liberty Point Resolves, was presenting this deed of sale and acknowledging it in open court in January 1775.[456] He next began appearing in the records of Chatham County.

In February 1778, Philip Herin first appeared in Chatham County documents when he proved a deed, being listed as a witness to said deed from November 18, 1773.[457] He appeared in a similar role in the May 1778 records when he proved a deed that he had witnessed in March.[458] In November 1778, he received a land warrant for 550 acres and another for 250 acres.[459] Unlike his Cumberland County warrant, he did get patents for his two Chatham County tracts, the 550 acre parcel in July 1779 and the 250 acre parcel in March 1780.[460] In the meantime, he began regularly appearing as a chain carrier in the plans of survey for other people's parcels.[461] He also appeared in a couple of Revolutionary War pay vouchers as well, first receiving twelve shillings for two bushels of corn in May 1782.[462] He then received £7 10s. in June 1783, though what this payment was for is not specified.[463]

Philip Herin continued his land speculation in 1785, purchasing 400 acres from Henry Bray in August.[464] On August 9, 1787, he purchased an additional 200 acres from the state, then on August 16, he sold his 550 acre tract.[465] In May 1789, he sold the same 200 acres he had purchased in 1787 to a Jacob Routh.[466] By November, he was dead.[467]

According to the claims of John Hay & Co., Philip Herin had a debt of £31 7s. 8d. from January 1, 1776, at their Cross Creek store, and the notes on his name give his location as Chatham and that his debt was "bonded with interest 11 Augt. 1785."[468] In 1804, their Special Agent William Duffy provided the following information after attempting to collect this debt: "Colonel John Hogan of Orange [County] says he was well acquainted with P. Heron. He killed himself by jumping out of a window in the Year 1792. He was always a poor man, drank to excess and was never solvent."[469]

William Herin

William Herin, brother of Philip Herin, was a blacksmith. In 1774, he received the sum of £10 16s. 2d. from the estate of John Brownlow for smithing work he had previously completed for Brownlow: hasps and staples, shoeing a wagon, making a chain, and shoeing three horses.[470] He was listed as a resident of Cumberland County in 1776 debt records.[471] By 1778, he was living in Bladen County and owned several hundred acres of land on the north and the east sides of the Great Marsh.[472]

At some point in 1785, William Herin abruptly moved his family to Edgefield County, South Carolina.[473] In February 1785, he purchased his last 100 acres in Bladen County from his neighbor, and fellow-blacksmith, Henry Messer, bringing his grand total to at least 500 acres.[474] By the end of August 1785, he was in South Carolina and received reimbursement for a claim of "provisions & forage for Continentals & militia in 1781 & 1782."[475] Between February and November 1785, Herin sold 300 acres of land to James Council (Arthur Council's younger brother), because on November 15, 1785, Council sold the land to a Hugh Brown.[476] In May 1786, the Bladen County Sheriff James Samuel Purdie, seized another 200 acres of Herin's land and sold two 100 acre tracts at auction in order to pay for a judgement awarded against William Herin (along with the court costs).[477]

William Herin remained settled in Edgefield, South Carolina, for the rest of his life. He returned to North Carolina at least once, in July 1793, to sell the remaining lands in Chatham County belonging to his brother, Philip Herin, as Philip's "heir at Law."[478] There is no indication that he ever returned to Bladen or Cumberland Counties. William Herin died sometime between August 29, 1820, the date of his will, and February 5, 1821, the date the will was proved and entered for probate.[479] His will lists the names of five sons and six daughters, as well as two enslaved persons, but nothing about a spouse so it is likely she died before he did.[480]

Samuel Hollingsworth

Samuel Hollingsworth came from a family of Quakers and was a descendant of Valentine Hollingsworth who came to America with William Penn.[481] Valentine's grandson, Stephen, headed to North Carolina in 1735 and settled in Bladen County.[482] He built a church on the mouth of the Cape Fear and was ordained at Welsh Neck Baptist in 1750, and he had the following children: John, Samuel, and Issac.[483] His son, Samuel, lived in Bladen County and was a planter who was involved in the turpentine industry.[484] Samuel Hollingsworth had the following children with an unknown spouse: Jacob, Enoch, Issac N., John, Samuel Jr., and two daughters (names unknown).[485] In 1804, he married a second time to Sarah Murphy.[486]

Samuel became the guardian of William Carver's children on July 30, 1772, after their father died in 1769.[487] By 1774, he returned the legacies needed to be paid to Sampson and William Carver, ending his guardianship with William and Sampson.[488] He continued to serve as the guardian for some of the Carver children until 1785.[489]

Samuel, like some other signers, appears to have had money troubles, and in January 1791, he lost a suit to Tunis Hood and had to pay £33 1s. 0d.[490] Previously, in the July 1790 term, Thomas Hadley sued Samuel Hollingsworth and Robert Raiford, and they had to pay him twenty-five pounds along with damages.[491] He was also listed in the Claims of British Merchants after the Revolution as "living...insolvent," in 1783.[492]

Yet Samuel apparently had enough money to contribute multiple times to the war effort: the Treasurer's and Comptroller's book 'B' lists Samuel Hollingsworth as being paid £4,475 in currency for provisions and forage that he provided to North Carolina for the war effort in November 1780.[493] He also claimed £28 12s. between October 1781 and July 1783 and £20 5s. by 1784.[494]

Samuel appears in the 1779 Bladen County Tax list with a substantial amount of property: seven enslaved persons, eleven horses, and thirty-four cattle. At this time, he was still the guardian of five Carver children as well.[495] In the 1786 Bladen County tax list he had eight enslaved persons, and by 1789, he still had five enslaved persons and property worth £2,000.[496] It seems improbable that he had multiple enslaved persons and thousands of pounds in property between 1779 and 1789 and yet somehow couldn't afford to pay his British creditors. He was also the guardian of Margaret and Sylvius Wilson in 1787, which is also improbable if he was poor.[497]

However, this could be explained by the fact that insolvency was not the same thing as being broke or bankrupt. Insolvency could just mean that the assets available to pay creditors are insufficient to cover the debt. Anyone could become insolvent—"all bankrupts were insolvent, but few insolvents were bankrupt."[498] If anything, Hollingsworth's insolvency and his property indicates that he had success; you could only amass a large debt if you had had success.[499] Samuel could have been playing the system, as leading New York lawyer Robert Troup told British creditors that it was easy to commit fraud when it came to insolvency, and often not worth the effort to get the creditor's money back.[500]

In 1789, Samuel led a petition before the state General Assembly to annex part of Bladen County into Cumberland County, which was granted.[501] So by the next year, Samuel lived in Cumberland County and is listed in the 1790 Census as being in a household of twenty-two, with five other males aged sixteen and older, two males under sixteen, three females, and ten enslaved persons.[502] Around the same time, Samuel was also engaged in lawsuits with the Carver family. In October 1791, he brought a suit regarding the administration of Samuel Carver's estate (the Samuel he had previously been guardian of), claiming he was due some payment. The jury found in favor of the defendant, in part because the statute of limitations had expired.[503] In the same term, he brought a suit against Jesse Carver, a younger sibling of the Carvers. The jury found Jesse not guilty as well for the same reason.[504]

Samuel died in 1814 from a snake bite.[505] According to the *Raleigh Sentinel* in 1875, Hollingsworth "killed the snake and carried it to the house, where he died, in six hours after the bit [*sic*]."[506] The family had descendants in the area for years afterward.[507]

John Jones

Like many of his contemporaries, John Jones was a planter. He first appears in the records of Cumberland County on the 1767 list of taxables.[508] That same year he was also issued a patent for 138 acres of land in the county.[509] When Col. James Moore gathered troops in Cumberland County to join the Patriot cause in 1776, he was one of the twenty-four signers who joined the militia company of signer Arthur Council.[510] In 1778 and 1779 he filed two more land entries, though neither was patented until 1799.[511] After that, the available records do not make it clear which John Jones was the signer.

Martin Leonard

During December 1772, Martin Leonard, the "Rope Maker," appears in Cumberland County records, signing a deed with John Stevens so that Leonard can gain land around Yadkin Road and Upper Cross Creek.[512] A month later, on January 30, 1773, the transfer was sealed and completed, with the deed proven by Michael King and Joseph Sloan.[513] The next year, on April 30, Leonard was granted a license to keep a tavern at his home. His securities for the license included "Walter Morray" (most likely the signer Walter Murray) and well-known Fayetteville native, James Gee.[514] A few months later, in July, he gained an apprentice boy named John Gray, who was five years old at the time.[515] Leonard was civically active in Cumberland County during his earlier years; he took part in juries and acted as a security to other members in the community.[516]

He was a participant in the Revolutionary War, serving under Capt. Arthur Council; written as "Martin Lennerd," he fought at the Battle of Moores

Creek Bridge under Col. Richard Caswell.[517] On October 29, 1778, Martin Leonard gained another license to keep a tavern at his house in Cumberland County.[518] Leonard, during the same year, signed a petition that became a House Bill for the North Carolina General Assembly.[519] The bill requested the unification of the two townships, Cross Creek and Campbellton. The unification would rename the two towns into Upper and Lower Campbellton and authorize the construction of a new jail and courthouse.[520]

By 1780, Martin Leonard left Cumberland County and moved to New Hanover County: "Removed himself from this County [Cumberland] before or about the year 1781...had at that time a good estate..."[521] He was listed as a resident in the Wilmington taxables during the April 1780 session.[522] After the Battle of Elizabethtown on August 27, 1781, a Lt. Col. Jacob Leonard helped command Brunswick inhabitants and Patriots to create an encampment above Wilmington to cut off supplies between the British Army and Tories, though it is unknown if he was related.[523] This same encampment would also prevent self-emancipators from joining the British Army.[524]

Yet, in 1782, Leonard's name was listed as a person of interest under "The Bill," which gathered suspected traitors and put them to trial.[525] Martin Leonard was the defendant in the trial against the State, and he originally was able to be released from pre-trial custody through recognizance; however, this decision was forfeited, since he did not appear during the June 1782 court session.[526] In May 1783, Leonard received a pay voucher for his prior military service.[527]

Peter Messer (Forgotten Signer)

Peter Messer was a blacksmith in Cumberland County.[528] He owned land by Blounts Creek and also had land near what is now Person Street in downtown Fayetteville.[529] Based on an early map of Campbellton, he also owned a lot by the Cape Fear River, near a lot held by John Brownlow.[530] He was the son of Henry and Hannah Messer, and his father also appeared to be a blacksmith.[531] His siblings were William and Dorothy Messer.[532] He may not have been in great financial shape early on, as in August of 1764, in a suit relating to James Council vs. John Kindell, it was said that "Peter Messer, garnishee, declared he was indebted to Kindell for £4 15s. 0d. proc. and had in his possession an old pot, broad ax, drawing knife and weeding hoe, property of the defendant."[533] Peter was married to Hannah, whose maiden name was likely

Terrell.[534] He served as a private under Capt. Arthur Council at the Battle of Moores Creek Bridge.[535]

After signing the Liberty Point Resolves, he later signed the July 1777 oath to bear allegiance to North Carolina against King George III.[536] In 1779, he served as a road overseer, and in January 1781, he was appointed to be a patroller with George Blocker on the northeast side of the Cape Fear River in the Campbell District.[537] Around this point, he seemed to own a considerable amount of property, being listed in the 1780 Campbellton tax lists as owning 476 acres of land, £1,899 pounds, five enslaved persons, four horses, and sixteen cattle.[538] Not much is known about him after that.

Thomas Moody

While Thomas Moody signed the Resolves, during the Revolution it appears that he lived in Onslow County. In April 1781, Moody enlisted for one year in Onslow County, North Carolina, and he served in the 3rd NC Regiment under Captain Samuel Jones.[539] He later fought in the battle of Eutaw Springs, South Carolina.[540] In 1782, Moody reenlisted in the first company of the South Carolina Continental Troops under the command of Captain Felix Warley.[541] He remained with this company in Charleston, South Carolina, until he was discharged from military service in May 1783.[542] During his service, he became a friend of Isaac Hammond, a free African American man from Cumberland County who also served in the 3rd NC Regiment under Captain Jones. Moody later verified Hammond's war service on his widow's pension claim in 1831.[543]

Following the war, Thomas Moody returned from South Carolina to live in Cumberland County. He is recorded as having lived in Cumberland County in all census records from 1790 to 1830.[544] Thomas Moody lived in Cumberland County with his wife, Mariam Moody.[545] Moody also had a daughter named Rebecca who died on October 11, 1810.[546]

After the Revolution, Moody and two others created a boating business, the Yankee Boat Company with Alexander Campbell and Paris I. Tillinghast, and they moved goods on barges up and down the Cape Fear between Wilmington and Fayetteville.[547] Thomas Moody also owned enslaved persons, and one of the enslaved individuals, Sip, ran away in 1807; Thomas took an ad out in the *Wilmington Gazette* offering a reward for his return.[548] Revolutionary war pension records record the date of death for Thomas Moody as January

3, 1832.[549] However, a church record records his burial date as December 7, 1831.[550]

Walter Murray

Not much is known about Walter Murray's personal life, though he was probably a Scottish Highlander.[551] Murray was a zealous Patriot who was involved in accusations concerning the Patriot zeal of other signers. Murray, John Matthews, and a Mr. William Rand charged Robert Rowan of Toryism, which Rowan had to refute in a letter to Governor Caswell.[552] Murray's fervor perhaps stemmed from an incident that summer where Rowan had led the placating of a mob that had seized the salt supplies at Cross Creek. Rowan had agreed to sell the salt to the mob at market price, provided they take a loyalty oath to the state.[553] Murray thought "the rioters were Loyalists" and disagreed with how Rowan handled the situation.[554] Robert Rowan was not the only signer who Murray testified against as being a Tory. In the July 1777 term, Walter Murray and James Dyer testified under oath that William Gillespie had spoken seditious words against the state. Gillespie defended himself and had relatives write letters to the governor protesting his innocence.[555]

In 1777, Murray joined other signers in signing an oath promising allegiance to North Carolina and against Great Britain.[556] He also signed the petition for the unification of Cross Creek and Campbellton in 1778, served as a justice of the peace for the county in 1776–1777, and was a major in the Cumberland County militia in 1781–1783 under Col. James Emmet.[557] He served as head of District Three when they laid the county out in districts in 1778, was the justice for that district, and served as justice for the April 1778–1782 County Court.[558] Later in 1778, he also served as county coroner.[559] In the 1780 taxables for the Campbellton district, he was listed as holding 640 acres of piney land, a lot in Upper Campbellton, a horse, and nine cattle.[560]

Maurice Nowlan (Loyalist)

Maurice Nowlan was an Irish native who came to New York around 1770.[561] By 1774, he had settled in Cross Creek as a freeholder and successful merchant.[562] He married the only daughter of William White around 1773 and built an "elegant dwelling house" in Cross Creek, which held eight mahogany tables and over 400 "valuable books."[563]

Maurice signed the Resolves, and after July 1775, he joined the Patriot military company in Cross Creek, which was led by Robert Rowan. Nowlan later said he joined Rowan's company because "the commander was his Country Man and his friend."[564] Nowland was appointed assistant lieutenant, and Vardy's tavern appeared to serve as a favorite place of resort for patriots in the area.[565]

While part of the Patriot force, Nowlan and fellow Loyalist signer Aaron Vardy were ordered by Rowan to join a party to intercept an emissary of Governor Martin. The posse came upon Capt. Walter Cunningham at Alexander McKay's home and took the letter he was carrying from Governor Martin to James Cotton, a Loyalist leader in Anson County.[566] Nowlan soon revealed his Loyalist sympathies and joined General McDonald as a captain, helping to raise a group of Scottish Highlanders to fight for the Crown.[567]

He fought as a Loyalist at the Battle of Moores Creek Bridge, where he was captured.[568] An April 20, 1776, report in the State and Colonial Records of North Carolina says that "Morris Nowlan" took up arms "as Captain of a Company, twenty men for the purpose aforesead" and that he lived "in Cross Creek."[569] According to *Loyalists in the Southern Campaign of the Revolutionary War*, he was "on half pay from 1776" and was a captain among the Loyalists, serving under other officers for the Regiment of North Carolina Highlanders.[570] Nowlan's claim said that he owned 1,200 acres in two tracts near Cross Creek, a house at Cross Creek, and four enslaved persons, among other property. Nowlan later lied on his Loyalist claim to the British government, saying he "never signed any association or took any oath to the Americans."[571] Like Vardy, Nowlan had participated in Patriot activities in 1775, from militia drill to the signing of the Resolves.[572]

After his capture, the Provincial Congress had ordered that Nowlan's horse and account books be delivered to them, but Patrick Travers refused to hand them over to the appointed commissioners, and the Provincial Congress had to pressure him to turn over Nowlan's confiscated property.[573] The state had appointed Cumberland Commissioners to take inventories of the estates of Tories, but Travers stalled on giving Nowlan's property to them until prodded.[574]

Nowlan spent time in multiple jails before escaping from a jail in Reading, Pennsylvania, in October 1780, after four years of imprisonment, first heading to New York.[575] He went to Charleston in 1781 to raise a company of North Carolina Highlanders but failed.[576] When Charleston evacuated, he went to England.[577] With the end of the war, he had lost 800 acres in Guilford County, two tracts containing 1,210 acres within seven miles of Cross Creek, and a lot with a house and outbuildings in Cross Creek, along with four horses and a boat he would use to transport goods to Wilmington.[578] His inventory claim with the British government also included the following enslaved individuals: Lupia, Maria, Elice, and a girl named Phillis.[579] His total claim was £4,373 10s. 5d.[580] After escaping to Great Britain, his claim said, "He is now embarrassed by many difficulties and is in dread each night that the revolving day will bring fresh calamities to the ruin of himself and family."[581]

John Oveler

Oveler ran a tavern from his house in Cumberland and renewed his tavern license in Cumberland County in 1775, in Cross Creek in 1778, and in Lower Campbellton in 1779.[582] John Oveler was a wealthy business owner in Cross Creek. The 1780 tax list shows John Ovelar (Oveler) as possessing "3 Negroes... 100 acres 'B' land Bladen County... Lot & House in Upper Campbellton & two lots in Lower Campbelton... 3 horses and 15 cattle."[583] Locations for some of this land recorded within the 100 acres sat "lying in the North side of the Horse Pen Branch, a branch of the great swamp Beginning At a Pine," and later another 300 acres were located "on the South West side of Harrisons Creek Swamp, beginning at a pine on the East side of the lake bay about half a mile below where Benjamin Lansdale Lived."[584]

John Oveler, however, primarily lived in Bladen County, North Carolina, with his wife, Elizabeth Oveler.[585] He operated a ferry on the Cape Fear, as seen in records from May 23, 1765, "On motion of Wm. Mouat, ordered that a road be laid out by John Rea, overseer of the road from Peter Lord's ferry to the street at the courthouse in Campbellton and that he with his company maintain the same and that Robert Bennerman and his company clear a road to John Oviller's ferry."[586]

John Parker

John Parker first appeared in Cumberland County records in the early 1770s. In a September 1772 land survey for a "John McLarren & Archd. McGoogen," the land is described as being "back of the Land John Parker

Lives on."[587] In January 1773, John and Kader Parker, along with fellow signer Micajah Terrell, submitted a land entry for 300 hundred acres which was surveyed in December 1773.[588] John also purchased 440 acres of land from Micajah and Hannah Terrell in February 1773, which Hannah Terrell had received from her father Samuel Goodman.[589] This land would later play a role in some of his descendants ascribing an incorrect date of death for John.[590]

By trade, John Parker was a carpenter.[591] He ended up settling in Cumberland County and appears in many court records over the years until he died in 1802.[592] Kader, however, returned to Edgecombe at some point, and he died in 1807.[593] In the twentieth century, John was mistakenly purported to have died in Cumberland County in 1818.[594] The reason for this is likely based on an 1818 probate estate case file under his name.[595] The document in the file is simply the record of distributing 407 acres of land among John Parker's heirs at the prompting of David Howie, who had purchased three of the ten shares in the land and wanted his portion duly recorded.[596]

James Pearl (Forgotten Signer)

After signing the Liberty Point Resolves, James Pearl was an active soldier in the Continental Army. On February 27, 1776, he was listed as a sergeant under Capt. Arthur Council and Col. Richard Caswell, and later under Capt. Robert Rowan and Col. Ebenezer Folsome.[597] In November of the same year, Pearl was commissioned as an ensign and served under Capt. John Walsh of the 8th NC Regiment (Wilmington District) in the Continental Line.[598] In November 1777, he was nominated (and approved) to be promoted from ensign directly to first lieutenant, skipping over second lieutenant, to fill the position vacated when 1st Lt. William Singletary resigned on October 26, 1777.[599] He served in this position under Capt. William Dennis in the 8th NC Regiment but then was transferred to the 1st NC Regiment in June 1778.[600] In July 1780, he was promoted to captain and commanded his own company until he retired from service in 1783.[601]

Throughout the war, James Pearl played a variety of important roles. As a sergeant he fought in the Battle of Moores Creek Bridge while serving in the company of fellow signer Capt. Arthur Council.[602] As a lieutenant, Pearl is referenced in a letter from Lt. Col. Hardy Murfree to Governor Burke as part of the officers that were entitled to clothing:

> The Board reported that the officers who drew in Charlestown and Captain Mills Jones, Lieutenants Wilkinson and Pearl and Dr. Fergus were entitled to their proportion and the others were not.[603]

As a captain, he is mentioned as bringing new recruits and a resupply of much-needed clothing to Gen. Jethro Sumner: "If Captain Pearl arrives safe with the drafts from this county, he will deliver you a cask containing sixty three pairs soldiers shoes..."[604]

Because he served until the end of the war, Pearl was acknowledged through the "List of Officers of the Late War Who Continued to the End Thereof or Were Deranged by Acts of Congress" as being eligible for membership in the Society of the Cincinnati.[605] After the war, records show Pearl helping other soldiers in receiving payments for their service. For example, in 1786, he "empowered" William Lord to adjust his claims and receive about £235.[606] He also conducted statements to witness for other individuals' time in the war or helping with the account of soldiers' pay.[607]

James Pearl is recorded in court sessions and deeds after the war as well. In November 1786, Pearl sold an enslaved girl named "Buzza" to Duncan McFarland in Richmond County with the stipulation that Pearl would have two months to redeem her, but in July 1787, the deed was proved in court and recorded.[608] In 1788, he participated in court cases against Hector McNeill and Patrick Travers.[609] In a court case on October 30, he won a lawsuit against John Willkings.[610] On October 28, 1789, Pearl was licensed to keep a ferry at Sproal's Ferry.[611] In a motion started by Mr. Spiller, the order was rescinded immediately in the next year, and the appeal was granted to Spiller.[612] Between the years of 1793–1796, Pearl attended multiple court sessions to sue Nathaniel Folsom, claiming an act of covenant was performed and acts of insolvency.[613] In 1797, Pearl signed a petition meant for the governor to save William Dale, accused of horse stealing, from the death penalty.[614]

Thomas Rea (Forgotten Signer)

Hardly anything has been found on Thomas Rea/Pea. He is not listed in either the county's court minute abstracts or the deed abstracts for the period. There was a Thomas Rea who lived in Perquimans and one in Chowan, but there does not seem to be a way to trace these individuals back to Cumberland's Thomas Rea.[615] Historian Duane Meyer spells his name as Thomas

Rhea and says that he was probably a Highland Scot, but Meyer does not cite any source to back up his claim.[616]

Robert Rowan

Col. Robert Rowan was the first signer and was a prominent military and civic leader in early Cumberland County.[617] Some have claimed that he was a major in the French and Indian War, but in fact, evidence shows that Rowan was a lieutenant at the end of the French and Indian War in 1762, under Col. Hugh Waddell, while another gentleman had been a major.[618] The next year, in Bladen County, Rowan was appointed the deputy clerk of the Inferior Court of Pleas and Quarter Sessions for Johnston County, and became close to Richard Grove, who he had served with in the French and Indian War.[619] After Richard Grove died around 1766, Rowan was named the administrator of his estate, and soon after married Grove's widow, Susanna (Greer).[620] His first child with Susanna was born around 1767, and his first son, Robert Rowan Jr., was born around 1771.[621] Starting around this time, he also served as Cumberland County sheriff for a number of years, and later as a judge of the local Court of Pleas and Quarter Sessions.[622]

As early as June 1770, Rowan demonstrated himself as an early supporter of the Patriot cause in America, being one of the Cumberland County representatives of the Sons of Liberty in North Carolina along with Walter Gibson and Farquhard Campbell.[623] He then represented Campbellton in the General Assembly from 1773 to 1775, and by April 1775, he was a member of the Second Provincial Congress.[624]

Rowan has been regarded as the leader behind the Liberty Point Resolves and was the first person to sign the document.[625] The *Raleigh Weekly Sentinel* said that Rowan "was to the signers of the Cumberland declaration in 1775 what Jefferson was to the signers of the national declaration in 1776."[626]

After signing the Resolves and serving as a delegate at the Third Provincial Congress in August 1775, Rowan was appointed a captain in the 1st NC Regiment under Col. James Moore in the North Carolina Continental Line until June 29, 1776, when he resigned.[627] During his service, Rowan's company blocked the Highlanders from marching to Wilmington over Rockfish Creek and probably helped round up prisoners after the Battle of Moores Creek Bridge.[628] Nine other signers were under Rowan in the Continental Line following the battle while the prisoners were being held at Campbellton.[629]

Eyewitness Hugh McDonald, who was fourteen at the time, gave Rowan credit for more than just participating in the battle at Moores Creek:

> Robert Rowan was the first officer that raised a company of men on Cape Fear in defense of his country when General McDonald raised the Royal standard in Fayetteville and collected many hundred of the Scotch in order to join Governor Martin at the mouth of Cape Fear. Capt. Rowan raised a company of minutemen and joined the minutemen under Col. Lillington, and Col. Caswell, and were in search of the army of the Tories, and hearing that General McDonald was marching in haste to join Govr. Martin, the Americans entrenched themselves near Moores Creek on the road in which Genl. McDonald and his Tories were marching. Capt. Rowan projected the plan of uncovering the Bridge in the night [at Moores Creek] and greasing the sleepers with soft soap and tallow, and when the Tories came to the Bridge about break of Day they attempted to cross on the sleepers, the Americans let the front get near the bank on the opposite side when they fired on them with their Artillery and musketry and swept them all off the Bridge, and the whole army was driven back in confusion.[630]

McDonald's account awarded Rowan credit for the Patriot victory at the Battle of Moores Creek Bridge. Is this true? The National Park Service account of the battle by Charles Hatch says that Caswell had directed his men to uncover the bridge but does not specify where the idea came from.[631] Historian Hugh Rankin also only says that Caswell ordered the sleepers covered with soap and tallow.[632] It is plausible that one of his officers, such as Rowan, suggested it to him, which is made more plausible by Rowan's prior relationship with Caswell dating back to 1763 (Caswell had been on his bond for his clerk position in Johnston County), and at Moores Creek, Rowan was a captain, and captains often served as aides-de-camp for colonels, such as Colonel Caswell. Considering that Hugh McDonald, the writer of the account crediting Rowan had originally served as a Loyalist, he would probably not be biased *for* Rowan. The most plausible outcome is that Rowan came up with the plan that led to the Patriot victory at Moores Creek.

Later that year, Rowan's company served at the Breech Inlet Naval Battle in South Carolina in June, and also the Battle of Fort Moultree.[633] Rowan then joined Phillip Alston and Col. Jeduthun Harper as commissioners of an Iron Works in Cumberland, and Rowan and Peter Mallett took custody of a supply of salt at Cross Creek in 1776. Rowan later wrote a letter to Gen.

John Ashe on July 30, 1777, where he described how "with a small company of volunteers I quelled a mob of about 140 persons" who "came here with a design...of taking the salt by force, and paying what price they thought proper...we seized the greatest number, & upon their taking the oath to the State, and appearing very penitent, we allowed them what salt they wanted at the market price."[634] This same month, Rowan and eleven other Liberty Point Resolves signers signed a loyalty oath from the state where they promised to "bear faithfull [*sic*] and true Allegiance to the State of No. Carolina and will to the utmost of my power Support, maintain and defend the independend [*sic*] Government thereof, against George the Third..."[635] Rowan also was the first individual to sign a Test Oath in 1777, which was an oath designed to exclude Roman Catholics from public office.[636]

Around this time, Rowan was accused of being a Tory by fellow signer Walter Murray and other leading town officials, because he had opposed "the ruling faction" and criticized the harsh measures that Cumberland County Patriots were dealing out on Tories in the region.[637] This was a serious accusation, as a new General Assembly law said that anyone who fought for the British Crown, or provided aid comfort, or other support to the British if convicted by the evidence of two or more witnesses would be "guilty of High-Treason, and shall suffer Death without the Benefit of Clergy, and his or her Estate shall be forfeited to the State."[638]

Rowan defended himself in a letter to Governor Caswell, saying that William Rand "has falsely and maliciously reported that I had turned Tory" and went on to say that Walter Murray and John Matthews had been:

> drawn over by the artifices of Rand [and now] look upon me as an obstacle to their designs, that they will not have it in their power to tyranise over the people in the manner they would wish, while I am in the least degree of credit with them. They know that I abhor tyranny in every shape, and therefore are determined to strike at me, and all those that I have any influence with. This is evident, they have attempted it already, and marked me and all my friends as Tories—(I would much rather at this time be called a Horse thief).[639]

Rowan said that his actions proved that he is not a Tory, and that he had been doing more work for independence than those who had accused him of being a Tory: "I fancy it would be difficult to find many people in my situation, that exerted themselves more in the defense of the Country, but I have never made a merit of it, in doing my utmost, I only did my duty, and am ready to do it again, when there may be occasion, I am only unhappy to live to be trampled upon by those that did nothing."[640]

Rowan claimed that Phillip Alston (who had just served with Rowan as a commissioner of the iron works) was one of the ringleaders of the slur against him. He also stated that Murray and Matthews could not think him an enemy to the American cause, since they were there with the salt mob and had seen how he defended the state against the mob.[641] Rowan goes on to note that Alston had arrested Conner Donnel and accused him of treason, and Alston had said that even if the justices released Donnel, Alston would put him back in jail. Rowan then told Alston that he would be a tyrant if he did that, which "threw him into a violent passion," and caused Alston to act with "personal resentment and malice."[642] Rowan said that "Mr Alston seems to rule them [the Cumberland court] all, and a greater tyrant is not upon earth according to his power, and it is much to be lamented, that about two or three years ago, no Gentleman that had the least regard for his character would have kept this hectoring, domineering, person company."[643]

However, Rowan *did* have active ties to some who were later accused of being Loyalists. Moore County genealogist George Willcox even suggests that Rowan had "been an integral part of a group of Loyalists who dominated the politics of Cumberland for many years" and that Rowan, while a Patriot, "had been so closely associated with the loyalists that he was accused of being a Tory."[644] He claims that Rowan was angry that he had been beaten for County clerk by William Rand, while Alston was simply a "hard nosed" patriot who "effectively" dealt with his country's enemies during the independence struggle.[645]

Rowan did have prior connections with some prominent Cumberland County Loyalists; in 1773, he was a member of the House along with Farquhard Campbell and Alexander McAllister, both of whom became Loyalists.[646] When he was a member of the 1775 Provincial Congress, he was joined by Farquhard Campbell, Thomas Rutherford, Alexander McKay, James Hepburn, Alexander McAllister and David Smith, of whom only David Smith was a Patriot throughout the whole war.[647] While Rowan was clearly a Patriot, demonstrated by his signing of the Resolves, intercepting a letter to Governor Martin, plus his heroic actions at Moores Creek and throughout the war, in this instance he was not aggressive enough for Alston's liking, leading to their conflict.

This was not Rowan's last run-in with Phillip Alston. The next year, in 1778, Governor Caswell promoted Rowan to colonel of the Cumberland militia regiment (after David Smith had resigned), as Caswell said he wanted "a diligent, & active officer," one who was "well acquainted with the different Manners and Customs of the People in that County and one whose past conduct and knowledge in Military matters will give him weight with those people," and then recommended Rowan in April 1778.[648] Caswell had previously served with Rowan at Moores Creek, and had a relationship with him, which helps explain Rowan's nomination. However, his promotion passed over Lieutenant Colonel Philip Alston, which infuriated Alston. Alston promptly petitioned the General Assembly, saying that Rowan's selection injured him, as "in right of his office as Lieutenant Colonel he ought to have succeeded to the office of Colonel."[649] Alston said that Rowan had "by means of some unfair Representation was at the last Session of the Genl. Assembly appointed to the Command of the Regiment of Militia for sd [said] County in exclusion of the petitioner and with a disregard to the Common line of Preferment in Military arrangements" and Alston "humbly hopes for his Proper Promotion so that the said Robt. Rowan Esqr. may be superseded" in August 1778.[650]

As a result of the complaint, Rowan then decided to resign his commission that very month, August 1778, leading to Alston's appointment.[651] This same year, Rowan joined the General Assembly and introduced the bill which led to Campbellton and Cross Creek combining into Upper and Lower Campbellton, which later became Fayetteville in 1783, and then served as one of the first commissioners of the town.[652] In 1779, he was appointed the deputy commissary of military stores and the deputy clothier general by the General Assembly for the state.[653] In this role, he supplied both General Gates and later General Greene of the Continental Army.[654]

Rowan's war conduct shows that rather than being a Tory, "his zeal and activity in the cause of liberty" [Rowan] provoked the Tories to make many efforts to get him in their power," including threatening his wife, all to no avail.[655] The Loyalists finally captured Rowan later in the war, along with Theophilus Evans and Thomas Sewell: "they all three were locked up in an old house near Cross Creek and a guard set over them with intention to hang them at 10 o'clock next day. They showed no uneasiness but appeared resigned to their fate. The guard seeing them so contented thought there no danger of their escape, being weary fell asleep."[656] At this, Rowan and the others "contrived to get the ropes loose with which they were tied, when they all made their escape by climbing up the chimney. As soon as they reached the ground, each one aimed for the American camp with all the speed he could, and they separately arrived there in perfect safety."[657]

In December 1780, while still serving in his role of deputy clothier general for the state, Continental Army Gen. Nathaniel Greene wrote to Rowan, asking if he could supply clothes for Greene's army. Greene informed him that "the state of the army is such, with respect to clothing and shoes, that I wish to see and consult with you upon some plan for securing a supply, particularly of the later articles."[658] During the war, Rowan was also one of the commissioners who would take possession of confiscated property from Loyalists in Cumberland.[659]

Rowan owned numerous enslaved persons, and in 1781, when the British passed through Cross Creek, Rowan "found that the greater part of his slaves had fled to the British and he asked [Thomas] Cabeen to accompany him to Wilmington to recover them."[660] In the previous year's tax assessment (1780), Rowan was listed as owning seven enslaved persons along with five horses, twenty-one cattle, and numerous lots in Campbellton, along with 214 acres by the Cape Fear River. His total property value was £13,730.[661]

Later in 1781, when a band of Tories passed through Cross Creek, not only did Rowan's enslaved people go with the British, but Rowan himself also was captured. John Ramsey wrote to General Burke on August 21, 1781, telling him that on August 14, 1781, Cross Creek "fell a Prey to the Tories. Their Number was said to be between Six and Seven Hundred, and they took Fifty Prisoners, amongst which are Cols. Emmet[,] Rowan[,] Messrs. Cochran[,] Winslow," among others, and that they had left Cross Creek, and Fanning was now heading toward Wilmington.[662]

When Upper and Lower Campbellton became Fayetteville in 1783, Robert Rowan was one of the first directors of the town, and his duty was "to regulate the streets and keep the same clean and in repair, and to prevent all encroachments thereon, or nuisances in any part of the said town, and to do everything for the good government thereof agreeable to the directions of this Act."[663]

He also kept his financial obligations. Starting in December 1775, North Carolina had closed its courts to creditors who refused to take oaths to the Patriot cause, which put American debtors out of reach of British creditors.[664] However, this had ended in 1783, and at the Treaty of Paris, American representatives agreed to Article Four, which said there would be no restrictions on British creditors recovering debt from Americans after the war.[665] Now American debtors were on the hook, and because of numerous factors, many labored to pay British creditors.[666] But Rowan had competently maintained his finances, and while British merchants struggled to reclaim owed money from many Americans, they did not face this issue with Rowan; the merchants state that "[Rowan] actually paid since the war."[667]

Despite Rowan's busy life, he still had the time to serve as the guardian for multiple orphans as well: William and Richard Watson in October 1774, Margret and William Simpson in 1785, and William Sproal in 1787, along with having another orphan, Nancy Poston, eleven, bound to him in 1772 until she turned eighteen.[668] Rowan owned a considerable amount of property in Fayetteville, and Rowan Street is believed to be named for him.[669] Rowan was also the stepfather of Congressman William Barry Grove, son of Richard and Susanna, and William served as a Cumberland delegate at the North Carolina Ratification Convention and later served in the US Congress.[670] Grove had also fought hard in a losing effort to make Fayetteville the state capital.[671] He was known as "Rowan's boy" and carried on his law practice in his stepfather's colonial mansion.[672] Rowan had a home in Fayetteville on Rowan Street but lived at his plantation at Hollybrook, which was three to four miles from Cross Creek on what is now Old Wilmington Road, near the Cape Fear River.[673]

After the war, Rowan again served in the General Assembly in 1785 and then was nominated for the Brigadier General position for the district of Fayette militia in 1787, though he lost out to Richard Clinton.[674] He also served as a commissioner for purchasing tobacco for Fayetteville, under a General Assembly law that regulated the sale of tobacco.[675] Rowan was later praised for his work in this position, with the merchants of Fayetteville extolling "the careful and praiseworthy conduct of Robert Rowan, Esq., in the Business of Purchasing Tobacco for the use of the public."[676] In 1792, Rowan was mentioned in a Treasury Department letter to Alexander Hamilton as being qualified for the Treasury Department's Office of Inspector for the First Survey of North Carolina.[677] In February 1798, President John Adams nominated Rowan to be the Commissioner of Loans for all of North Carolina.[678] Commissioners would manage federal debt on a state-by-state basis.[679] After being appointed, Rowan wrote back to President Adams on March 13, saying that he would "endeavor to execute to the best of my knowledge and ability...it is my best inclinations to prove myself worthy of your approbation."[680] He held that post until his death later that year.[681]

Rowan died on October 26, 1798, and at his death it was supposedly said that he "was an early and steady friend to American Independence. In Domestic & private life he was affectionate[,] sincere[,] generous[,] & cheerful."[682] In 1972, his remains were moved to Cross Creek Cemetery #1 by the Daughters of the American Revolution (DAR), which has a local chapter named after him: the Colonel Robert Rowan Chapter.[683]

Robert and Susanna had the following children: Robert Jr. (the eldest), Thomas, Suzanne (married John Hay), Julia (married John Lewis Taylor, first justice of North Carolina's Supreme Court), and Jane (married to Dr. Alexander MacQueen).[684] As of 1791, Rowan owned 242 acres and seven enslaved persons.[685] When Rowan died, he owned cattle, horses and sheep, and his enslaved individuals (Dick, Phillis, Ceasar, Jim, and Hollis) were given to his wife Susanna. His eldest son, Robert Jr., was cut out of the will, with Robert Sr. saying, "lastly I give and bequest to my eldest son Robert, one shilling the reason of this bequest will be well known to the world."[686] Theophilus and David Evans were witnesses to his will, and were frequent associates of him in life.[687]

David Shepherd

David Shepherd, like several other signers, made his living running his own tavern.[688] In February 1776, he was also one of the twenty-four signers who served in the militia company led by signer Arthur Council during the Battle of Moores Creek Bridge.[689] While he may have participated in other militia activity throughout the remainder of the war, the records show that he remained in Fayetteville and became an active and well-known member of the community. In July 1777, he was one of the men who swore and signed the Oath of Allegiance in court.[690] During that same court session he was appointed as overseer of the road from Cross Creek to Campbellton.[691] He was also chosen as one of three commissioners who were charged with laying out a road reaching from the mouth of Locks Creek to "William Lord's ferry road," and working the "hands" (i.e., enslaved persons) to establish the same.[692]

It appears that in the summer of 1777, David Shepherd had recently moved. On the last day of the July session he "prayed lisence [*sic*] to keep a tavern at his new dwelling house in Campbleton."[693] His request was granted and fellow signers John Oveler and Lewis Bowell were named as securities for him.[694] While the location eventually changed he continued to operate a tavern until the 1820s, with the last one being on Liberty Point itself.[695]

Throughout the years, David Shepherd participated in the annual celebrations of Independence, most notably during the thirtieth anniversary of the signing in 1805.[696] For this Fourth of July celebration, he provided a "sumptuous Dinner" for fellow signer Capt. James Dick's company of riflemen and other guests, at which dinner Capt. Dick presided over as president.[697] He also continued to be active in the community and he was known to keep the memory of the Liberty Point Resolves alive.[698] He last appears in the Cumberland County court records in 1826 when he sold some land to "James Millar [*sic*]" on March 11 of that year.[699] An article published in an 1830 edition of the *North-Carolina Journal*, which discusses the Liberty Point Resolves, was picked up by the *Raleigh Register*, and in a portion defending the veracity of the document, the author specifies "it has not been two years since David Shephard [*sic*], one of the signers, died in this place [i.e. Fayetteville]," thus establishing his death in 1828 or 1829.[700]

Charles Stevens

There are numerous accounts of a Charles Stevens purchasing land in Cumberland County from the 1760s to 1770s.[701] In 1772, Charles Stevens sold "one Negroe fellow Named Cesar about twenty years of age," to Farquhard Campbell for £63 14s.[702] In 1772, after the death of Neill Curry, Charles Stevens was put in charge of selling the effects of Neill Curry's estate and administering those funds to "discharge the funeral expenses of the deceased and the surplus, if any, be paid to Richd. Lyon and Co…"; additionally, some of the funds would be used to support the care of Curry's infant son.[703] Then in January 1775, we see "Margaret Carroll, a mulatto girl, bound to Charles Stevens till age 18."[704] Another signer, Lewis Barge, stated that, "Charles Stevens an inhabitant of Cumberland county died about the year 1780 insolvent[;] he had always been considered as a person not worthy of credit."[705]

Given the large amount of land exchanged by and through Charles Stevens, that claim from Lewis Barge may be false. It is possible that this comment derived from a personal dispute between Stevens and Barge, and it is also possible that this Charles Stevens is in fact being mistaken for another. In May 1770, the Wilmington District Superior Court held a case in which it was determined that "Charles Stephens of Cumberland County" was mistaken for another Charles Stephens, who was indicted for petty larceny.[706] Not much else is known about Charles Stevens.

John Stevenson (Forgotten Signer)

John Stevenson (sometimes written as Stevens) was a tailor.[707] He is listed in the 1777 tax list as being valued at £1,315, and in the 1767 tax list he appears to have lived alone.[708] There were other men named John Stevens who appear in numerous deed entries from the time period, but are most likely not him, as they do not appear to be the same individual as the one on the 1767 tax list. He also signed the 1777 Oath with the Act of Assembly saying they would support North Carolina against the Crown.[709] Nothing else is known about him.

Micajah Terrell

Micajah Terrell was born April 22, 1746, in North Carolina and was the son of Timothy Terrell and Mary Martin.[710] He married Hannah Goodman, and in February 1773, the two appear in a Cumberland County deed selling 440 acres of land to fellow signer John Parker, the land being part of the 640 acres previously conveyed to Hannah by her father, Samuel Goodman.[711] Micajah Terrell and the Parker brothers, John and Kader, submitted a land entry for 300 acres in Cumberland County in January 1773, which was patented on July 25, 1774.[712] Micajah Terrell and the Parkers appear in other Cumberland County records as well, though there is no indication as to whether there is a familial connection or if it is only fraternal.[713]

Micajah Terrell was a member of the Cumberland County militia early on and served under fellow signer Arthur Council in August 1775.[714] He later served under fellow signer Robert Rowan for a time as well.[715] After the war, he continued to accumulate land and grow his family.[716] By 1792, he had ten children: five boys and five girls.[717] Shortly after 1800, Micajah Terrell and his family moved to Natchez, Mississippi.[718] His will of October 1805 was probated in the court session of January 1806 in Adams County, Mississippi.[719]

Aaron Vardy (Loyalist)

Aaron Vardy was originally from England and came to America and settled at Cross Creek in 1770, where he was a tavern keeper (his wife appears to have been named Frances).[720] He was granted a license to a tavern in Cumberland

County in 1774, and it was renewed the next year.[721] He also served as a patroller in Cross Creek in 1774.[722] After the Battle of Lexington and Concord, he signed the Liberty Point Resolves, and later accompanied some Patriots on the way to intercept a letter to Governor Martin. When questioned later about his support of the Patriots in 1775, he claimed that he "never took any oath or signed any Association to the Americans," but that at times the Americans, led by Robert Rowan, compelled him to help them, such as on that November 1775 endeavor to intercept the letter.[723] Yet the British did not let him off the hook so easily: "Being further questioned as to his conduct prior to Jan 1776 and Governor Martin's instructions to him—Says Governor Martins instructions to him were to remain quiet and with respect to his acting in the manner he did in in intercepting Governor Martin's letter he resisted it and denied his having a horse to ride on but was at last forced to submit."[724]

Fellow Loyalist Maurice Nowlan stated that to his knowledge, Vardy was loyal and that he had been coerced into intercepting that letter by "Mr. Robert Rowan of Cross Creek," but Nowlan thought that it "was no detriment to the British cause" and that Vardy "did not at the time show any reluctance to going."[725] Nowlan also admitted that two or three times, he and Vardy were mustered with a company at Cross Creek for manual exercises but that it was "not in favor of Gr [*sic*] Britain."[726] Nowlan confirmed that in 1776, Vardy joined the Loyalists and ever since then was attached to Great Britain, and that Vardy's wagon and four horses were captured at Moores Creek.[727] Governor Martin himself vouched for Aaron Vardy after his death in 1785, saying that "he understood he was among the people who first took part with Great Britain" and regarding his interception of the letter that Cunningham was carrying, Martin "does not infer any thing against the loyalty of the claimant."[728]

Vardy joined the Loyalists in January 1776 and was a captain and served as wagon-master under General MacDonald.[729] At Moores Creek Bridge he was taken prisoner and spent time in jail at Halifax, North Carolina. Vardy was then sent to Fredericktown, Maryland, as a prisoner of war at the end of April 1776.[730] He lost 200 hundred acres in Anson County for his Loyalist ties, along with his horses and other supplies.[731]

After being "confined to a Dungeon," he "finally escaped with great hazard and with the utmost difficulty through wild woods and mountains," making his escape on September 23, 1776, with six other Tories.[732] Vardy was described as: "An Englishman, about six feet high, a very strong well made man, ruddy complexion, has short brown curled hair, had an old brown broad cloth coat & jackett, a pair of leather breeches, stocking shoes and an old hat."[733]

On his journey back to North Carolina, Vardy claimed he had "nothing to subsist on for 5 weeks but wild roots and herbs and was almost perished with hunger before he got among the friends to Government in that province."[734] The Patriots had put a price on his head, so he hid out in the woods and swamps for the next eighteen months. He did not like hiding out, but "what grieved him more than all his sufferings was the close confinement of his wife by the Rebels which they did to prevent her giving any intelligence to your Memorist. At length being tired of leading a Forest life and hearing that the Royal Army had got possession of Philadelphia he immediately concluded to alter his name and travel through the country in disguise which he effected to his entire [*sic*] satisfaction and got safe to that city."[735] After Moores Creek, Vardy discovered that his family was being watched during his imprisonment, and that his escape had made it difficult for them.[736]

In January 1779, he was made wagon master in the Southern District for four years and then assistant agent for army vessels in the Expeditionary Force, and in 1780, he joined General Cornwallis in North Carolina and became part of the North Carolina Highland Regiment, with the rank of captain.[737] He then bought land in British territory in Florida near St. Augustine, not thinking that the province would be given to the Spanish in 1783.[738] He owned a schooner called the *Edward* which was used by the British army at Charleston but sunk in service in August 1782 when Vardy "was aboard her with 4 negroes."[739] His Loyalist claim was made in 1784 by Alexander McKay, Connor Bond, and Daniel McNabb regarding his estate. He had owned 200 acres in Anson County, a personal estate in Cumberland, and a plantation, house, and 100 acres in St. Augustine, Florida.[740] All told, his loyalist claim was for £764 7s. 10½d.[741]

Robert Varner

Robert Varner served in the Revolutionary War as part of the 1st NC Regiment under Captain Henry Dixon.[742] He first joined the service on March 28, 1776, and was commissioned at the rank of ensign.[743] He received his first promotion to second lieutenant on July 7, 1776, and his second promotion to first lieutenant on March 8, 1777.[744] By the summer of 1779 he was running the company assigned to the regimental commander (Lt. Col. William

Lee Davidson at the time) and held the position of "Captain-Lieutenant."[745] This position carried the authority of a captain and the pay of a lieutenant and allowed the regimental commander to focus on the regiment as a whole without having to run the day-to-day operations of the company.[746]

It would seem that Captain-Lieutenant Varner abused the authority of his position, because on August 25, 1779, he was the subject of a Court of Inquiry for "playing Cards in Camp contrary to General, Brigade, and Regimental Orders, encouraging the soldiers in the same practice by certain expressions when he was President of a Brigade Court-Martial on the trial of prisoners for that crime, and not sending for evidence against the prisoners charged with playing Cards, and for allowing the Court to set them free for want of evidence before Lieutt Dickinson (who went for evidence and desired the court to wait) could return with the evidence."[747] The Court of Inquiry determined the charges were justly founded and serious enough to warrant a court-martial.[748] Captain-Lieutenant Varner was placed under arrest, and he was tried at the General Court-Martial held on September 21, 1779.[749] At this court he was formally charged with repeatedly violating orders by playing cards and with "conniving at and encouraging the same practice among the soldiers," both of the charges the Court of Inquiry had deemed to be justified. In addition to these charges, he was also charged with "playing Cards in camp since his Arrest in contempt of orders" and (more seriously) with "breaking his Arrest."[750]

Under the Articles of War, the fourth charge alone was grounds for Varner to be cashiered (the equivalent of receiving a dishonorable discharge).[751] It almost goes without saying that the court found Varner to be guilty. They stated the first and third charges were breaches of General Washington's orders issued January 8, 1778, the second charge was a violation of section 18 article 5 of the Articles of War, and the fourth charge was a violation of section 14 article 20, so the court sentenced Varner to be cashiered.[752] Washington himself confirmed the sentence of the court and ordered it to take place immediately.[753] He was cashiered on October 1, 1779.[754]

Robert Varner obtained a land warrant for 1,280 acres after his time in the war.[755] He then served as the deputy quarter master of the port of Fayetteville, having been appointed by Quarter Master General of North Carolina, Robert Burton.[756] He was taken prisoner by the British army at Brown Marsh in Bladen County around 1781, and died shortly after his capture.[757]

In December of 1791, Robert Burton petitioned the General Assembly for the return of some missing funds. Robert Varner had been granted three warrants by Burton before his capture. Burton believed the British destroyed the warrants, and he did not receive his payments, totaling £30,000. The General Assembly determined the above to be true and directed the comptroller give Burton a certificate for the missing funds.[758]

Onesiphorous West (Forgotten Signer)

Before living in North Carolina, Onesiphorous West lived in Massachusetts. He was the ninth child of Stephen and Susannah (nee Jenney) West. His siblings included: Hannah, Mary, Samuel, Anne, Almy, Stephen, Bartholomew, and Susannah.[759] Between late 1738 and early 1739, West married Zilpha Wood in Dartmouth, Massachusetts.[760] The couple had five children between 1739–1746: two sons and three daughters. The children were named Zephaniah, Anstice, Hannah, Eunice, and Jacob.[761] In 1740, West went to court to claim that Edward Kirbey from Newport trespassed and damaged West's barn and property; Kirbey denied the accusation but the jury awarded damages to West.[762] The situation was brought up again in a later court session, in which judgment was affirmed alongside added costs.[763] On March 20, 1744, West was chosen as a leather sealer, most likely in relation to his occupation as a saddler.[764]

He later left Massachusetts without his wife, as Zilpha's father openly acknowledged her husband's departure: "provided that she [Zilpha] should be reduced to want and her husband does not return to take care of her..."[765] He wrote his will about 1773 and made further adjustments after her death in 1778. With her death in Bristol County, the amount of his property owed to her then passed to her children as part of his will.[766] Onesiphorous, however, had moved to North Carolina, showing up by 1763 in New Bern. He also appeared in these North Carolina records with a new wife, a woman named Margaret.[767] Onesiphorous and Margaret West were found in other parts of North Carolina as well, including Anson County. During this occasion, executors of William Hoggatt's estate sold 100 acres to West, with Margaret as a witness. Right after, West sold the same land to James Auld.[768]

After he joined the Cross Creek community, West signed an early petition to the General Assembly of North Carolina, joining the argument for better roads for the town. This same petition also requested for Cross Creek and Campbellton to be instead called Upper and Lower Campbellton to ease confusion.[769] On January 25, 1776, "Onisipherus" West took over the administration of Sarah Allen's estate and "entered into court an inventory of the estate."[770] Three years later in November, Onesiphorous' marriage to Margeret (formerly Lawson from a prior marriage), granted him more property through her late husband's will. He acquired 400 acres in Craven County by Swift Creek, and he received more land in the New Bern area.[771] On January 25, 1785, he became Fayetteville's overseer for Matthew's Bridge; his responsibility was to repair his half of the bridge if there was ever an issue. During this time span, in 1786, he went to court against John McNeill. He won the case and earned monetary payments of an estimate of forty-three pounds.[772] In 1788, he was replaced as the road overseer by Stephen Gilmore.[773] Later in April that year, West was once again in court against John McNeill, since McNeill desired to overturn the decision; McNeill was discharged from his bail.[774] By 1790, West still lived in Cumberland County, with two other older men and one woman living with him.[775] Onesiphorous West died in 1793, attended to by his daughter, Rebecca West, before he passed away.[776]

Thomas White (Forgotten Signer)

Thomas White's name appears early in 1754, in which he signed a petition to Arthur Dobbs, the governor of North Carolina. The petition requested that the "Commissioners of the Several Districts" in New Hanover County would be instructed to build better, standardized roads to help both travelers and county inhabitants. The request was stated to be especially helpful after the ferries were established alongside the Cape Fear River, so that transportation between the river and townships could be easier.[777]

He lived in Bladen County by 1747, where he is described as a planter. He sold half an acre of land in Brunswick to George Richardson of Brunswick for five shillings sterling.[778] In 1761, White sold 200 acres of land to a William Howe.[779] On August 13, 1782, White released 136 acres to another purchaser, a Joseph Wood, for twenty pounds in Bladen County.[780] Later in July 1785, Thomas White paid twenty-five pounds to Robert Green for "more or less" 100 acres, starting at a branch of Pughs Marsh in Bladen County (currently Little Marsh Swamp in Robeson County). Both men are acknowledged as living in Cumberland County at this time, although the deed itself was proved in Bladen in August 1786.[781] Years later, on February 6, 1798, Thomas White identified himself as residing in Cumberland County for a Robeson County bill of sale. In the document, he sold a twenty-year-old enslaved man named Bob to one Neill W. Alphin and stated he had previously purchased this enslaved person from William Russell in Campbellton.[782]

Similar to other signers of Cumberland County, he served as a lieutenant under Capt. Arthur Council in February 1776.[783] He most likely served under Col. Richard Caswell too about the same time.[784] During April of the same year, White served as a first lieutenant under Captain Council again and returned in January 1779, serving as captain in the 5th NC Regiment.[785] He left the service afterward that same year in December.[786] He lived in Cumberland County, appearing in the 1800 North Carolina Census.[787] White later started a tanning and currying business in Fayetteville with John Egan.

> THOMAS WHITE & JOHN EGAN, Inform the public in general, and their friends in particular, that they propose carrying on the TANNING and CURRYING business in this town, and that they will give eash or leather for hides, or tan by the share—Currying on reasonable terms...[788]

Thomas White died by December 1802, as mentioned in the newspaper by Isabella White during an advertisement for a lost horse on December 10th.

> Strayed, or was stolen from the lot of Thomas White, late of Fayetteville, dec. about the 11th of Sept. last, a dark Roan Mare, branded G. D. on the buttock of the mounting fide...has been worked in the waggon of the dec. and will probably bear the mark of the traces, and she is well known about Fayetteville. The above reward will be paid on delivery of her to the subsriber, or a much greater Reward if she was stolen and the thief can be convicted.[789]

Similarly, Isabella White was appointed as the executrix for Thomas White by the Court of Pleas and Quarter Sessions of Cumberland County.[790] He is buried at the historically registered Cross Creek #1 Cemetery in Fayetteville, North Carolina.[791]

William White

William White the signer has previously been confused with another William White from Cumberland County, who was the father-in-law of fellow signer Maurice Nowlan.[792] William White the father-in-law actually died in 1774, and his will from that date stated that he gave his "granddaughter Catrain Knowlan rest of my estate at age 18, with reversion to my nephew James White son of my brother James dec'd."[793] William White the signer does make an appearance in the records, being appointed as a patroller in the district of Campbellton, along with fellow signer James Dick and two others, in July 1777.[794] He is also listed as a debtor in the claims of John Hay & Co. with a debt from 1 January 1776, and his residence given as Cross Creek.[795] Unfortunately, the note from the special agent who came to collect the debt stated, "Died about the year 1783 or 4 leaving no estate."[796]

John Wilson

The records do not reveal much about the signer John Wilson but reveal more about his uncle and his father. In fact, the 1790 Census of Cumberland County shows three different John Wilsons, two of which lived in Fayetteville.[797] What we can determine about the signer John Wilson, however, is in part through his father Sylvanus. John and Sylvanus Wilson first appeared in the Cumberland County records in the mid-1760s when Sylvanus received two separate 200-acre land grants in October 1765.[798] Then, on the 1767 list of taxables for Cumberland County, Sylvanus appeared along with his brother John (uncle of the signer John Wilson) and were the only Wilsons listed.[799] This John cannot be the signer, because John the signer would have been too young at this time, having been born in 1756.[800] According to the 1780 tax list, Sylvanus had clearly done well and increased his net worth so that his taxable property totals £125,000 (what is being assessed is not recorded), whereas no John is listed at all (his brother John having died by this time and his son John was still a part of his household).[801] In 1783, other Wilsons first appeared on the list of taxables, though only one John and one Sylvanus.[802] For whatever is being assessed in this year, Sylvanus is shown to have £1,760 of taxable property and John only £100.[803]

More of their circumstances can be understood by turning to the records of claims by British merchants after the war and the reports generated by their agents. The 1799 report of an agent for John Hay & Co. shows that for a debt from December 14, 1775, "John and Sylvanus Wilson paid with Int[erest]: Jan:25.1786;" the agent specifies, however, that the payments he records in his list "have been paid in deprecated Paper money."[804] Once again, this is John the brother of Sylvanus and not John the son of Sylvanus. The younger John would not yet have been twenty-one and under British common law would not have been able to write a promissory note (i.e., an IOU).[805] An 1800 report by an agent for William Campbell & Co. shows that John Wilson, and an unspecified "Blyth," had "a debt anew" with a date of July 1, 1784, and the note from the agent states "both dead 1788 insolvent."[806] Around 1804, another agent for John Hay & Co was sent to collect on what was still owed based on the value of the original debts and not the face value of the previously collected paper money. His note on the December 1775 debt of John and Sylvanus Wilson states that, "They are both dead. Sylvanus died about 16 years [ago], solvent, but since then his Estate has been rendered insolvent by reason of a decree in Equity in favor of the Ex[ecuto]rs of Robert Hogg."[807]

Confirmation that this is the correct Sylvanus Wilson, and by extension the correct John, is found in the records of deeds for January 1790 when Sheriff Thomas Armstrong sold the land of Sylvanus Wilson to John Sibley in order to cover a debt against the executors of Sylvanus Wilson's estate.[808] In the May 1791 marriage contract between John Sibley and Mary Winslow, this land is further specified as the exact land that Sylvanus Wilson was granted in 1765.[809] A final piece of evidence identifying the signer John Wilson can be found on a petition to the North Carolina General Assembly dated January 31, 1795, (almost twenty years after Sylvanus' brother John died).[810] The petition is requesting reimbursement for the costs associated with providing firewood for the General Assembly at their previous meeting in Fayetteville, and it is signed by a John Wilson with a signature that matches the one on the Liberty Point Resolves.[811] Thus, by incorporating the records of Sylvanus Wilson, we learn which John Wilson in these records was his brother and which was his son. This distinction also leaves open the possibility that the signer John Wilson is the same John Wilson who married a daughter of fellow signer Lewis Barge, as the Barge family has suggested.[812]

Notes

1. Lewis, *NC Patriots* 2(2):42.

2. Moss, Roster of Patriots, 11.

3. According to the Revolutionary War Pension Project (a collaboration between the National Park Service and the National Archives and Records Administration), "[r]ecords kept by militias were incomplete at best" (National Park Service, "Revolutionary War Pension Files."

4. NC Land Grant Office, "Warrants, Surveys, and Related Documents—Washington County," roll 2, https://familysearch.org/ark:/61903/3:1:3QSQ-G9WV-BXMQ. Document reads: "State of North Carolina Washington County Octr. 9 1779 / No. 1911 } To the surveyor of the sd. County You are hereby Required to measure & lay of[f] according to law fifty acres of Land for Simeon Bundy on the Wt. Side of Gap Creek including a sink-hole with a black walnut tree in it, Given under my hand this 12 of Feby. 1780 ~ / John Carter E. T."

5. "Residences of the First Settlers of Watauga," 2. The City of Elizabethton purchased Big Spring in 1981, and the water treatment facility was completed in 1983.

6. Washington County, NC and TN, "Court Records," folder 4, p. 9, https://familysearch.org/ark:/61903/3:1:3Q9M-CS4Y-4YCC. Jonesborough has the distinction of being the first city in Tennessee and is still the county seat of Washington County.

7. NC Land Grant Office, *Land Patent Books*, 47:73, "Washington Co. File No. 283, Simon Bunday," https://nclandgrants.com/grant/?mars=12.14.20.283&qid=1145441&rn=1; Washington County, NC and TN, "Court Records," folder 7, p. 8, https://familysearch.org/ark:/61903/3:1:3Q9M-CS4Y-4Y9Y.

8. Washington County, NC and TN, "Court Records," folder 7, p. 8.

9. "Lewis Barge." This memorial includes pictures of Barge's tombstone in Cross Creek Cemetery #1; "DIED, In Child Bed"; "DIED, at Fayetteville"; Weaver Jr., *Barge Families*, 75.

10. Weaver Jr., *Barge Families*, 85.

11. Cumberland County, *Record of Deeds*, 2:264, "Martha Higgins & Thomas Wilkinson to Lewis Barge, 23 July 1763," https://familysearch.org/ark:/61903/3:1:3QS7-99DC-ZCWT.

12. Cumberland County, *Minutes*, B:114v, https://familysearch.org/ark:/61903/3:1:3Q9M-CS4G-MWGB-C.

13. Weaver Jr., *Barge Families*, 85.

14. "May 3: Remitting the Tax on Houses of Lewis Barge, Campbellton." As former British subjects most items in Colonial and post-Revolutionary America were valued in pounds (£), shillings (s.), and pence (d.), with £1 worth 20s. and 1s. worth 12d. (Miller, "Colonial Currency").

15. "Last Will of Lewis Barge Senr."

16. Cumberland County, *Minutes*, B:117v, https://familysearch.org/ark:/61903/3:1:3Q9M-CS4G-MWGB-3 (document reads: "Ordered that Lewis Barge be appointed Constable in the room & District of David Davis"); Weaver Jr., *Barge Families*, 91; *CSR*, 24:180; Weaver Jr., *Barge Families*, 91; *CSR*, 24:515.

17. Fields, *Abstracts of Minutes*, 1:136, 176, 284, 324; 2:1, 3, 16, 25, 34, 45, 62, 66, 79, 95, etc.

18. Johnson, *Hometown Heritage*, 1:166.

19. Weaver Jr., i, ix. He then revised and updated the book in 1999.

20. Weaver Jr., *Barge Families*, i.

21. Weaver Jr., *Barge Families*, 3.

22. Weaver Jr., *Barge Families*, 3.

23. Weaver Jr., *Barge Families*, 13.

24. Weaver Jr., *Barge Families*, 75–78.

25. Weaver Jr., *Barge Families*, 78–90. Weaver states that a great-grandson of Lewis and Mary Barge, Dr. Hubert Barge, passed on a tradition that her name was Mary Kelly. Weaver supports this with confirmation of documents listing her as Mary K. and their oldest son was George K. Barge. Based on the close connections between the Robeson and Barge families Weaver presents a possible argument that Christiana Barge was Christiana Robeson, and points to Thomas Robeson's involvement with helping with the children after Lewis Barge died, as well as the youngest being named John Robeson Barge.

26. Walker, *New Hanover County Court Minutes*, 1:76.

27. Walker, *New Hanover County Court Minutes*, 1:91.

28. Walker, *New Hanover County Court Minutes*, 1:100.

29. Walker, *New Hanover County Court Minutes*, 2:12.

30. Barnes, "Three Pounds Reward."

31. Walker, *New Hanover County Court Minutes*, 2:21.

32. Walker, *New Hanover County Court Minutes*, 2:26.

33. Norfolk (Independent City), *Record of Deeds*, 5:148–49, https://familysearch.org/ark:/61903/3:1:3Q9M-CSL6-49LW-L.

34. Marshall, "A Norfolk, Virginia, Clock Signed 'John Jones.'"

35. Bathgate, "The Subscriber Intends to Leave Petersburg."

36. "William Bathgate," in *Taxable Property in Cumberland County for 1777*, "List of Taxables," 2, line 10, record ID CR.029.701.001, State Archives of NC, https://familysearch.org/ark:/61903/3:1:3QSQ-G98M-Z66.

37. Cumberland County, *Minutes*, D:71v, https://familysearch.org/ark:/61903/3:1:3Q9M-CS4G-MWGW-X.

38. "William Bathgate" on deed from Robert Freeman to William Farrer (7 November 1789) as part of "Freeman, William & Tabbitha 1818," in Orange County, "Estate Records," roll 19, https://familysearch.org/ark:/61903/3:1:3QS7-99C6-P9XS.

39. Whisker, *Virginia Clockmakers and Watchmakers*, 10.

40. Whisker, *Virginia Clockmakers and Watchmakers*, 10.

41. Virginia Historical Society, "The Bank of the United States," 290.

42. Whisker, *Virginia Clockmakers and Watchmakers*, 10.

43. Norfolk (Independent City), *Record of Deeds*, 3:248r, https://familysearch.org/ark:/61903/3:1:3Q9M-CSL6-4QVY-4.

44. "Bathgate, William," in Hall, "Marriages and Obituaries, 1736–1820," roll 1, https://familysearch.org/ark:/61903/3:1:33SQ-GPF9-BKB.

45. Norfolk (Independent City), *Record of Deeds*, 5:148–49, https://familysearch.org/ark:/61903/3:1:3Q9M-CSL6-49LW-L.

46. Whisker, *Virginia Clockmakers*, 10.

47. Norfolk (Independent City), *Will Books*, 1:202, https://familysearch.org/ark:/61903/3:1:3QS7-L9PX-X9YM. One Will was a "fidler" and another Will was an oysterman; the inventory makes it unclear to which Will was the older man. In the "Sales of Negroes" section, Paul Proby purchased "Old Will" for £35.5, and Jacob Shuster purchased the other Will for £48 15s. and Simon for £61 10s. James Taylor bought Mathew for fifty pounds. Richard Spralley purchased the "Woman Affa" for forty-five pounds, while John Cam[p] bought Dina/Dianna for possibly £[117 15s.].

48. See note 44 above.

49. Cumberland County, *Record of Deeds*, 4:317, "William Blocker to James Dyer, 1 April 1771," https://familysearch.org/ark:/61903/3:1:3QS7-99DC-ZCKG.

50. Fields, *Abstracts of Deeds*, 2:25.

51. McBride, "Claims of British Merchants After the Revolutionary War," pt. 5, 110.

52. Fields, *Abstracts of Deeds*, 2:112.

53. *Heads of Families at the First Census*, 51.

54. Caruthers, *Old North State in 1776*, 105; Cumberland County, *Record of Deeds*, 4:248, "John Stevens & Wife to Lewis Bowel, 8 November 1770," https://familysearch.org/ark:/61903/3:1:3QSQ-G98M-X3BX.

55. *CSR*, 9:80.

56. Caruthers, *Old North State in 1776*, 105.

57. Caruthers, *Old North State in 1776*, 106.

58. Roebuck, "Cape Fear River Basin Debtors, 1752," 99.

59. McBride, "Claims of British Merchants After the Revolutionary War," pt. 5, 111.

60. *CSR*, 18:200.

61. *CSR*, 18:200.

62. *CSR*, 18:454.

63. *CSR*, 18:461.

64. CSR, 18:233–34; *Joint Standing Committees: Committee on Finance – Subcommittee No. 4 on Application of L 100,000 Emitted (Fraud) (Nov. 21–Dec. 27)*, https://digital.ncdcr.gov/Documents/Detail/joint-standing-committees-committee-on-finance-subcommittee-no.-4-on-application-of-l-100000-emitted-fraud-nov.-21-dec.-27/828307?item=828342; *Joint Standing Committees: Committee on Finance – Subcommittee No. 2 on the Treasury, Nov. 21–Jan. 5*, https://digital.ncdcr.gov

/Documents/Detail/joint-standing-committees-committee-on-finance-subcommittee-no.-2-on-the-treasury-nov.-21-jan.-5/837887?item=837888; *Joint Select Committees: Committee for Examinations of the State Prisoners, Dec. 11–18*, https://digital.ncdcr.gov/Documents/Detail/joint-select-committees-committee-for-examinations-of-the-state-prisoners-dec.-11-18/835735?item=835736.

65. "North Carolina, Revolutionary Pay Vouchers, 1779–1782," https://familysearch.org/ark:/61903/3:1:3QS7-99WW-MF65, image 907 of 1,035https://familysearch.org/ark:/61903/3:1:3QS7-99WW-MF65.

66. "North Carolina, Revolutionary Pay Vouchers, 1779–1782," https://familysearch.org/ark:/61903/3:1:3QS7-L9WW-MFW4, image 905 of 1,035https://familysearch.org/ark:/61903/3:1:3QS7-L9WW-MFH1.

67. First Census, "Lewis Bowell," population schedule for Fayetteville town (Cumberland), NC, Fayette District, 1790, NARA microfilm M637, roll 7, Records of the Bureau of the Census, RG 29, National Archives, Washington, DC, p. 107 (handwritten), line 24, https://familysearch.org/ark:/61903/3:1:33S7-9YY8-SLHT.

68. Bowell, "Strayed or Stolen."

69. "Bowell, Lewis 1795," in Cumberland County, "Estate Records," roll 4, https://familysearch.org/ark:/61903/3:2:77TD-JVHK.

70. Cumberland County, *Record of Deeds*, 4:248, https://familysearch.org/ark:/61903/3:1:3QSQ-G98M-X3BX.

71. "Bowell, Lewis 1795," in Cumberland County, "Estate Records," roll 4, https://familysearch.org/ark:/61903/3:2:77TD-JVHL.

72. Tidwell, *Roster of Revolutionary Soldiers*, 2:23; Cates, "Legislative Petitions, 1780–1781," 43.

73. Pruitt, Cumberland County, NC, Taxables, 2.

74. Fields, *Abstracts of Minutes*, 1:305. "Patrollers" were the result of a 1753 law directing county courts to appoint three freeholders in each district to patrol in search of freedom seekers and to search the dwellings of enslaved persons for contraband (Salemson, "Slave Patrols," NCpedia, https://www.ncpedia.org/slave-patrols).

75. *CSR*, 15:209–11.

76. NC Land Grant Office, *Land Patent Books*, 52:168; "Cumberland Co. File No.1880, Thomas Cabeen," https://nclandgrants.com/grant/?mars=12.14.51.1877.

77. "NC, Revolutionary Pay Vouchers," https://familysearch.org/ark:/61903/3:1:3QS7-L9WQ-9236, image 611 of 1022https://familysearch.org/ark:/61903/3:1:3QS7-L9WQ-9236.

78. Tidwell, *Roster of Revolutionary Soldiers*, 23.

79. Pruitt, *Cumberland County, NC, Taxables*, 34.

80. "July 4: Petition of Thomas Cabeen, 1781," State Archives of NC, https://digital.ncdcr.gov/Documents/Detail/joint-papers-june-july-1781-miscellaneous-petitions/834503?item=834542.

81. "July 4: Petition of Thomas Cabeen, 1781," State Archives of NC. It is probable that Cabeen and Rowan were accompanied by James Emmet, as Emmet wrote a letter to General Greene on April 4 saying that he was going to travel to recover some slaves that had gone with the enemy around the same time (*CSR*, 15:781).

82. "July 4: Petition of Thomas Cabeen, 1781," State Archives of NC.

83. See the section on Joshua Hadley for more on their behavior.

84. "July 4: Petition of Thomas Cabeen, 1781," State Archives of NC.

85. Cates, "Legislative Petitions, 1780–1781," 43. For more see Fowler, *Valley of the Scots*, 65.

86. "July 4: Petition of Thomas Cabeen, 1781," State Archives of NC.

87. Cumberland County, *Record of Deeds*, 7:314, "Thomas Cabeen to McIver & Dick, 28 December 1784," https://familysearch.org/ark:/61903/3:1:3QS7-8983-N6C5.

88. Fields, *Abstracts of Minutes*, 2:76.

89. Parker Jr., "Revolutionary Patriot," 1; "Dec. 29: Resolution Acquitting Sundry Inhabitants." See also Hamburger, *Law and Judicial Duty*, 556–57.

90. The others were Nathan Steadman Sr., Nathan Steadman Jr., Duncan Ockeltree, and Anthony Rosney (*CSR*, 18:28–29).

91. "Dec. 29: Resolution Acquitting Sundry Inhabitants."

92. "Dec. 29: Resolution Acquitting Sundry Inhabitants."

93. "Dec. 29: Resolution Acquitting Sundry Inhabitants."

94. Dec. 29: Resolution Acquitting Sundry Inhabitants."

95. Dec. 29: Resolution Acquitting Sundry Inhabitants."

96. *CSR*, 18:403, 406–7; See Hamburger, *Law and Judicial Duty*, 557–59.

97. York County, SC, *Minutes of the Court*, A:183, https://familysearch.org/ark:/61903/3:1:3Q9M-CSLK-V1JG.

98. First Census, "Thomas Cabeen," population schedule for Chester Township, SC, 1790, NARA microfilm M637, roll 11, p. 178 (handwritten), line 14, left column, https://familysearch.org/ark:/61903/3:1:33SQ-GYBZ-4CQ.

99. Second Census, "Thomas Cobean," population schedule for Chester Township, SC, Second Census, 1800, NARA microfilm M32, roll 47, p. 332 (typed), line 17, https://familysearch.org/ark:/61903/3:1:33SQ-GR8K-DHR.

100. Tidwell, Roster of Revolutionary Soldiers, 2:23.

101. "IN RE Estate of Thomas Cabeen," file 9, package 136, in archive no. 000012/.L 12021-000004, SC Archives, Columbia, SC, https://familysearch.org/ark:/61903/3:1:939L-FN5G-1.

102. "IN RE Estate of Thomas Cabeen."

103. "IN RE Estate of Thomas Cabeen."

104. "IN RE Estate of Thomas Cabeen."

105. "IN RE Estate of Thomas Cabeen."

106. "IN RE Estate of Thomas Cabeen."

107. "IN RE Estate of Thomas Cabeen."

108. "IN RE Estate of Thomas Cabeen."

109. "IN RE Estate of Thomas Cabeen."

110. Shepherd, "Gen. D. H. Hill," 366, https://archive.org/details/confederateveter25conf/page/366/mode/2up.

111. A. C. Avery in Peele, *Lives of Distinguished North Carolinians*, 525. Avery also says that Thomas Cabeen was Sumter's trusted scout during the Revolution and was "'the bravest man in his command,' as the General himself often declared," but we have found no corroborating documentation for that claim (525).

112. Fields, *Abstracts of Deeds*, 2:90.

113. Fowler, *They Passed This Way*, 34.

114. A search among land grant files returns many hits for John Carraway in Cumberland County, such as NC Land Grant Office, "Warrants, Surveys, and Related Documents—Cumberland County," roll 1, No. 106, https://familysearch.org/ark:/61903/3:1:3QS7-99WV-Y6SQ. According to the Tax Lists for 1780, he is also listed as owning 350 acres of land, eleven enslaved persons, five horses, and forty-three cattle, for a total property of £7,582 17s. 8d. (Pruitt, *Cumberland County, NC, Taxables*, 37).

115. Fields, *Abstracts of Minutes,* 1:103. Thomas's will lists Margaret Stewart as the administrator of the estate, as she was his wife. However, it then appears that she became John Carraway's wife. This most likely means that John took in Elizabeth because she was his stepdaughter (Cumberland County, *Minutes*, B:63v, https://familysearch.org/ark:/61903/3:1:3Q9M-CS4G-MWP5-H).

116. Fields, *Abstracts of Minutes*, 1:281.

117. Fields, *Abstracts of Minutes*, 1:318, 322.

118. NC DAR, *Roster of Soldiers*, 324; "NC, Revolutionary Pay Vouchers," https://familysearch.org/ark:/61903/3:1:3QS7-89WQ-6FD, image 976 of 991.

119. First Census, "John Carraway Sr," population schedule for Cumberland (excluding Fayetteville), NC, 1790, NARA microfilm M637, roll 7, p. 88 (handwritten), line 11, https://familysearch.org/ark:/61903/3:1:33SQ-GYY8-3W4B.

120. Fields, *Abstracts of Deeds*, 1:164; Lepine and Sherman, *Will Abstracts Cumberland County*, 32–33.

121. Wyche, "North Carolina Militia," 149.

122. "Carraway, John 1795," in Cumberland County, "Original Wills," https://familysearch.org/ark:/61903/3:1:3QS7-89GW-BYC8.

123. Doris Fort, email message to author, September 11, 2024.

124. Fields, *Abstracts of Minutes*, 1:305.

125. "Carver, Robert 1797," in Cumberland County, "Original Wills," https://familysearch.org/ark:/61903/3:1:3QS7-89GW-BRMG. Doris Fort, a descendant of one of the signers, says that her last name was Newberry.

126. "Carver, Robert 1797," in Cumberland County, "Original Wills," https://familysearch.org/ark:/61903/3:1:3QS7-89GW-BRMG.

127. NC DAR, *Roster of Soldiers*, 331.

128. Pruitt, *Cumberland County, NC, Taxables*, 38.

129. *Heads of Families at the First Census*, 38.

130. "Carver, Robert 1797," in Cumberland County, "Original Wills," https://familysearch.org/ark:/61903/3:1:3QS7-89GW-BRMG.

131. "Carver, Robert 1797," in Cumberland County, "Original Wills," https://familysearch.org/ark:/61903/3:1:3QS7-89GW-BRSZ, p. 2.

132. "Carver, Robert 1797," in Cumberland County, "Original Wills," 2.

133. "Carver, Robert 1797," in Cumberland County, "Original Wills," https://familysearch.org/ark:/61903/3:1:3QS7-89GW-BRMG. Other enslaved persons listed are Priss, Jimmy, George, Jack, Rachel, Lucy, Pompy, Nancy, Brite, Dick, Phillis, Abrim, Anney, Primus, and Pate.

134. NC Land Grant Office, *Land Patent Books*, 9:65; "Bladen Co. File No.783, Samuel Carver."

135. NC Land Grant Office, "Warrants, Surveys, and Related Documents – Bladen County," roll 1, "No. 1069 Carver, Samuel, 11 October 1751," https://familysearch.org/ark:/61903/3:1:3QS7-89WV-TXMW.

136. NC Land Grant Office, "Warrants, Surveys, and Related Documents – Bladen," roll 1, "No. 1069 Carver, Samuel."

137. "Carver, Samuel, 1758, Bladen," in NC Secretary of State, "Secretary of State Original Wills," https://familysearch.org/ark:/61903/3:1:3QS7-99GC-F93W-7.

138. "Carver, Samuel, 1758, Bladen."

139. "Carver, Samuel, 1758, Bladen."

140. "Carver, Samuel, 1758, Bladen."

141. Fields, *Abstracts of Minutes*, 1:206

142. Cumberland County, *Minutes*, C:12v, https://familysearch.org/ark:/61903/3:1:3Q9M-CS4G-MWP9-K.

143. T. D. McDowell Papers, case 1, folder 18: 1785–1786; case 1, folder 20: 1789.

144. T. D. McDowell Papers, case 1, folder 18: 1785–1786; case 1, folder 20: 1789.

145. "NC, Revolutionary Pay Vouchers," https://familysearch.org/ark:/61903/1:1:Q2WT-R9KK, image 638 of 1,012.

146. Fields, *Abstracts of Minutes*, 2:183.

147. Bladen County, *Record of Deeds*, 1:465–66, "No. 574 Sarah Willis to Samuel Carver, 30 May 1787," https://familysearch.org/ark:/61903/3:1:3QS7-L98M-FG1.

148. Bladen County, *Record of Deeds*, 1:465–66.

149. Bladen County, *Record of Deeds*, 1:465–66.

150. Bladen County, *Record of Deeds*, 1:465–66.

151. Cumberland County, *Trial Docket Fayetteville District Superior Court*, vol. 1, *1788–1795*, October Term 1791, docket 87, https://familysearch.org/ark:/61903/3:1:-3QS7-89Q8-Y7KV. Cornell Law School describes the "assumption of risk" as a legal defense technique, in which the defense argues that any risk and/or harm to the plaintiff is in part to the plaintiff's own acknowledgement of danger; therefore, the defendant has no responsibility in the matter (See "Assumption of Risk," *Legal Information Institute*, https://www.law.cornell.edu/wex/assumption_of_risk).

152. *CSR*, 23, *Laws, 1715–1776*, 32–33.

153. "Carver, Samuel, 1758, Bladen," roll 2, https://familysearch.org/ark:/61903/3:1:3QS7-99GC-F93W-7.

154. This narrative draws heavily on work by Doris Fort, a descendant of William Carver. The credit for this section goes to her.

155. Doris Fort, email message to author, September 11, 2024; S.8158, for William Carver, NC, NAID 54170226, in Revolutionary War Pension and Bounty Land Warrant Application Files, https://catalog.archives.gov/id/54170226.

156. S.8158, image 10, in Revolutionary War Pension and Bounty Land Warrant Application Files, https://catalog.archives.gov/id/54170226?objectPage=10.

157. Fort, email, September 11, 2024.

158. First Census, "William Carver," population schedule for Cumberland County (excluding Fayetteville town), NC, Fayette District, First Census, 1790, NARA microfilm M637, roll 7, Records of the Census, RG 29, p. 89 (handwritten), line 42, https://familysearch.org/ark:/61903/3:1:33SQ-GYY8-3W42; Second Census, population schedule for Cumberland County (excluding Fayetteville), NC, Fayetteville District," 1800, NARA microfilm M32, roll 31, Records of the Census, RG 29, p. 350 (handwritten), line 19, https://familysearch.org/ark:/61903/3:1:33S7-9R8C-GC7; Third Census, population schedule for Cumberland County, NC, Capt. Jackson's (3rd) District, Third Census, 1810, NARA microfilm M252, roll 39, Records of the Census, RG 29, p. 569 (handwritten), line 23, https://familysearch.org/ ark:/61903/3:1:33SQ-GYY8-SBCG; Fifth Census, population schedule for Cumberland County, NC, Rockfish, 1830, NARA microfilm M19, roll 120, Records of the Census, RG 29, p. 41 (handwritten), line 8, https://familysearch.org/ark:/61903/3:1:33S7-9YY6-9TNX.

159. S.8158, image 14, in Revolutionary War Pension and Bounty Land Warrant Application Files, https://catalog.archives.gov/id/54170226?objectPage=14; Lewis, *NC Patriots*, 2(2):153.

160. Lewis, *NC Patriots*, 2(2):152. Isom's father Robert was brother of the Carver brothers' father, William.

161. S.8158, image 3, in Revolutionary War Pension and Bounty Land Warrant Application Files, https://catalog.archives.gov/id/54170226?objectPage=3.

162. S.8158, in Revolutionary War Pension and Bounty Land Warrant Application Files, https://catalog.archives.gov/id/54170226.

163. S.8158, image 16, in Revolutionary War Pension and Bounty Land Warrant Application Files, https://catalog.archives.gov/id/54170226?objectPage=16.

164. S.8158, image 16, in Revolutionary War Pension and Bounty Land Warrant Application Files, https://catalog.archives.gov/id/54170226?objectPage=16.

165. Phoenix Lodge No. 8, "Cumberland Association."

166. Campbell, *Bladen County*, 2:237.

167. S.8158, image 10, in Revolutionary War Pension and Bounty Land Warrant Application Files, https://catalog.archives.gov/id/54170226?objectPage=10.

168. *Fayetteville Observer*, April 7, 1836, 3.

169. "Carver Senr., William 1836," in Cumberland County, "Estate Papers," roll 7, https://familysearch.org/ark:/61903/3:2:77TD-JL9M-9.

170. Moss, *Roster of Patriots*, 43.

171. *CSR*, 15:699–700; *CSR*, 11:716–17.

172. *CSR*, 11:788.

173. NC DAR, *Roster of Soldiers*, 31; *CSR*, 14:817–18.

174. Lewis, *NC Patriots*, 2(2):172; NC DAR, *Roster of Soldiers*, 31; *CSR*, 14:817–18.

175. NC DAR, *Roster of Soldiers*, 31.

176. Lewis, *NC Patriots*, 2(2):172.

177. *CSR*, 18:485–86.

178. W.1325, for Buckner Smith, NC, NAID 196649614, image 76, in Revolutionary War Pension and Bounty Land Warrant Application Files, https://catalog.archives.gov/id/196649614?objectPage=76

179. W.1325, for Buckner Smith, NC, NAID 196649614, image 76, in Revolutionary War Pension and Bounty Land Warrant Application Files, https://catalog.archives.gov/id/196649614?objectPage=76.

180. Hillsborough District Superior Court, "Estate Records," roll 1, https://familysearch.org/ark:/61903/3:1:3QS7-89L4-CHFG.

181. Councill, *Hodges Councill*, 60.

182. Pringle, *Register Book*, 21. Lucile Miller Johnson claimed he was born in South Carolina (*Hometown Heritage*, 1:168). While there are no records to refute this outright, it is unlikely because the first time his father Hardy Council appears in the records of South Carolina is in 1745, six years after Arthur Council was born (South Carolina Department of Archives and History, "Combined Alphabetical Index"; Rockwell, "Council, Arthur."

183. Pringle, *Register Book*, 21.

184. Cumberland County, *Record of Deeds*, 6:236, "Francis Pugh to Arthur Council, 3 May 1762," https://familysearch.org/ark:/61903/3:1:3QS7-898Y-LWFZ. Other historians have previously speculated that Arthur Council was born about 1755, but if

that were the case he would not have been able to purchase land in 1762 ("Arthur Council," Find a Grave, https://findagrave.com/memorial/118807630/arthur-council; the modern headstone shown simply gives 1755 and 1777 as his approximate birth and death dates).

185. Charleston County, *Record of Deeds*, 4E:365, "Arthur Council to Henry Mills, 24 March 1773, https://familysearch.org/ark:/61903/3:1:3Q9M-CSK7-RH3C.

186. Arthur Council was a witness to deeds (Cumberland County, *Record of Deeds*, 2:303, 350, 490, 573; 4:258; 5:100), proved deeds in court (Cumberland County, *Minutes*, C:12v), served on juries (Cumberland County, *Minutes*, B:104r, https://familysearch.org/ark:/61903/3:1:3Q9M-CS4G-MWPQ-C; B:111v, https://familysearch.org/ark:/61903/3:1:3Q9M-CS4G-MWP3-R; B:113v, https://familysearch.org/ark:/61903/3:1:3Q9M-CS4G-MWP4-X), carried survey chains (NC Land Grant Office, "Cumberland County," roll 3, "Peter Messer 66 7/10 acres, 11 June 1767," https://familysearch.org/ark:/61903/3:1:3QS7-99WK-CWD7), settled tobacco inspector's books (Cumberland County, *Minutes*, C:39r, https://familysearch.org/ark:/61903/3:1:3Q9M-CS4G-MWGD-7, C:47v, https://familysearch.org/ark:/61903/3:1:3Q9M-CS4G-MWGR-V), administered estates (Cumberland County, *Minutes*, C:23r, https://familysearch.org/ark:/61903/3:1:3Q9M-CS4G-MWG2-H), and was on a committee to inquire into the conduct of insurgents (*CSR*, 10:594, https://familysearch.org/ark:/61903/3:1:3Q9M-CSSR-V8BS).

187. *CSR*, 22:411–12.

188. Lewis, "Capt. Arthur Council."

189. *CSR*, 10:501.

190. *CSR*, 10:502, 505, 518; 520.

191. *CSR*, 11:828. The few pages of his manuscript that have survived are now known as the Hugh McDonald Papers and are kept in the State Archives of North Carolina (Hugh McDonald Papers, https://digital.ncdcr.gov/Documents/Detail/hugh-mcdonald-papers-1776-1777/424262).

192. Hugh McDonald Papers, 5; *CSR*, 11:830–31. The cause of death was likely due to illness or disease as there were no military engagements in the area during the time the 6th NC Regiment remained there.

193. "Arthur Council (1739–1777)"; *CSR*, 11:834.

194. Councill, *Hodges Councill*, 20, 50, 61–62.

195. Lewis, *NC Patriots*, 1: 334–35; Lewis, "1st NC Regiment."

196. Cumberland County, *Record of Deeds*, 17:373, "6 May 1799," https://familysearch.org/ark:/61903/3:1:3QS7-998N-WXPH.

197. Cumberland County, *Record of Deeds*, 17:373, "6 May 1799."

198. Hartmann, "Munro's Doctrines," 479.

199. "Joseph De L'espine," 1.

200. "Joseph De L'espine," 1.

201. South Carolina Secretary of State, *Columbia, SC, Mortgages*, DDD: 62, https://familysearch.org/ark:/61903/3:1:3Q9M-CSLV-G3WQ-P.

202. Charleston County, *Miscellaneous Records*, 156, https://familysearch.org/ark:/61903/3:1:939L-J89D-LP.

203. Charleston County, *Miscellaneous Records*, 156, https://familysearch.org/ark:/61903/3:1:939L-J89D-LP.

204. Decisions, Examinations, Army and Navy, 46–47 (handwritten).

205. Berenson et al., "Francisca de Paula Petronita Fontanet; Joseph Delespine; Frances Jane Delespine; Christian Jacob Bernhard Boye," in *Florida Pioneer Biographies*, https://fsgs.org/florida-pioneer-biographies/francisca-de-paula-petronita-fontanet-joseph-delespine-frances-jane-delespine-christian-jacob-bernhard-boye/.

206. Massengale, reply to "Edward I Munro 1732 Inverness, Scotland," Genealogy.com, September 30, 2006. https://www.genealogy.com/forum/surnames/topics/munro/1678/; Berenson et al., "Francisca de Paula Petronita Fontanet."

207. Berenson et al., "Francisca de Paula Petronita Fontanet." The claims of the younger De Lespine resulted in two precedent-setting Supreme Court cases regarding land claims in former Spanish territories: United States v. Delespine's Heirs, et al. (1838), in which it was confirmed that De Lespine's claim for 43,000 acres of land was valid; and United States v. Delespine's Heirs (1841), in which De Lespine's claim for 92,160 acres was rejected (37 U.S. 654 (1838), https://loc.gov/resource/usrep.usrep037654/; 40 U.S. 319 (1841), https://loc.gov/resource/usrep.usrep040319/).

208. Georgia Society DAR, *Thronateeska Chapter*, 235, https://familysearch.org/ark:/61903/3:1:3QHK-Q35R-G89.

209. "Obituary. Mrs. Harriet DeLespine Munro," 104, *Georgia Historic Newspapers*, https://gahistoricnewspapers.galileo.usg.edu/lccn/sn91099152/1872-07-03/ed-1/seq-4/. Inaccurate statement about arriving with the Comte d'Estaing's fleet omitted from the first sentence.

210. Cumberland County, *Record of Deeds*, 7:314, "Thomas Cabeen to McIver & Dick, 28 December 1784," https://familysearch.org/ark:/61903/3:1:3QS7-8983-N6C5.

211. Fields, *Abstracts of Minutes*, 1:274.

212. "Fayetteville—On Saturday Last"; "At a Late Meeting of the Inhabitants of This Town."

213. "Returns of the Election for Members of the Next General Assembly of North Carolina."

214. "NC, Revolutionary Pay Vouchers," https://familysearch.org/ark:/61903/3:1:3QS7-L9W8-XQFLhttps://familysearch.org/ark:/61903/3:1:3QS7-L9W8-XQFL, image 233 of 999; https://familysearch.org/ark:/61903/3:1:3QSQ-G9W8-XQHJ https://familysearch.org/ark:/61903/3:1:3QSQ-G9W8-XQHJ, image 231 of 999.

215. "NC, Revolutionary Pay Vouchers," https://familysearch.org/ark:/61903/3:1:3QSQ-G9W8-XQHXhttps://familysearch.org/ark:/61903/3:1:3QSQ-G9W8-XQHX, image 234 of 999.

216. "Forty-Seven Republicans Met at the House of William Dick."

217. "Patriotism." The USS *Chesapeake* was intercepted by the HMS *Leopard* to seek the return of deserters from the Royal Navy. The American commander refused to submit to being boarded so the *Leopard* attacked. This resulted in three US sailors killed and eighteen wounded. The *Leopard* then sent a boarding party onto the *Chesapeake* and seized four men, three of whom were American-born ("USS *Chesapeake*– HMS *Leopard* Affair").

218. During an occasion when he may have carried his zeal too far, he participated in the horsewhipping of fellow signer Thomas Cabeen to keep him from "corrupting the morals" of the community. See the Thomas Cabeen section for more information.

219. *CSR*, 24:513.

220. *CSR*, 24:514.

221. *CSR*, 24:695.

222. Cumberland County, *Record of Deeds*, 7:272, "Mark Russell to James Dick, 8 September 1784, https://familysearch.org/ark:/61903/3:1:3QS7-L983-NDRC.

223. Cumberland County, *Record of Deeds*, 11:454, "Mark Russell to James Dick, 13 April 1791," https://familysearch.org/ark:/61903/3:1:3QS7-898Q-ZW49.

224. Cumberland County, *Record of Deeds*, 16:71, "Findley MacRae to Duncan MacRae, 9 February 1796," https://family search.org/ark:/61903/3:1:3QS7-L9DC-DQPC.

225. "DIED- On the 1st Inst."; Third Census, "James Dick," population schedule for Fayetteville, 1810, p. 620 (penned), https://familysearch.org/ark:/61903/3:1:33S7-9YY8-S6VN.

226. Cumberland County, *Record of Deeds*, 26:111, "James Dick to David Mitchell, 14 February 1811," https://familysearch.org/ark:/61903/3:1:3QSQ-G98M-DQ1R.

227. "American Independence"; Cumberland County, *Record of Deeds*, 32:381, "Mark Russell to John L. Hadley, 25 October 1817," https://familysearch.org/ark:/61903/3:1:3QS7-998M-K8Q.

228. Cumberland Association Papers, https://dc.lib.unc.edu/cdm/ref/collection/02ddd/id/446855.

229. Cumberland Association Papers, SHC Z box 106, folder 1, scan 9, https://dc.lib.unc.edu/cdm/ref/collection/02ddd/id/446842.

230. Pruitt, *Cumberland County, NC, Taxables*, 97; "Tax Lists, Cumberland County, 1767," 4, line 25, State Archives of NC, https://digital.ncdcr.gov/Documents

/Detail/tax-lists-cumberland-county-1767/ 355294?item=355328; "Doyle Daniel" on estate inventory of "McConnell, James 1771," in Cumberland County, "Estate Records," roll 19, p. 1, line 34, left column, https://familysearch.org/ark:/61903/3:2:77TD-V3T7.

231. "[Claim of] John Hay and Company. 22 Jan., 1799."

232. "Dunn, David - South Carolina - Fifth Regiment," in *Compiled Service Records*, Revolutionary War Records, RG 93, https://catalog.archives.gov/id/142067361.; Moss, *Roster of South Carolina Patriots*, 1:275.

233. Dunn, "2092C."

234. Moss, *Roster of South Carolina Patriots,* 67. J. D. Lewis says that Edmondson was a private who fought at Moores Creek and was in Arthur Council's unit (*NC Patriots*, 2(2):271).

235. Pruitt, *Cumberland County, NC, Taxables*, 97.

236. Pruitt, *Cumberland County, NC, Taxables*, 47.

237. McBride, "Claims of British Merchants After the Revolutionary War," pt. 5 , 112.

238. Fields, *Abstracts of Deeds*, 2:27; Cumberland County, *Record of Deeds*, 4:331–33, "George Cooper & Wife to William Farmer, 25 October 1768," https://familysearch.org/ark:/61903/3:1:3QSQ-G9DC-ZSYR.

239. NC Land Grant Office, "Warrants, Surveys, and Related Documents – Bladen County," roll 34, "Warrant no. 246 – Benjamin Elwell & Joseph Locke, 11 January 1773," https://familysearch.org/ark:/61903/3:1:3QS7-89WV-YG3B; "Son in Law Benjamin Elwell," in Bladen County, *Wills*, vol. 1. 522, item 3, https://familysearch.org/ark:/61903/3:1:939L-JG94-29.

240. NC Land Grant Office, "Warrants, Surveys, and Related Documents – Bladen County," roll 34, "Surveyd. for Joseph Lock & Benjamin Elwell, 25 June 1773," https://familysearch.org/ark:/61903/3:1:3QSQ-G9WV-YLG1. In his 1781 will, Joseph Lock bequeathed his half of this land to his son Leonard, and it is Leonard's name that is written with Benjamin Elwell's on the back of each copy of the survey (Bladen County, *Wills*, 1:522, item 6, https://familysearch.org/ark:/61903/3:1:939L-JG94-29; NC Land Grant Office, "Warrants, Surveys, and Related Documents – Bladen County," roll 34, https://familysearch.org/ark:/61903/3:1:3QS7-L9WV-YGWY and https://familysearch.org/ark:/61903/3:1:3QS7-L9WV-YG94).

241. "Benjamin Elwell," in *Taxable Property in Cumberland County for 1780*, "List of Taxables," 75, line 22, record ID CR.029.701.001, State Archives of NC, https://familysearch.org/ark:/61903/3:1:3QS7-898M-Z965.

242. *Amount of the Tax of Cumberland County for 1783*, "List of Taxables 1777–1783," https://familysearch.org/ark:/61903/3:1:3QSQ-G98M-Z99F.

243. "Benjamin Elwell," in *Amount of the Tax of Cumberland County for 1783*, "List of Taxables 1777–1783," p. 2, line 24, right column, https://familysearch.org/ark:/61903/3:1:3QS7-L98M-Z9HK.

244. NC Land Grant Office, "Bladen County," roll 10, "Entry no. 69, 3 February 1784," https://familysearch.org/ark:/61903/3:1:3QS7-L9WV-B931-F; NC Land Grant Office, *Land Patent Books*, 70:346; "Bladen Co. File No. 4372, Benjamin Elwell," NC Land Grants and Data, https://nclandgrants.com/grant/?mars=12.14.33.4370&qid=1233159&rn=1.

245. Second Census, "Benja. Elwell," population schedule for Bladen, NC, Capt. Lock's (10th) District, 1800, NARA microfilm M32, roll 31, Records of the Census, RG 29, National Archives, p. 153 (handwritten), line 15, https://familysearch.org/ark:/61903/3:1:33SQ-GR8C-5HL.

246. Fourth Census, "Benjn. Elwell," population schedule for Bladen, NC, 1820, NARA microfilm M33, roll 82, pp. 154–55 (typed), line 30, https://familysearch.org/ark:/61903/3:1:33S7-9YTB-SJSW. There is no record on this census for the Elwell family and the number of enslaved or free persons on their property; therefore, it is unknown what changes were made to these two specific populations on the census.

247. "Sheriff Sales," 3.

248. "Elwell Benjamin," in *Registers of Enlistments in the United States Army*, 7:50, line 88, https://familysearch.org/ark:/61903/3:1:33SQ-G1RN-SB1. This Benjamin Elwell was listed as a lieutenant under Capt. J. Nicolson and remarked to be thirty-five years old. He experienced "weekly RR" in Elizabethtown, NC.

249. "Elwell Ferry (I-84)."

250. "Elwell Ferry (I-84)."

251. "Elwell Ferry (I-84)."

252. Fields, *Abstracts of Deeds*, 2:103, 128.

253. Fields, *Abstracts of Deeds*, 1: 132, 185; Cumberland County, *Record of Deeds*, 2:554, "John Dukemineer to John Elwell, 9 March 1765," https://familysearch.org/ark:/61903/3:1:3QS7-898M-D7NR.

254. Lewis, *NC Patriots*, 2(2):279.

255. "Death of Mrs. Lucy Carver," 3.

256. Fields, Abstracts of Minutes, 1:312.

257. "John Elwell," in *Taxable Property in Cumberland County for 1780*, "List of Taxables," 75, line 10, record ID CR.029.701.001, State Archives of NC, https://familysearch.org/ark:/61903/3:1:3QS7-898M-Z965.

258. See note 210 above.

259. "John Elwell," in *Amount of the Tax of Cumberland County for 1783*, "List of Taxables 1777–1783," 2, line 6, left column, https://familysearch.org/ark:/61903/3:1:3QS7-L98M-Z9HK.

260. First Census, "John Elwell," population schedule for Cumberland (excluding Fayetteville town), NC, 1790, NARA microfilm M637, roll 7, p. 91 (handwritten), line 2, https://familysearch.org/ark:/61903/3:1:33S7-9YY8-S21T.

261. Fourth Census, "John Elwell," population schedule for Cumberland, NC, Captain Newberry's (12th) District, 1820, NARA microfilm M33, roll 83, Records of the Census, RG 29, National Archives, line 32, https://familysearch.org/ark:/61903/3:1:33SQ-GYYJ-9BG5.

262. "Cumberland Centennial," 1.

263. Fields, *Abstracts of Minutes*, 2:241; Cumberland County, *Minutes*, vol. 1787–1791, 29 April 1789, https://familysearch.org/ark:/61903/3:1:3Q9M-CSKV-S96H-Q.

264. Cumberland County, *Minutes*, vol. 1787–1791, 30 July 1789, https://familysearch.org/ark:/61903/3:13Q9M-CSKV-S9FY-D; Fields, *Abstracts of Minutes*, 2:257.

265. Cumberland County, *Minutes*, vol. 1791–1797, 11 January 1792, https://familysearch.org/ark:/61903/3:1:3Q9M-CSKV-S9D1-1.

266. "John Elwell."

267. "Died," 3.

268. See note 234 above.

269. *CSR*, 11:716.

270. NC DAR, Roster of Soldiers, 34.

271. Lewis, *NC Patriots*, 1:370.

272. Fields, *Abstracts of Deeds*, 2:155.

273. *CSR*, 15:559; Lewis, *NC Patriots*, 1:370.

274. *CSR*, 19:663, 704.

275. *CSR*, 22:549–50.

276. *CSR*, 22:566–67.

277. "From John Ramsey, 21 August 1781"; *CSR*, 22:570–71.

278. NC Land Grant Office, "Warrants, Surveys, and Related Documents – Davidson County, Tennessee," roll 2, "File No. 249, James Emmet (Military Warrant No. 365)," 14 March 1786, https://familysearch.org/ark:/61903/3:1:3QS7-89WN-5DCW.

279. Fields, *Abstracts of Minutes*, 2:63; Cheney Jr., *North Carolina Government 1585–1979*, 213.

280. "History of Sheriffs." On April 19, 1784, the General Assembly voted to divide Cumberland County in two, forming Moore County and Fayette County. This was enacted on 4 July of that year. Three months later, on October 22, 1784, the act was repealed, the boundary line between the counties was redrawn, and Fayette County was changed back to Cumberland while parts of Moore County remained (Olds, "Fayette County Existed Brief Period 4 Months; Fred Olds Recalls Past").

281. Studebaker, *History of Eagle Lodge*, 4; "A Short History of the Founding of Phoenix Lodge No. 8."

282. Studebaker, *History of Eagle Lodge*, 4.

283. "A Short History of the Founding of Phoenix Lodge No. 8."

284. McBride, "Claims of British Merchants After the Revolutionary War," pt. 4, 21; McBride, "Claims of British Merchants After the Revolutionary War," pt. 6, 197.

285. Mann, *Republic of Debtors*, 48–49.

286. Fields, *Abstracts of Minutes*, 2:200.

287. "Emmet, James 1787," in Cumberland County, "Original Wills," roll 3, https://familysearch.org/ark:/61903/3:1:3QS7-L9GW-BJ25.

288. Cumberland County, "Original Wills," roll 3, https://familysearch.org/ark:/61903/3:1:3QS7-L9GW-BJ25.

289. Cumberland County, "Original Wills," roll 3, https://familysearch.org/ark:/61903/3:1:3QS7-L9GW-BJ25.

290. Cumberland County, "Original Wills," roll 3, https://familysearch.org/ark:/61903/3:1:3QS7-L9GW-BJ25.

291. DeLancey Evans Papers, DeLancey Evans to Mrs. Wm G. Holmes, (Nee) Rebecca Locke Evans, 25 November 1926, p. 6, box 1, folder 9: correspondence, 1926, scan 46, DeLancey Evans Papers, Wilson Special Collections Library, https://dc.lib.unc.edu/cdm/ref/collection/02ddd/id/486469. Between 1909 and 1931, DeLancey Evans of Virginia set out to create a family history of the Evans family of Cumberland County. A collection of correspondences from this search are held at the Southern Historical Collection at the University of North Carolina and the biographies for David and Theophilus Evans draw heavily from this work. David's siblings, in order of birth, were Josiah, Jonathan, George, Mary, Sarah, John, Theophilus, Ann, and Rebecca.

292. DeLancey Evans Papers, David Evans line, folder 14: undated, scan 65, https://dc.lib.unc.edu/cdm/ref/collection/02ddd/id/486778.

293. DeLancey Evans Papers, David Evans line, folder 14: undated, scan 65.

294. DeLancey Evans Papers, family notes, folder 12: undated, scan 10, https://dc.lib.unc.edu/cdm/ref/collection/02ddd/id/486584.

295. Haun, *North Carolina Revolutionary Army Accounts*, 1:6–7, 30.

296. "American Independence."

297. "American Independence."

It is suspected that Robert Rowan and James Emmet were among those captured prisoners who were rescued at the battle, though there is no documentary proof of this.

298. "Battle of Elizabethtown Culminated at the Tory Hole."

299. Pruitt, *Cumberland County, NC, Taxables*, 38.

300. Gibbons, "Cumberland County Deed Book 13 (1794–98)," pt. 1, 343.

301. Fields, *Abstracts of Minutes*, 1:227; "Evans, George 1773," in Cumberland County, "Original Wills," roll 3, https://familysearch.org/ark:/61903/3:1:3QS7-L9GW-BNMV.

302. "Rowan, Robert 1799," in Cumberland County, "Original Wills," roll 7, https://familysearch.org/ark:/61903/3:1:3QSQ-G9G4-S1MR.

303. DeLancey Evans Papers, folder 9, scan 46, https://dc.lib.unc.edu/cdm/ref/collection/02ddd/id/486469.

304. "Cumberland Centennial."

305. DeLancey Evans Papers, folder 9, scan 46, https://dc.lib.unc.edu/cdm/ref/collection/02ddd/id/486469. See the David Evans section for more info on the siblings of Theophilus Evans.

306. DeLancey Evans Papers, folder 12, scan 10, https://dc.lib.unc.edu/cdm/ref/collection/02ddd/id/486584.

307. "Theophilus Evans."

308. DeLancey Evans Papers, Evans to Mrs. Holmes, 25 November 1926, p. 10, folder 9, scan 50, https://dc.lib.unc.edu/cdm/ref/collection/02ddd/id/486473.

309. Bill to Divide Anson County; Cates, "Legislative Petitions, 1779," 141–42. The signatures between this and the Resolves are not an exact match but are close enough that it is more likely than not that this is the same person.

310. NC DAR, *Roster of Soldiers*, 379.

311. Hugh McDonald Papers, 12, https://digital.ncdcr.gov/Documents/Detail/hugh-mcdonald-papers-1776-1777/424262?item=424312.

312. Fields, *Abstracts of Deeds*, 2:66, 145.

313. "Cumberland Centennial."

314. DeLancey Evans Papers, folder 12, scan 27, https://dc.lib.unc.edu/cdm/ref/collection/02ddd/id/486601; folder 9, scan 47, https://dc.lib.unc.edu/cdm/ref/collection/02ddd/id/486470.

315. *CSR*, 24:635.

316. *CSR*, 24:635.

317. "Evans, Theophilus 1822," in Cumberland County, "Original Wills," roll 3, https://familysearch.org/ark:/61903/3:1:3QS7-L9GW-BNH7.

318. "Evans, Theophilus 1822," in Cumberland County, "Original Wills," roll 3, https://familysearch.org/ark:/61903/3:1:3QS7-L9GW-BNH7.

319. DeLancey Evans Papers, "Extract of the Records of the Evans Family," p. 2, folder 13: undated, scan 36, https://dc.lib.unc.edu/cdm/singleitem/collection/02ddd/id/486660/rec/36; p. 18, folder 13, scan 28, https://dc.lib.unc.edu/cdm/singleitem/collection/02ddd/id/486652/rec/28.

320. DeLancey Evans Papers, Letter from H. T. Ivy, undated, folder 12, scan 29, https://dc.lib.unc.edu/cdm/singleitem/collection/02ddd/id/486603/rec/29.

321. DeLancey Evans Papers, folder 9, scan 50, https://dc.lib.unc.edu/cdm/ref/collection/02ddd/id/486473.

322. *CSR*, 24:180; Parker Jr., "City Owes its Existence to Revolutionary Patriots," 1; "Cumberland Centennial." The other commissioners were Peter Mallet, Robert Cochran, Lewis Barge, Daniel Southerland, James Patterson, and Robert Rowan.

323. Fields, *Abstracts of Minutes*, 1:295. The two securities for the second license were James Dick and John Oveler.

324. LMJ Collection, untitled document, folder 83.

325. Johnson, *Hometown Heritage*, 1:170. See also "Rebecca *Evans* Brownlow Fletcher."

326. Johnson, *Hometown Heritage,* 1:170. See also Lewis, *NC Patriots*, 2(1):377, 303; *CSR*, 14:391–92.

327. *CSR*, 14:392.

328. *CSR*, 14:411–12, 446.

329. Johnson, *Hometown Heritage*, 1:170. After John Brownlow died in 1775, they divided up his property, which included enslaved persons. Polly received Cloe, her youngest child (young Cloe,) and Sall, while Rebecca Brownlow received Ben and Cloe's eldest daughter (not named) (Fields, *Minutes*, 1:251).

330. Pringle, *Register Book*, 21.

331. Pruitt, *Cumberland County, NC, Taxables*, 33.

332. Fowler, *Valley of the Scots*, 64.

333. Fowler, *Valley of the Scots*, 64.

334. Fowler, *Valley of the Scots*, 64.

335. Fowler, *Valley of the Scots*, 64.

336. Wood, "Crises of Authority," 68–69.

337. "Cumberland Centennial."

338. Fowler, *Valley of the Scots*, 64. See also pension application of Daniel McLellan: S.7208, for Daniel McLellan, NC, NAID 144193728, in Revolutionary War Pension and Bounty Land Warrant Application Files, https://catalog.archives.gov/id/144193728.

339. "Cumberland Centennial."

340. Linn, "Revolutionary War Claims," pt. 4, 228.

341. Linn, "Revolutionary War Claims," pt. 4, 228. George may have had a relative named John Fletcher. John was from Cumberland and served as a captain under Col. Thomas Matthews in 1779, then a captain under Col. James Emmet in 1781 (Lewis, *NC Patriots,* 2(2):302).

342. "James Gee."

343. *CSR*, 18:406–7.

344. *CSR*, 18:406–7.

345. Fields, *Abstracts of Deeds*, 2:8.

346. NC Land Grant Office, "Warrants, Surveys, and Related Documents – Cumberland County," roll 22, "No. 0171 Gee, James, 17 November 1768," https://familysearch.org/ark:/61903/3:1:3QS7-L9WV-TCRT.

347. Fields, *Abstracts of Deeds*, 2:8.

348. Fields, *Abstracts of Minutes*, 1:195.

349. Cumberland County, *Record of Deeds*, 4:420–21, "John Newberry to James Gee, 23 September 1766," https://familysearch.org/ark:/61903/3:1:3QS7-99DC-ZCCN; Fields, *Abstracts of Deeds*, 2:37.

350. Fields, *Abstracts of Deeds*, 2:93.

351. Fields, Abstracts of Minutes, 1:229.

352. Cumberland County, *Minutes*, C:43r, https://familysearch.org/ark:/61903/3:1:3Q9M-CS4G-MWGQ-Y.

353. Fields, *Abstracts of Minutes*, 1:257.

354. Fields, *Abstracts of Minutes*, 1:272.

355. Fields, *Abstracts of Minutes*, 1:272.

356. Fields, *Abstracts of Minutes*, 1:279, 304, 308.

357. Fields, *Abstracts of Deeds*, 2:155; Fields, Abstracts of Minutes, 2:45.

358. Fields, *Abstracts of Minutes*, 2:66, 68.

359. Fields, *Abstracts of Minutes*, 2:295.

360. Pruitt, *Abstracts of Land Entrys– Cumberland County*, 176.

361. MacKethan, "Turning the Pages."

362. Fletcher, "The Gees of Cumberland County," 96; Hill, "Confederate Women's Home

363. Fletcher, *The Gee Family*, 96.

364. "Cumberland Centennial," 1; "The Patriot Gee and His Brave Wife," 6; "An Anniversary," 3.

365. Fletcher, *The Gee Family*, 101. The information about which Gee this story references may have been mixed up, as Captain Charles Gee also has the same story within Marion's Brigade (See O'Kelley, *"Unwaried Patience & Fortitude,"* 546).

366. "The Patriot Gee and His Brave Wife"; Boddie, *Marion's Men*, 2.

367. NC DAR, *Roster of Soldiers*, 340, 380.

368. New Hanover County, *Record of Deeds*, H:200–1, https://familysearch.org/ark:/61903/3:1:3QSQ-G983-6H21.

369. LMJ Collection, "James Gee," folder 7; Fletcher, *The Gee Family*, 96.

370. MacKethan, "Turning the Pages."

371. MacKethan, "Turning the Pages."

372. "The Patriot Gee and His Brave Wife."

373. "The Patriot Gee and His Brave Wife."

374. Heitman, *Historical Register*, 248.

375. Ervin, *South Carolinians in the Revolution*, 83.

376. Meyer, *Highland Scots*, 144.

377. Fields, *Abstracts of Minutes*, 1:276

378. Fields, *Abstracts of Minutes*, 1:276; Fields, *Abstracts of Minutes*, 1:272. See also *CSR*, 24:10, for the 1777 legislation decreeing that if any persons should be caught opposing or dispiriting the new United States government or giving aid to the British, and have their charges proven in court with two or more witnesses, they would be imprisoned during the war. Alongside imprisonment, the charged individuals would have to forfeit half of their property and goods to the State.

379. *CSR*, 11:744–46.

380. *CSR*, 11:744.

381. *CSR*, 11:744.

382. *CSR*, 11:746.

383. Cumberland County, *Record of Deeds*, 7:419, "Mark Cole & Wife Deed to William Gillespie, 5 March 1779," https://familysearch.org/ark:/61903/3:1:3QS7-99DC-XDLH.

384. Cumberland County, *Record of Deeds*, 7:419, https://familysearch.org/ark:/61903/3:1:3QS7-99DC-XDLH.

385. Cumberland County, *Minutes*, vol. 1787–1791, 30 July 1789, https://familysearch.org/ark:/61903/3:1:3Q9M-CSKV-S9FY-D.

386. "Galespie, William 1794," in Cumberland County, " Original Wills," roll 3, https://familysearch.org/ark:/61903/3:1:3QS7-L9GW-BV7K.

387. "Galespie, William 1794," in Cumberland County, "Original Wills," roll 3, https://familysearch.org/ark:/61903/3:1:3QS7-L9GW-BV7K.

388. "Galespie, William 1794," in Cumberland County, "Original Wills," roll 3.

389. "Galespie, William 1794," in Cumberland County, "Original Wills," roll 3.

390. Holcomb, *Greer and Related Families*, 1.

391. J. W. Cooper, "Letter from J. W. Cooper to His Son," 14 August 1856, Simpsonville, SC, in Holcomb, *Greer and Related Families*, 95.

392. Holcomb, Greer and Related Families, 1, 95.

393. Cumberland County, *Record of Deeds*, 8:172, "John James to Thomas Greer, 5 August 1755," https://familysearch.org/ark:/61903/3:1:3QS7-L98Q-7Q16.

394. Holcomb, *Greer and Related Families*, 2.

395. Cumberland County, *Record of Deeds*, 13:272, "Thomas Greer to William B. Grove, 29 October 1795," https://familysearch.org/ark:/61903/3:1:3QS7-99DC-DP4L.

396. Cumberland County, *Record of Deeds*, 3:50, "James Crawford to Ed Fanning, 14 June 1765," https://familysearch.org/ark:/61903/3:1:3QSQ-G9DC-Z33Q. This deed was registered by Richard Grove on 10 October 1766 and is the last document

in the record bearing his signature. The next item in this deed book ("Elijah Keelam to Walter Gibson, 4 November 1766," https://familysearch.org/ark:/61903/3:1:3QS7-99DC-ZZDK) shows Thomas Rutherford as the new clerk of court; Cumberland County, *Record of Deeds*, 5:124, "Robert Rowan to Mitchel Carol, 20 November 1770," https://familysearch.org/ark:/61903/3:1:3QS7-89DC-X36Q. This 1770 deed is signed by Robert Rowan and witnessed by Susanna Rowan, confirming they are married by this time.

397. Clark, "Notes on the Post Revolutionary War History of the Liberty Point Resolves," https://dc.lib.unc.edu/cdm/singleitem/collection/02ddd/id/446808/rec/18.

398. "Greer, Thomas 1783," in Cumberland County, "Original Wills," roll 3, https://familysearch.org/ark:/61903/3:1:3QS7-L9GW-BN8G.

399. "Greer, Thomas 1783," in Cumberland County, "Original Wills," roll 3, https://familysearch.org/ark:/61903/3:1:3QS7-L9GW-BN8G.

400. Cumberland County, *Minutes*, vol. 1787–1791, "30 January 1790," https://familysearch.org/ark:/61903/3:1:3Q9M-CSKV-S9F5-R.

401. Blackstone, "Of Title by Descent," 200–40; Baird, "Wills, Intestates, & Probate."

402. Cumberland County, *Record of Deeds*, 2:573, "Stevens & Walsh to Greer & Grove, 28 August 1764," https://familysearch.org/ark:/61903/3:1:3QSQ-G9DC-Z3SY.

403. Cumberland County, *Record of Deeds*, 5:68–70, "Robert Greer to John Brownlow, 10 June 1772," https://familysearch.org/ark:/61903/3:1:3QS7-99DC-XN8R.

404. See note 346 above.

405. Cumberland County, *Record of Deeds*, 6:339–40, "Robert Greet to Robert Rowan, 16 March 1775," https://familysearch.org/ark:/61903/3:1:3QSQ-G98Y-LWZP.

406. *CSR*, 10:943, https://familysearch.org/ark:/61903/3:1:3Q9M-CSSR-V86S.

407. Buck, "Washington's Encampment on the Neshaminy," 275; DAR, "Historic Site: Moland House." On a side note, it was while encamped at Neshaminy that a young Gilbert du Motier, Marquis de La Fayette, presented himself to George Washington and was commissioned as a major general and attended his first Council of War (DAR, "Historic Site: Moland House"; "Council of War, 21 August 1777").

408. *CSR*, 12:491.

409. *CSR*, 12:491.

410. Continental Congress, "Articles of War," in *Journals of the Continental Congress*, 5:803.According to these Articles of War, an officer could only be cashiered for the following reasons: using "traitorous or disrespectful words against the authority of the United States in Congress assembled, or the legislature of any of the United States in which he may be quartered" (§ II, art. 1); signing a "false certificate, relating

to the absence of either officer or private soldier" (§ IV, art. 4); making "a false muster of man or horse" or if he were to "willingly sign, direct, or allow the signing of the muster-rolls, wherein such false muster is contained" (§ IV, art. 5); making a "false return" regarding the number of forces under his command "or of arms, ammunition, clothing, or other stores" said forces have (§ V, art. 1); "knowingly, receive and entertain" someone who has deserted from another unit, or after discovering someone has deserted failing to "immediately confine him, and give notice thereof to the corps in which he last served" (§ VI, art. 3); challenging another officer or a soldier to a duel (§ VII, art. 2); willfully neglecting or refusing to turn over "to the civil magistrates" any officer or soldier accused of a capital crime or use of violence or committing any offense against a civilian, or willfully neglecting or refusing to aid and assist "the officers of justice in apprehending such person or persons" (§ X, art. 1); protecting an individual from creditors by claiming he is a soldier or non-commissioned officer (NCO) when that is not true, or protecting an actual soldier or NCO from creditors beyond the scope or level "allowed by a resolution of Congress" passed on December 26, 1775 (§ X, art. 2); embezzling or misusing any money provided to pay his soldiers or to enlist men (§ XII, art. 4); being drunk on duty (§ XIII, art. 5); breaking confinement without liberty if arrested (§ XIV, art. 20); and for cowardice (§ XIV, art. 22).

411. "Articles of War," § XIV, art. 22, in *Journals of the Continental Congress*, 5:804, https://www.loc.gov/resource/llscdam.lljc005/?sp=389.

412. *CSR*, 12:491.

413. *CSR*, 12:491.

414. "North Carolina, 8th Regiment, 1777, Jacket 9," image 4, NAID 503390974, NAID 503390974, in Revolutionary War Rolls, War Department Collection of Revolutionary War Records, RG 93. https://catalog.archives.gov/id/503390974; "Rispiss, Richard - North Carolina - Eighth Regiment," NAID 141374594, image 2, in *Compiled Service Records*, https://catalog.archives.gov/id/141374594. The same board of officers who recommended Robert Greer for promotion to first lieutenant also recommended fellow signer James Pearl from ensign to first lieutenant, completely skipping over second lieutenant.

415. *Journals of the Continental Congress*, 11:550–51, https://www.loc.gov/resource/llscdam.lljc011/?sp=137.

416. Washington, "General Orders, 15 May 1778"; "Orders for March from Valley Forge, 17 June 1778"; "George Washington to Jonathan Trumbull, October 1, 1777, with Order of March," image 3, in George Washington Papers, https://www.loc.gov/resource/mgw4.044_0535_0538/. This draft order of march, created 28 May 1778, was mistakenly filed with the October 1777 letter to Jonathan Trumbull (see editorial note for "Orders for March from Valley Forge, 17 June 1778").

417. "NC, Revolutionary Pay Vouchershttps://familysearch.org/ark:/61903/3:1:3QS7-L9W8-N7FD, images 129–34 of 970.

418. First Census, "Robert Greer," population schedule for Cumberland (excluding Fayetteville), NC, 1790, NARA microfilm M637, roll 7, p. 91 (handwritten), line 50, https://familysearch.org/ark:/61903/3:1:33S7-9YY8-S21T. No records have been found identifying the names of these enslaved persons.

419. Cumberland County, *Record of Deeds*, 14:154–55, "Robert Greer Agreement Thomas Greer, 22 August 1792," https://familysearch.org/ark:/61903/3:1:3QSQ-G98M-DQY9; Cumberland County, *Record of Deeds*, 12:197–98, "Robert Greer to Thomas Greer, 28 August 1792," https://familysearch.org/ark:/61903/3:1:3QS7-8983-NP9T.

420. Cumberland County, *Record of Deeds*, 18:14–16, "Robert Greer to Stephen Beck, 2 October 1799," https://familysearch.org/ark:/61903/3:1:3QS7-L98N-WXBP.

421. "Greer, Robert 1800," in Cumberland County, "Estate Records," roll 12, https://familysearch.org/ark:/61903/3:2:77TD-JT9Y-5.

422. Hadley, "Captain Joshua Hadley."

423. "Hadly, Thomas 1791," in Cumberland, County "Estate Records," roll 13, https://familysearch.org/ark:/61903/3:2:77TD-JBH7e; Hadley, *Notes on the Quaker Family of Hadley*, 39. His siblings were Jane, John, Simon, Benjamin, Mary (called Polly), Jesse, and Thomas. According to Chalmers Hadley, the junior Thomas was the youngest of these siblings and he married Margaret Parker, the daughter of signer John Parker (43).

424. "The Tragic Death of a Patriot of '76."

425. "The Tragic Death of a Patriot of '76"; Healton, *A Hadley Genealogy*, 43–45.

426. Healton, *A Hadley Genealogy*, 43–45.

427. "The Tragic Death of a Patriot of '76."

428. Hadley, *Notes on the Quaker Family of Hadley*, 41.

429. NC DAR, *Roster of Soldiers*, 36.

430. NC DAR, *Roster of Soldiers*, 36.

431. "American Independence."

432. Robertson, "To Major General Andrew Jackson."

433. Robertson, "To Major General Andrew Jackson."

434. "Gen. James Robertson and the Corps of Invincibles."

435. Hadley, *Notes on the Quaker Family of Hadley*, 46; Cane Creek Monthly Meeting, *Minutes*, 1:81.

436. Caruthers, *Old North State in 1776*, 166. In 1781, Thomas Hadley was in his home when a group of Scots surrounded his home in the night. Thomas barricaded the door and his wife and daughters assisted in hiding the valuables. Thomas ran upstairs and shouted out his window for the assistance of Frank Cooly and Andrew Beard. One of the Scotsmen (allegedly McAlpin) heard the shout and shot Thomas. They then rushed into the house and stabbed his body with a sword. Afterwards

they took the youngest son away to a nearby island where they "subjected him to barbarous treatment" ("The Tragic Death of a Patriot of '76").

437. Lynch, *Our Valiant Men*, 80.

438. Hadley, *Notes on the Quaker Family of Hadley*, 41.

439. Hadley, "Captain Joshua Hadley"; "Proud Descendants of Revolutionary War Hero Gather in Williamson County."

440. Healton, *A Hadley Genealogy*, 43–45.

441. Healton, *A Hadley Genealogy*, 43–45.

442. Sumner County, *Minutes*, 394, "William Payton Ass.ee &c vs. Joshua Hadley & Benjamin Rawlings, 7 June 1808," https://familysearch.org/ark:/61903/3:1:3QHV-D3CD-B3X9.

443. Sumner County, *Record of Deeds*, 11:338–39, "Joshua Hadley to John L. Hadley, 24 March 1827," https://familysearch.org/ark:/61903/3:1:3Q9M-CS4V-GSM2-Z.

444. Lynch, *Our Valiant Men*, 80.

445. "Capt Joshua Hadley."

446. His name is also spelled Phillip as well as Herring, Herrin, Her(r)en, or Her(r)on in the records.

447. NC Land Grant Office, *Land Patent Books*, 23:255, "Cumberland Co. File No. 1509, Philip Herring and Nathl. Holton," https://nclandgrants.com/grant/?mars=12.14.51.1508&qid=1147004&rn=80.

448. Cumberland County, *Record of Deeds*, 3:452, "Philip Herin to Nathaniel Hoton, 6 November 1769," https://familysearch.org/ark:/61903/3:1:3QS7-99DC-ZC27.

449. Cumberland County, *Record of Deeds*, 7:111, "James Hogg to James Burges, 24 February 1783," https://familysearch.org/ark:/61903/3:1:3QS7-8983-NXJG; Cumberland County, *Record of Deeds*, 4:391, "Philip Herren to Miran Clark, October 1771," https://familysearch.org/ark:/61903/3:1:3QS7-898M-X3GJ.

450. NC Land Grant Office, "Warrants, Surveys, and Related Documents – Cumberland County," roll 22, "No. 540 Phillip Herrin 200 acres, 25 November 1771," https://familysearch.org/ark:/61903/3:1:3QS7-99WV-TZDK.

451. NC Land Grant Office, "Warrants, Surveys, and Related Documents – Cumberland County," roll 22, "No. 540, January 1773," https://familysearch.org/ark:/61903/3:1:3QS7-L9WV-TZ52.

452. See note 377 above.

453. NC Land Grant Office, "Warrants, Surveys, and Related Documents – Cumberland County," roll 22, "Surveyd. For Phillip Herring Thirty five acres, 16 September 1772," https://familysearch.org/ark:/61903/3:1:3QSQ-G9WV-T87Z.

454. Cumberland County, *Minutes*, C:12v, https://familysearch.org/ark:/61903/3:1:3Q9M-CS4G-MWP9-K.

455. Cumberland County, *Minutes*, C:40v, https://familysearch.org/ark:/61903/3:1:3Q9M-CS4G-MWP7-Pe.

456. Cumberland County, *Minutes*, C:39r, https://familysearch.org/ark:/61903/3:1:3Q9M-CS4G-MWGD-7.

457. Chatham County, *Record of Deeds*, B:120, "Benjamin Landrum and Elizabeth His Wife to Joseph Moore, 18 November 1773," https://familysearch.org/ark:/61903/3:1:3QSQ-G987-34XG.

458. Chatham County, *Record of Deeds*, B:169, "Joseph Lyon to John Luttrell, 1 March 1778," https://familysearch.org/ark:/61903/3:1:3QS7-9987-34D3.

459. Chatham County, "Land Entries, 1778–1795," 1 roll, "No. 171 Phillip Herrin 550 Acres" and "No. 172 Phillip Herrin 250 Acres," https://familysearch.org/ark:/61903/3:1:939L-JZ9W-Q6.

460. NC Land Grant Office, *Land Patent Books*, 30:162, "Chatham Co. File No. 163, Philip Herring," https://nclandgrants.com/grant/?mars=12.14.44.163&qid=1147062&rn=1; *Land Patent Books*, 32:246, "Chatham Co. File No. 261, Philip Herring," https://nclandgrants.com/grant/?mars=12.14.44.261&qid=1147062&rn=4.

461. NC Land Grant Office, "Warrants, Surveys, and Related Documents – Chatham County," roll 2, "Surveyed for William Alston, 18 March 1779," https://familysearch.org/ark:/61903/3:1:3QSQ-G9WK-9549; roll 1, "Surveyed for Danial Yarnall, 25 March 1779," https:/familysearch.org/ark:/61903/3:1:3QS7-89WK-9Y4H; roll 2, "Surveyed for Samuel Stewart, 20 January 1780," https://familysearch.org/ark:/ 61903/3:1:3QS7-99WK-9BDN; roll 2, "Surveyd. for Henry Bray, 20 January 1780," https://familysearch.org/ark:/61903/3:1:3QS7-99WK-99MH-Z. At the time surveyors used a device known as a Gunter's Chain for measuring out plots of land. This chain, named after Edmund Gunter, the English mathematician who developed it, was exactly 66 feet long and made up of 100 links that were each 7.92 inches long. Because of this specific measurement, one square chain was 484 square yards, ten square chains was an acre, and eighty chains was a mile. Surveyors would employ two people to be "chain carriers," where one would keep an end of the chain in place with a stake while the other stretched it out along the azimuth the surveyor directed. Once the chain reached its full length another stake would be placed in that end, the first stake would be taken up, and the chain would be moved up to stretch out from the new stake and continue to follow the directions of the surveyor (Coquillon, "Practicing Measurement with Historic Surveying"; "Surveyor's Chain").

462. "NC, Revolutionary Pay Vouchers," https://familysearch.org/ark:/61903/3:1:3QSQ-G9W8-J9S5, image 381 of 884.

463. "NC, Revolutionary Pay Vouchers," https://familysearch.org/ark:/61903/3:1:3QS7-L9W8-J977, image 383 of 884. There is no indication that he had any further involvement in the Revolutionary War.

464. Chatham County, *Record of Deeds*, D:37, "1 August 1785," https://familysearch.org/ark:/61903/3:1:3QS7-8987-QDP6.

465. Chatham County, *Record of Deeds*, D:452, "State of NC No. 790, https://familysearch.org/ark:/61903/3:1:3QS7-8987-QDFK; Chatham County, *Record of Deeds*, D:360, https://familysearch.org/ark:/61903/3:1:3QS7-9987-Q8DM.

466. Chatham County, *Record of Deeds*, D:568, https://familysearch.org/ark:/61903/3:1:3QS7-L987-Q8Z3.

467. Chatham County, "Deeds, Bills of Sale, Inventories of Estates & Wills," roll 1, p. 58, "An Inventory of the Estate of Phillip Herrin decd., November 1789," https://familysearch.org/ark:/61903/3:1:3QS7-L98M-879D; Chatham County, "Deeds, Bills of Sale, Inventories of Estates & Wills," roll 2, p. 125, "An Accot. of the Sale of the Estate of Philip Herren Deceased, 29 November 1789," https://familysearch.org/ark:/61903/3:1:3QS7-L9GC-69NP-W.

468. "John Hay and Co, Jan 1799," 154–55, line 28.

469. McBride, "Claims of British Merchants After the Revolutionary War," pt. 11, 245.

470. Other signers that received items from the estate of John Bronlow include Robert Rowan, Arthur Council, Lewis Barge, Philip Herin, Lewis Bowell, Theophilus Evans, and James Gee ("Brownlow, John 1772," in Cumberland County, "Estate Records," roll 4, https://familysearch.org/ark:/61903/3:2:77TD-JV9N-G).

471. "John Hay and Co, Jan 1799."

472. Pruitt, *Abstract of Land Entries*, 38, 57, 91.

473. Bladen County, *Record of Deeds*, 25:355, "James Council to Hugh Brown, 15 November 1787," https://familysearch.org/ark:/61903/3:1:3QSQ-G98M-645Y; Salley Jr., *Stub Entries*, 4:270 270, https://familysearch.org/ark:/61903/3:1:3Q9M-CSFF-L5LV.

474. Bladen County, *Record of Deeds*, 25:355, https://familysearch.org/ark:/61903/3:1:3QSQ-G98M-645Y.

475. Salley Jr., *Stub Entries*, 4:270.

476. Bladen County, *Record of Deeds*, 25:355, https://familysearch.org/ark:/61903/3:1:3QSQ-G98M-645Y.

477. Bladen County, *Record of Deeds*, 12:571–72, "James Purdie to James Council, 10 May 1786," https://familysearch.org/ark:/61903/3:1:3QS7-898M-FSFX; Robeson County, *Record of Deeds*, 5:113, "Jas. S. Purdie to Hugh Brown, 10 May 1786," https://familysearch.org/ark:/61903/3:1:3QS7-998Q-7SKC.

478. Chatham County, *Record of Deeds*, G:115–16, "William Herrin to Benjamin and Thomas Tyson, 19 July 1793," https://familysearch.org/ark:/61903/3:1:3QS7-8987-3C84.

479. Edgefield County, Probate Records, box 14, pkg. 508, "Wm Herrin Will John Herrin Exor," https://familysearch.org/ark:/61903/3:1:3Q9M-C9YB-F9ZN-6.

480. Edgefield County, Probate Records, box 14, pkg. 508, "Wm Herrin Will John Herrin Exor," https://familysearch.org/ark:/61903/3:1:3Q9M-C9YB-F9ZN-6. The names of the children were John, Margaret, Catharine, Elizabeth, Nancy, Henry, Mary, Hannah, Dolly, Philip, William Jr., and Peter. The names of the enslaved persons were Handy and Delsy. For whatever reason William Herin only left $1 each to Henry, Mary, Hannah, Dolly, Philip, William Jr., and Peter.

481. Hollingsworth, "General History"; descendant Cathrine Marsh Cashwell, email message to author, August 6, 2025.

482. Cashwell, email, August 6, 2025; Bladen County, *Wills*, 2:550, https://familysearch.org/ark:/61903/3:1:939L-JWSZ-3H; Weis, *Colonial Clergy*, 64; Chowan County, "Suits Dismissed and Miscellaneous Court Papers, 1687–1783," roll 17, https://familysearch.org/ark:/61903/3:1:3QS7-89GF-K3XD

483. Weis, *Colonial Clergy*, 64; Marsh and Cashwell, *The History of the Cape Fear Baptist Church*, 18–19.

484. Campbell, *Bladen County*, 1:25; Cashwell, email, August 6, 2025.

485. Cashwell, email, August 6, 2025.

486. "Samuel Hollingsworth Senr. & Saml. Carver."

487. Fields, *Abstracts of Minutes*, 1:201, 206, 215, 226, 241.

488. Fields, *Abstracts of Minutes*, 1:241. A legacy is described in guardianship records as the "property or money bequeathed to someone in a will" (see "Glossary of Genealogical Terms"). The two Carver siblings received the rest of their assigned properties and exited guardianship officially in court. This process may have been similar to exit processes for apprenticed orphans who received "freedom dues" through North Carolina orphan laws (see Watson, "Orphanage in Colonial North Carolina," 112).

489. Fields, *Abstracts of Minutes*, 2:98.

490. Fields, *Abstracts of Minutes*, 2:274–75.

491. Fields, Abstracts of Minutes, 2:297.

492. McBride, "Claims of British Merchants After the Revolutionary War," pt. 6, 195.

493. "Samuel Hollingsworth," in Comptroller's Office Accounts, p. 274, line entry 324.

494. Haun, *NC Revolutionary Army Accounts*, 4:470, 479.

495. T. D. McDowell Papers, document case 1, folder 12: 1779.

496. T. D. McDowell Papers, case 1, folder 18: 1785–1786; case 1, folder 20: 1789.

497. Fields, *Abstracts of Minutes*, 2:90.

498. Mann, *Republic of Debtors*, 46.

499. Mann, *Republic of Debtors*, 26.

500. Mann, *Republic of Debtors*, 33.

501. "Bill to Add Part of Bladen County to Cumberland (with Petition)." Hollingsworth was the second person to sign.

502. First Census, "Samuel Hollingsworth," population schedule for Cumberland (excluding Fayetteville), NC, 1790, NARA microfilm M637, roll 7, p. 92 (handwritten), line 25, https://familysearch.org/ark:/61903/3:1:33S7-9YY8-S21T.

503. Cumberland County, *Trial Docket Fayetteville District Superior Court*, vol. 1, October Term 1791, docket 87, https://familysearch.org/ark:/61903/3:1:3QS7-89Q8-Y7KV. Statute of limitations in North Carolina was for seven years at the time (*CSR*, 23:32–33).

504. Cumberland County, *Trial Docket Fayetteville District Superior Court*, vol. 1, October Term 1791, docket 89, https://familysearch.org/ark:/61903/3:1:3QS7-89Q8-Y7KV.

505. Stewart, *Descendants of Valentine Hollingsworth*, Sr, 140.

506. "Cumberland Centennial."

507. Stewart, *Descendants of Valentine Hollingsworth, Sr*, 141–42. See also "Col. J. G. Hollingsworth Dead," 3.

508. Pruitt, *Cumberland County, NC, Taxables*, 100.

509. NC Land Grant Office, *Land Patent Books*, 23:24, "Cumberland Co. File No. 1428, John Jones," https://nclandgrants.com/frame/?fdr=41&frm=438.

510. Lewis, *NC Patriots*, 2(2):515; Moss, *Roster of Patriots*, 119.

511. NC Land Grant Office, *Land Patent Books*, 105:2–3, "Cumberland Co. File No. 3606, John Jones" and "Cumberland Co. File No. 3607, John Jones," https://nclandgrants.com/frame/?fdr=74&frm=18.

512. Cumberland County, *Record of Deeds*, 6:41–42, "Deed of Sale John Stevens to Martin Leonard, 2 December 1772," https://familysearch.org/ark:/61903/3:1:3QS7-898Y-G6P.

513. Cumberland County, *Record of Deeds*, 6:41–42, https://familysearch.org/ark:/61903/3:1:3QS7-898Y-G6P.

514. Fields, *Abstracts of Minutes*, 1:229.

515. Fields, *Abstracts of Minutes*, 1:234.

516. Fields, *Abstracts of Minutes*, 1:285, 310, 325. Lewis Bowel[l] was granted a license to have a tavern on January 30, 1779. His securities included Martin Leonard and James Dick.

517. Lewis, *NC Patriots*, 1:561; "Moores Creek Bridge."

518. Fields, *Abstracts of Minutes*, 1:325.

519. Cates, "Legislative Petitions, 1778," 47–48.

520. Cates, "Legislative Petitions, 1778," 47–48.

521. McBride, "Claims of British Merchants After the Revolutionary War," pt. 4, 23.

522. *CSR*, 15:192.

523. Caruthers, *Old North State in 1776*, 102; Lewis, "Brunswick County Regiment of Militia."

524. Caruthers, Old North State in 1776, 102.

525. Turner, "A Bill to Bring Traitors to Trial, 1782," 421.

526. Newman, "Cases Heard Before Wilmington District Superior Court, Summary Information," pt. 5, 147.

527. "NC, Revolutionary Pay Vouchers," https://familysearch.org/ark:/61903/3:1:3QS7-L9WB-8LFP, images 634–35 of 923.

528. Fields, *Abstracts of Deeds*, 1:304–5; Fields, *Abstracts of Minutes*, 1:126.

529. NC Land Grant Office, "Warrants, Surveys, and Related Documents – Cumberland County," roll 22, 0354 "Mackie, Robt.; Robt. Bannerman & Peter Messur, 26 October 1765," https://familysearch.org/ark:/61903/3:1:3QS7-L9WV-TD9H; MacMillan, *Fayetteville About 1770*.

530. Potts, *A Map of Campbelton*.

531. Robeson County, *Wills: 1783–1851*, 3:49, https://familysearch.org/ark:/61903/3:2:77T2-232Y. His dad gave him his smith tools and land when he died and was from Robeson County.

532. Fields, *Abstracts of Deeds*, 1:389–90; Pruitt, *Cumberland County, NC, Taxables*, 101.

533. Fields, *Abstracts of Minutes*, 1:157.

534. Cumberland County, *Record of Deeds*, 6:136, "Peter Messer to John Turner, 27 April 1774," https://familysearch.org/ ark:/61903/3:1:3QSQ-G98Y-L4W5. She was *probably* Hannah Terrell, since this deed asks her to give up the land for her dowery, and Peter Messer had originally bought the land from the Terrell's, which implies she was married to him.

535. Lewis, *NC Patriots*, 2(2):650.

536. Fields, *Abstracts of Minutes*, 1:270.

537. Fields, *Abstracts of Minutes*, 1:319, 2:40.

538. Pruitt, *Cumberland County, NC, Taxables*, 39.

539. Lewis, *NC Patriots*, 1:515; S.41,892, for Thomas Moody, NC, NAID 196271254, image 7, in Revolutionary War Pension and Bounty Land Warrant Application Files, Records of the VA, RG 15, https://catalog.archives.gov/id/196271254?objectPage=7.

540. S.41,892, image 10, in Revolutionary War Pension and Bounty Land Warrant Application Files, Records of the VA, RG 15, https://catalog.archives.gov/id/196271254?objectPage=10.

541. "Moody, Thomas - South Carolina - First Company," in *Compiled Service Records*, Revolutionary War Records, RG 93, https://catalog.archives.gov/id/142071533.

542. S.41,892, image 4, in Revolutionary War Pension and Bounty Land Warrant Application Files, https://catalog.archives.gov/id/196271254?objectPage=4.

543. Crane, "FILI To Pay Tribute to 'The Old Fifer,'" 1d.

544. First Census, "Thomas Moody," population schedule for Cumberland (excluding Fayetteville), NC, 1790, NARA microfilm M637, roll 7, p. 95

(handwritten), line 37, https://familysearch.org/ark:/61903/3:1:33SQ-GYY8-3WHJ; Second Census, population schedule for Fayetteville (Cumberland), NC, 1800, NARA microfilm M32, roll 31, p. 373 (handwritten), line 26, https://familysearch.org/ark:/61903/3:1:33S7-9R8C-G6Q; Third Census, population schedule for Fayetteville, NC, Fayetteville District, 1810, NARA microfilm M252, roll 39, Records of the Census, RG 29, National Archives, p. 620 (handwritten), line 17, https://familysearch.org/ark:/61903/3:1:33S7-9YY8-S6VN; Fourth Census, population schedule for Fayetteville, NC, 1820, NARA microfilm M33, roll 83, p. 210 (typed), line 21, https://familysearch.org/ark:/61903/3:1:33S7-9YYJ-S996; Fifth Census, population schedule for Fayetteville, NC, Fayetteville District, 1830, NARA microfilm M19, roll 120, Records of the Census, RG 29, National Archives, p. 92 (handwritten), line 15, https://familysearch.org/ark:/61903/3:1:33S7-9YY6-9T4J.

545. Cumberland County, *Record of Deeds*, 20:220, "Thomas Moody & Mariam Moody His Wife to Paris J Tillinghast Junr., 11 July 1804," https://familysearch.org/ark:/61903/3:1:3QS7-898N-WFL6.

546. First Presbyterian Church, "Minutes, Church Records, and Sermons, 1792–1957," roll 3, "Births, Deaths, and Marriages 1809–1835," https://familysearch.org/ark:/61903/3:1:3Q9M-CSVY-WSJV-7.

547. "The Boating Business," 1; see also "Steamboat Henrietta for Sale 6 June 1827," 3; "Mercantile Reports," 3; and Oates, *The Story of Fayetteville*, 192.

548. "Ran Away."

549. "Moody, Thomas," in Ledgers of Payments, 1818–1872, roll 2, "Volume B: Revolutionary War Pensioners Act of 1818," Records of the Accounting Officers of the Department of the Treasury, RG 217, National Archives, p. 332 (handwritten), line 5, https://familysearch.org/ark:/61903/3:1:3QS7-99WB-Z9J2.

550. St. John's Episcopal Church, *Parish Register*, 2:57, https://familysearch.org/ark:/61903/3:1:3Q9M-CSVY-C5W6.

551. Meyer, *Highland Scots*, 144.

552. *CSR*, 11:626–31.

553. Hilldrup, "The Salt Supply of North Carolina," 402–3

554. Hilldrup, "The Salt Supply of North Carolina," 402–3.

555. Fields, *Abstracts of Minutes*, 1:276. For more, see the section on William Gillespie.

556. Fields, *Abstracts of Minutes*, 1:270.

557. House Bills (April 21): Bill for Regulating Campbellton and Erecting Public Buildings (with Petition); Lewis, *NC Patriots*, 2(1):522, 617, 651; House Resolution for Appointing Field Officers of Cumberland County. See also Johnson, *Hometown Heritage*, 1:168–69.

558. Fields, *Abstracts of Minutes*, 1:289–90, 317; 2:22, 37.

559. Fields, Abstracts of Minutes, 1:303.

560. Pruitt, *Cumberland County, NC, Taxables*, 33.

561. GBAO, *American Loyalists*, 47:194.

562. GBAO, *American Loyalists*, 47:194; Clark, "Resolves Signers Fought with Loyalists," E1. A 'freeholder' was someone who owns property rather than rents it (Harris and Harris, *Ancestry's Concise Genealogical Dictionary*, 101).

563. Clark, "Resolves Signers Fought with Loyalists," E1.

564. GBAO, *American Loyalists*, 47:205.

565. "White, William (Cumberland County)"; Clark, "Resolves Signers Fought with Loyalists," E1.

566. Clark, "Resolves Signers Fought with Loyalists," E1.

567. Decisions, Examinations, Army and Navy, 1789, 46–47 (handwritten).

568. GBAO, *American Loyalists*, 47:194.

569. *CSR*, 10:597.

570. Clark, *Loyalists in the Southern Campaign of the Revolutionary War*, 1:426.

571. GBAO, *American Loyalists*, 47:195.

572. GBAO, *American Loyalists*, 47:281.

573. *CSR*, 10:964–65.

574. *CSR*, 10:972.

575. GBAO, *American Loyalists*, 47:194.

576. GBAO, *American Loyalists*, 47:195.

577. GBAO, *American Loyalists*, 47:195.

578. Moss, *Roster of Loyalists*, 63; GBAO, *American Loyalists*, 47:192.

579. GBAO, *American Loyalists*, 47:191. However, Nowlan also claimed that Elice had been sold by him in 1775, so her inclusion in the list was a mistake (GBAO, *American Loyalists*, 47:198).

580. GBAO, *American Loyalists*, 47:193.

581. Coldham, American Migrations, 645.

582. Fields, *Abstracts of Minutes*, 1:263, 310; 2:15.

583. Pruitt, *Cumberland County, NC, Taxables*, 34.

584. NC Land Grant Office, "Warrants, Surveys, and Related Documents – Bladen County," roll 5, "John Oveler One Hundred, 18 May 1778," https://familysearch.org/ark:/61903/3:1:3QS7-89WV-BS8X; "Warrants, Surveys, and Related Documents – Bladen County," roll 10, "Survey'd for John Oveler Three Hundred Acres, 27 June 1776," https://familysearch.org/ark:/61903/3:1:3QS7-99WV-B9MZ-J.

585. Bladen County, NC, *Record of Deeds*, vol. 1738–1779, 191, "John Oviler & Wife to Richard Smith, 8 August 1770," https://familysearch.org/ark:/61903/3:1:3QS7-L98M-69VV.

586. Fields, *Abstracts of Minutes*, 1:176-177.

587. NC Land Grant Office, "Warrants, Surveys, and Related Documents – Cumberland County," roll 3, "Surveyd. for John McLarren & Archd. McGoogen, 18 September 1772," https://familysearch.org/ark:/61903/3:1:3QSQ-G9WK-CH4P.

588. See note 328 above.

589. Cumberland County, *Record of Deeds*, 3:96, "Micajah Terrel to John Parker, 24 February 1773," https://familysearch.org/ark:/61903/3:1:3QS7-998Y-L4X5.

590. Parker, *Parker Family*, 20; "Parker, John 1818," in Cumberland County, "Estate Records," roll 27, https://familysearch.org/ark:/61903/3:2:77TD-VD36; "Parker, John 1802," in Cumberland County, "Estate Records," roll 27, https://familysearch.org/ark:/61903/3:2:77TD-VD3D.

591. "Dawson, John 1793," in Cumberland County, "Estate Records," roll 8, https://familysearch.org/ark:/61903/3:2:77TD-JG9V-M.

592. "Parker, John 1802," in Cumberland County, "Estate Records," roll 27, https://familysearch.org/ark:/61903/3:2:77TD-VD3D.

593. "Parker, Kader 1807," in Edgecombe County, "Estate Records," roll 31, https://familysearch.org/ark:/61903/3:1:33S7-91QY-6R3.

594. Parker, *Parker Family*, 20.

595. "Parker, John 1818," in Cumberland County, "Estate Records," roll 27, https://familysearch.org/ark:/61903/3:2:77TD-VD36.

596. "Parker, John 1818," in Cumberland County, "Estate Records," roll 27, https://familysearch.org/ark:/61903/3:2:77TD-VD3X.

597. Lewis, *NC Patriots*, 2(2):744–45; "Moores Creek Bridge."

598. *CSR*, 10:944.

599. "North Carolina, 8th Regiment, 1777, Jacket 9," image 4, NAID 503390974, NAID 503390974, in Revolutionary War Rolls, War Department Collection of Revolutionary War Records, RG 93. https://catalog.archives.gov/id/503390974; *CSR*, 16:577. The same board of officers who recommended James Pearl for promotion also recommended fellow signer Robert Greer for promotion to first lieutenant.

600. Lewis, *NC Patriots*, 2(2):744; NC DAR, *Roster of Soldiers*, 44; *CSR*, 16:577.

601. Lewis, *NC Patriots*, 2(2):744; NC DAR, *Roster of Soldiers*, 44.

602. Moss, Roster of Patriots, 163.

603. *CSR*, 16:260.

604. *CSR*, 15:568–69.

605. *CSR*, 18:485–86. Only two other signers have the honor of this distinction: Captain Joshua Hadley and Lieutenant John Clendenin.

606. Linn, "Revolutionary War Claims," part 7, 30.

607. Linn and McBride, "Private Petitions," pt. 1, 151; McBride, "Revolutionary War Service Records and Settlements," 212; *CSR*, 17:206, 215, 220, 227, 233.

608. Richmond County, *Record of Deeds*, B:175, https://familysearch.org/ark:/61903/3:1:3QS7-998Q-S6CN; Richmond County, *Minutes*, 1:128, https://familysearch.org/ark:/61903/3:1:3Q9M-CSTM-SSCM-B; Richmond County, *Minutes*, 1:55, https://familysearch.org/ark:/61903/3:1:3Q9M-CSLZ-BS7F-9.

609. Fields, *Abstracts of Minutes*, 2:202, 205.

610. Fields, *Abstracts of Minutes*, 2:223.

611. Fields, *Abstracts of Minutes*, 2:265.

612. Fields, *Abstracts of Minutes*, 2:275.

613. Cumberland County, *Trial Docket Fayetteville District Superior Court*, vol. 1, dkt. 142, Apr. 1793, https://familysearch.org/ark:/61903/3:1:3QS7-99Q8-Y72Q; dkt. 104, Oct. 1793, https://familysearch.org/ark:/61903/3:1:3QS7-99Q8-Y7J5; dkt 76, Apr. 1794, https://familysearch.org/ark:/61903/3:1:3QS7-99Q8-Y7T2; dkt. 61, Oct. 1794, https://familysearch.org/ark:/61903/3:1:3QS7-L9Q8-Y7GB; dkt. 52, Apr. 1795, https://familysearch.org/ark:/61903/3:1:3QS7-89Q8-Y7LH; vol. 2, *Oct 1795–Apr 1804*, dkt. 36, Oct. 1795, https://familysearch.org/ark:/61903/3:1:3QSQ-G9Q8-YQD8; dkt. 29, Apr. 1796, https://familysearch.org/ark:/61903/3:1:3QS7-89Q8-YQVS; dkt. 23, Oct. 1796, https://familysearch.org/ark:/61903/3:1:3QS7-89Q8-YQGY.

614. *CSR*, 19:933.

615. Perquimans County, "Estate Records," roll 37, https://familysearch.org/ark:/61903/3:1:3QS7-L9CD-BVN5; Chowan County, "Estate Records," roll 48, https://familysearch.org/ark:/61903/3:1:33S7-9RVY-37P.

616. Meyer, *Highland Scots*, 144.

617. Rowan was an active member of Cumberland who signed numerous documents, enough that it was later said that his "hand writing is as well known to all the old settlers, as the face of any man in the community" ("American Independence").

618. *Apr. 29: Report on Petition of Robert Rowan and Others (Rejected). CSR*, 5: xi. There is reference to a Major Rowan, but he is not the same as *Cumberland's* Rowan (*CSR*, 5:131, 136).

619. *CSR*, 6: 992–93; "Governor Arthur Dobbs: Bond of Rowan, July 19, 1763,"; *Apr. 29: Report on Petition of Robert Rowan and Others (Rejected).*

620. Fields, *Abstracts of Deeds*, 1:181; 2:33.

621. Holcomb, *Greer and Related Families*, 3.

622. *CSR*, 9:572; *CSR*, 22:545; "History of Sheriffs." Based on Fields's *Abstracts of Minutes* and *Abstracts of Deeds* records, Rowan served as sheriff *at least* from 1770 to 1771 and in 1774 (Fields, *Abstracts of Deeds*, 2:11, 16, 135; *Abstracts of Minutes*, 1:233). Rowan was a judge for at least the following years according to the local court minute books: 1772, 1774–75, 1778, 1780, 1782, 1784–88, and 1790 (Fields, *Abstracts of Minutes*, 1:190, 207, 223, 252, 299; 2:40, 62, 74, 107, 165, 190, 270).

623. *South Carolina Gazette*, July 5, 1770, 3.

624. *CSR*, 9:745, 776, 1179; Cheney Jr., *North Carolina Government 1585–1979*, 56–57.

625. *CSR*, 10:29–30; Clark, in Cumberland County Bicentennial Commission, *Bicentennial News*, 2; Liberty Point, Jack Crane Collection, Cumberland County Public Library.

626. "Cumberland Centennial."

627. Lewis, *NC Patriots*, 1:3; Hay and Whitaker, *Rosters of Soldiers from North Carolina in the American Revolution*, 603; *CSR*, 10:955.

628. Clark, in Cumberland County Bicentennial Commission, *Bicentennial News*, 2.

629. Haun, *NC Revolutionary Army Accounts*, 1:7. They were Simon Banday, John Clendenin, Arthur Council, David and Theophilus Evans, George Fletcher, Joshua Hadley, Micajah Terrell, and Thomas White.

630. Hugh McDonald Papers, State Archives of NC, https://digital.ncdcr.gov/Documents/Detail/hugh-mcdonald-papers-1776-1777/424262?item=424312, 12.

631. Hatch Jr., *The Battle of Moores Creek Bridge*, 38.

632. Rankin, *The Moores Creek Bridge Campaign*, 34.

633. Lewis, *NC Patriots*, 1:231; Camin, "Revolutionary War Pension Applications at the NC Archives," *NCGS Journal* 11, no. 1 (1985): 16.

634. *CSR*, 11:387–88, 394–96; *CSR*, 12:325; *CSR*, 11:560–61; Clark, in Cumberland County Bicentennial Commission, *Bicentennial News*, 2.

635. Fields, *Abstracts of Minutes*, 1:270. The following Liberty Point individuals also signed: Lewis Barge, Lewis Bowell, Theophilus Evans, George Fletcher, James Gee, Martin Leonard, Peter Messer, John Oveler, James Pearl, David Shepherd, and Charles Stevens. In 1782, Rowan signed another loyalty oath that was quite like this one (Fields, *Abstracts of Minutes*, 1:190).

636. Fields, *Abstracts of Minutes*, 1:269. This test oath was signed by twenty residents and said that the signers "declare that I do believe that there is not any Transubstantiation in the Sacrament of the Lords Supper or in the Elements of Bread and Wine at or after the Consecration thereof by any person whatsoever."

637. Richards, "John Adams and the Moderate Federalists," *NC Historical Review* 43, no. 1 (1966): 21. See also *CSR*, 11:627–31. This was also perhaps partly in response to how Rowan had handled a mob that had tried to take salt from Cross Creek. Gov. Caswell and others said they were Tory mobs who were only pretending to get salt, while Rowan disagreed (see Hilldrup, "The Salt Supply of North Carolina," 393–417 and *CSR*, 11:603).

638. *CSR*, 24:9–10.

639. *CSR*, 11:627, 629.

640. *CSR*, 11:630.

641. *CSR*, 11:629–30.

642. *CSR*, 11:628. Alston's overzealousness for the Patriot cause and his hotheadedness would continue; later in the war he captured a Loyalist at the rear of David Fanning's forces in July 1781 and instantly put him to death (*CSR*, 22:550). In 1786, Alston had to give up his seat in the General Assembly because he had been indicted for murder (*CSR*, 20:32, 69).

643. *CSR*, 11:629.

644. Willcox, *A History of the House in the Horseshoe*, 254.

645. Willcox, *A History of the House in the Horseshoe*, 254, 113.

646. *CSR*, 9:574; Willcox, *A History of the House in the Horseshoe*, 81.

647. *CSR*, 10:164–66.

648. *CSR*, 13:403.

649. *CSR*, 12:860.

650. *Delmar Transcripts*, 170.

651. *CSR*, 12:860; Clark, in Cumberland County Bicentennial Commission, *Bicentennial News*, 4. Rowan later claimed that position anyway after Alston was taken prisoner in 1779 (*Delmar Transcripts*, 117; *CSR*, 1579–80, 156).

652. House Bills (April 21): Bill for Regulating Campbellton and Erecting Public Buildings (with Petition); *CSR*, 24:180, 695.

653. *CSR*, 13:903–4.

654. *CSR*, 14:387, 418, 446–47, 15:182.

655. Hugh McDonald Papers, 12, https://digital.ncdcr.gov/Documents/Detail/hugh-mcdonald-papers-1776-1777/424262?item=424312.

656. Hugh McDonald Papers, 12, https://digital.ncdcr.gov/Documents/Detail/hugh-mcdonald-papers-1776-1777/424262?item=424312.

657. Caruthers, *Old North State in 1776*, 174.

658. *CSR*, 15:182.

659. Fields, *Abstracts of Minutes*, 2:42.

660. "July 4: Petition of Thomas Cabeen, 1781"; Cates, "Legislative Petitions, 1780–1781," 43.

661. Pruitt, *Cumberland County, NC, Taxables*, 32–33.

662. "From John Ramsey, 21 August 1781"; *CSR*, 22:570. It is unclear if this is the same arrest as that previously, when Loyalists caught Rowan and Theophilus Evans. While the raid was associated with Loyalist David Fanning, it was the Loyalist commander McNiel who captured the men at Cross Creek (*CSR*, 22:566). See also Hairr, *Colonel David Fanning*, 107.

663. *CSR*, 24:515. Joining him as town directors for 1783 were Robert Cockran, James Patterson, Lewis Barge, Robertson Montford, James Burges, and John Ingrum.

664. Mathews, "Forgive Us Our Debts," 55.

665. Mathews, "Forgive Us Our Debts," 60; "Definitive Treaty of Peace Between the United States and Great Britain, 3 September 1783."

666. Mann, *Republic of Debtors*, 176.

667. McBride, "Claims of British Merchants After the Revolutionary War," pt. 5, 115.

668. Fields, *Abstracts of Minutes*, 1:244; 2:104, 150; 1:199.

669. "Robert Rowan (circa 1738–1798)"; MacMillan, *Fayetteville About 1770*; Fields, *Abstracts of Deeds*, 2:191–93, 238; "Reminiscences of Fayetteville in the Olden Times," 3. Rowan owned property on what is now Rowan/Grove street, based on the following deed map, and there are multiple deed entries showing that Rowan and his stepson William owned plots in downtown Cross Creek, which is strong circumstantial evidence that Rowan street was named after Robert, though as of yet we have not found a primary source document that expressly says that the street was named for him. It was already called Rowan Street when Rowan was alive, as shown in his will.

670. "Greer, Thomas 1783," in Cumberland County, "Original Wills," roll 3, https://familysearch.org/ark:/61903/3:1:3QS7-L9GW-BN8G; Parker, *Cumberland: Brief History*, 15; LMJ Collection, folder 47.

671. Richards, "John Adams and the Moderate Federalists," 22–24.

672. Richards, "John Adams and the Moderate Federalists," 23.

673. "History of Sheriffs."

674. Cheney Jr., *North Carolina Government 1585–1979*, 216; *CSR*, 20: 265, 442, 465.

675. *CSR*, 17:413, 416.

676. *CSR*, 18:212.

677. "Tench Coxe to Alexander Hamilton, 13 December 1792." (Original source: See Syrett, *The Papers of Alexander Hamilton*, 13:317–19).

678. "From John Adams to United States Senate, 12 February 1798."

679. "Genealogical and Biographical Research Part 2."

680. "To John Adams from Robert Rowan, 13 March 1798."

681. "To John Adams from Joshua Winslow, 27 October 1798."

682. "Col Robert Rowan."

683. Johnson, *Hometown Heritage*, 1:166.

684. "Rowan, Robert 1799," in Cumberland County, "Original Wills," roll 7, https://familysearch.org/ark:/61903/3:1:3QSQ-G9G4-SBXW. In 1787, Rowan sold the following enslaved individuals to Hay: Sampson, Kit, and Ben (Fields, *Abstracts of Minutes*, 2:182–83).

685. Fields, *Abstracts of Minutes*, 2:101.

686. "Rowan, Robert 1799," in Cumberland County, "Original Wills," roll 7, https://familysearch.org/ark:/61903/3:1:3QSQ-G9G4-S1MR.

687. "Rowan, Robert 1799," in Cumberland County, "Original Wills," roll 7, https://familysearch.org/ark:/61903/3:1:3QSQ-G9G4-S1MR.

688. Cumberland County, *Minutes*, vol. 1801–1804, "11 May 1803," "Tavern License Granted to David Shepperd," https://familysearch.org/ark:/61903/3:1:-3Q9M-CSKV-S9J3-5; "The Fourth of July at Fayetteville"; "Town of Fayetteville."

689. Moss, *Roster of Patriots*, 192.

690. Fields, *Abstracts of Minutes*, 1:270. The oath can be viewed at https://familysearch.org/ark:/61903/3:1:3Q9M-CS4G-MWGD-R.

691. Fields, *Abstracts of Minutes*, 1:275.

692. Fields, *Abstracts of Minutes*, 1:277.

693. Fields, *Abstracts of Minutes*, 1:277–78. The document can be viewed at https://familysearch.org/ark:/61903/3:1:3Q9M-CS4G-MWGQ-5.

694. Fields, *Abstracts of Minutes*, 1:277–78.

695. "Multiple Classified Advertisements."

696. "The Fourth of July at Fayetteville."

697. "The Fourth of July at Fayetteville." This military dining tradition is known as a Mess Night, though today is most often referred to as a "Dining-In" or "Dining-Out" depending on if there are guests present other than the military organization, or "members of the mess." The President of the Mess is the commanding officer of the organization, and it is his (or her) duty to assemble the mess and enforce the formalities and traditions of the mess (Garvin, "Conduct of the Mess"; "Guide to the Military Dining-In"; Civil Engineer Corps Officers Naval School, *Mess Night Manual*).

698. "It Gives Us Pleasure to Lay the Following Before Our Readers."

699. Cumberland County, *Record of Deeds*, 37:35, "David Shepherd to James Millar, 11 March 1826," https://familysearch.org/ark:/61903/3:1:3QS7-99DC-8WFY.

700. "Mr. Jefferson and North Carolina."

701. Cumberland County, *Record of Deeds*, 2:589, "Edward Dunfield to Charles Stevens, 28 September 1764," https://familysearch.org/ark:/61903/3:1:3QS7-898M-D7VB; *Record of Deeds*, 3:184, "Drurry Francis to Charles Stevens, 24 August 1767," https://familysearch.org/ark:/61903/3:1:3QSQ-G9DC-Z39Z; *Record of Deeds*, 3:456, "Charles Stevens to Moore Stevens, 17 July 1769," https://familysearch.org/ark:/61903/3:1:3QS7-89DC-ZSPQ; *Record of Deeds*, 7:276, "Charles Stevens to William Armstrong, 17 April 1778," https://familysearch.org/ark:/61903/3:1:3QSQ-G983-N6QT.

702. Cumberland County, *Record of Deeds*, 5:155, "Charles Stevens to Ferqd. Campbell, 20 April 1772," https://familysearch.org/ark:/61903/3:1:3QS7-99DC-XNMH.

703. Fields, *Abstracts of Minutes*, 1:196, 214.

704. Fields, *Abstracts of Minutes* 1:252.

705. "Further Report on Claim of John Hay and Co. To Debts Due in North Carolina [n.d.], [1800]," State Archives of NC, 66-67 (handwritten), line 2.

706. "Charles Stevens," in Wilmington District Superior Court, *Minutes*, record ID SR 398.8, 165.

707. Parker, *Cumberland: Brief History*, 12; see also Fields, Abstracts of Deeds, 1:86.

708. Pruitt, *Cumberland County, NC, Taxables*, 6, 103.

709. Fields, *Abstracts of Minutes*, 1:270.

710. Dicken, *Terrell Genealogy*, 236; Barnhill, *Richmond, William, and Timothy Terrell*, 28.

711. Cumberland County, *Record of Deeds*, 6:96, "Micajah Terrell to John Parker, 24 February 1773," https://familysearch.org/ark:/61903/3:1:3QS7-998Y-L4X5.

712. NC Land Grant Office, "Warrants, Surveys, and Related Documents – Cumberland County," roll 3, "Surveyd. for John Parker Kedar Parker and Micajah Terrill, 3 December 1773," https://familysearch.org/ark:/61903/3:1:3QSQ-G9WK-C3QR; NC Land Grant Office, *Land Patent Books*, 26:147, "Cumberland Co. File No. 1724, John Parker, Kedar Parker, and Micajah Terrell," https://nclandgrants.com/grant/?mars=12.14.51.1722&qid=1180474&rn=84.

713. Cumberland County, *Minutes*, D:54r, https://familysearch.org/ark:/61903/3:1:3Q9M-CS4G-MWG6-S.

714. Dicken, *Terrell Genealogy*, 236.

715. Dicken, *Terrell Genealogy*, 236.

716. Cumberland County, *Record of Deeds*, 10:382, "Saml. Johnson Govr. to Micajah Terrell, 18 May 1789," https://familysearch.org/ark:/61903/3:1:3QS7-9981-H7NT-B; Dicken, *Terrell Genealogy*, 236.

717. Dicken, *Terrell Genealogy*, 236–37; Barnhill, *Richmond, William, and Timothy Terrell*, 28–29. His children were James, Archibald, Timothy, Hannah, Samuel, Winnifred, Martin, Elizabeth, Sarah, and Mary.

718. Dicken, *Terrell Genealogy*, 236.

719. Adams County, *Will Records*, 1:18, https://familysearch.org/ark:/61903/3:1:3QS7-L9QD-Z99C-M; Adams County, *Orphans Court Minutes*, 1:61, https://familysearch.org/ark:/61903/3:1:3QS7-L9Q8-2RRW. Fun fact: Micajah Terrell is of royal descent and his line can be traced back to the grandfather of Alfred the Great and to William the Conqueror (Dicken, *Terrell Genealogy*, 4–5; Barnhill, *Richmond, William, and Timothy Terrell*, xii–xv).

720. "John Hay and Co, Jan 1799," 170 (handwritten), line 9.

721. Fields, *Abstracts of Minutes*, 1:225, 253. In Vardy's Loyalist claim, one sworn witness (Robert Nelson) confirmed that Vardy "kept a Tavern at Cross Creek & was in a thriving way," while another (Neil McArthur) testified that Vardy's tavern "was principally frequented by the Rebels it was not frequented by the Loyalists." Evidence, North Carolina, 1785–1786, American Loyalist Claims, Series 1, record ID AO12/34, National Archives of the UK, Kew, Surrey, England, pp. 196–97 (handwritten).

722. Fields, *Abstracts of Minutes*, 1:236.

723. GBAO, *American Loyalists*, 47:272.

724. GBAO, *American Loyalists*, 47:274.

725. GBAO, *American Loyalists*, 47:280–81. Nowlan says that he and Vardy were made to go on this expedition by Rowan.

726. GBAO, *American Loyalists*, 47:281.

727. GBAO, *American Loyalists*, 47:282, 270.

728. GBAO, *American Loyalists*, 47:284.

729. *CSR*, 10:597. Vardy said that he joined the Loyalists at "the risk of his life and fortune." (GBAO, *American Loyalists*, 47:266).

730. McLean, *Highland Scots*, 182–83.

731. Moss, *Roster of Loyalists*, 75–76; Clark, "Resolves Signers Fought with Loyalists," E2.

732. GBAO, *American Loyalists*, 47:267; McLean, *Highland Scots*, 192.

733. McLean, *Highland Scots*, 192.

734. GBAO, *American Loyalists*, 47:267.

735. GBAO, *American Loyalists*, 47:267–68. Vardy did not get to Philadelphia until 1778; it took him three years of hiding out (GBAO, *American Loyalists*, 47:273).

736. *CSR*, 10:549.

737. Clark, *Loyalists in the Southern Campaign*, 1:469.

738. GBAO, *American Loyalists*, 47:270.

739. Coldham, *American Migrations*, 652.

740. Coldham, *American Migrations*, 652; GBAO, *American Loyalists*, 47:270–71.

741. GBAO, *American Loyalists*, 47:271.

742. Heitman, *Historical Register*, 559; Lewis, "Lieutenants."

743. Heitman, *Historical Register*, 559.

744. Heitman, *Historical Register*, 559.

745. "General Orders, 31 August 1779."

746. Hagist, "Untangling British Army Ranks." This position was similar to the modern US Army's Headquarters and Headquarters Company (HHC) commander in combat arms battalions.

747. "General Orders, 31 August 1779."

748. "General Orders, 31 August 1779."

749. "General Orders, 1 October 1779."

750. "General Orders, 1 October 1779."

751. Continental Congress, "Articles of War," in *Journals of the Cont. Congress*, 5:804, https://tile.loc.gov/storage-services/service/ll/llscd/lljc005/lljc005.pdf. An

officer breaking confinement without liberty if arrested (§ XIV, art. 20) was to be cashiered.

752. "General Orders, 1 October 1779."

753. "General Orders, 1 October 1779."

754. Heitman, *Historical Register*, 559. Apparently he was reduced in rank as well, because the National Archives show that his rank upon discharge was once again ensign ("Varner, Robert - North Carolina - First Regiment, NAID 141367143," in *Compiled Service Records*, Revolutionary War Records, RG 93, https://catalog.archives.gov/id/141367143).

755. Linn and McBride, "Private Petitions," 160.

756. Linn, "Revolutionary War Claims," pt. 4, 41.

757. Linn, "Revolutionary War Claims," pt. 4, 41.

758. Linn and McBride, "Private Petitions," pt. 3, 109; "Petitions: Revolutionary War, 28 December 1791," https://digital.ncdcr.gov/Documents/Detail/petitions-revolutionary-war/797284?item=797438.

759. *Mesa, AZ, Genealogical Library Records*, vol. Caverly–Devinney, https://familysearch.org/ark:/61903/3:1:3Q9M-CSLG-N8H4.

760. Dartmouth, *Records of Town of Dart'th*, 29, https://familysearch.org/ark:/61903/3:1:3QS7-L97M-R5L4.

761. Dartmouth, *Dartmouth Records 1667–1844*, 181, https://familysearch.org/ark:/61903/3:1:3QS7-L979-CWCV.

762. Bristol County, *Minutes of Inferior Court of Common Pleas*, 4:381, https://familysearch.org/ark:/61903/3:1:3Q9M-CS41-Y93L-N.

763. Suffolk County, *Minutes of Superior Court*, vol. *October 1740*, action 164, https://familysearch.org/ark:/61903/3:1:3Q9M-CSZV-H9VV-D.

764. Dartmouth, *Records of Town of Dart'th*, 215, https://familysearch.org/ark:/61903/3:1:3QS7-997M-RPWK; see also Bristol, *Minutes of Inferior Court*, 4:381, https://familysearch.org/ark:/61903/3:1:3Q9M-CS41-Y93L-N.

765. Bristol County, "Probate Records A–Z 1690–1881," roll 348, "Wood, Sophia–Woodward, David," https://familysearch.org/ark:/61903/3:1:3Q9M-C9YR-PGSS.

766. Bristol County, *Probate Records*, 25:162, https://familysearch.org/ark:/61903/3:1:3Q9M-C9YR-X7ML.

767. Craven County, *Record of Deeds*, 11:306, https://familysearch.org/ark:/61903/3:1:3QS7-898M-Z72; Craven County, *Wills, Deeds, and Inventories: 1749–1766*, 346, https://familysearch.org/ark:/61903/3:1:3QSQ-G98M-X7V7.

768. Anson County, *Minutes*, vol. 1771–1776, 125, https://familysearch.org/ark:/61903/3:1:3Q9M-CSLV-P9ML-B; Anson County, *Record of Deeds*, K:294, "Onesiphorus West to James Auld, 18 May 1774," https://familysearch.org/ark:/61903/3:1:3QS7-99Z1-D4X8.

769. *CSR*, 15:209–11.

770. Fields, *Abstracts of Minutes*, 1:266.

771. Fields, *Abstracts of Deeds*, 2:156; Fields, *Abstracts of Minutes*, 2:34; Cumberland County, *Record of Deeds*, 7:49, "Francis Anderson to Onsephoru West, 1 November 1779," https://familysearch.org/ark:/61903/3:1:3QS7-99DC-XX3W.

772. Fields, *Abstracts of Minutes*, 2:175.

773. Fields, *Abstracts of Minutes*, 2:199.

774. Fields, *Abstracts of Minutes*, 2:202.

775. First Census, "Onesiphorus West," population schedule for Cumberland (excluding Fayetteville), NC, 1790, NARA microfilm M637, roll 7, p. 106 (handwritten), line 17, https://familysearch.org/ark:/61903/3:1:33SQ-GYY8-3W4Q.

776. "West, Onosophorous (Onesefores)," in Cumberland County, "Estate Records," 1758–1930, C.R.029508.76.

777. *CSR*, 5:166.

778. New Hanover County, *Record of Deeds*, C:148, "Thomas White to George Richardson, 5 June 1747," https://familysearch.org/ark:/61903/3:1:3QSQ-G983-NF5C.

779. Bladen County, *Record of Deeds*, vol. 1738–1779, 385–86, "No. 285 Thomas White To William Howe, 27 January 1761," https://familysearch.org/ark:/61903/3:1:3QS7-998M-69MM.

780. Bladen County, *Record of Deeds*, 19:436, "No. 39 Thomas White To Joseph Wood, 13 August 1782," https://familysearch.org/ark:/61903/3:1:3QS7-998M-C3M8.

781. Bladen County, *Record of Deeds*, 1:211, "No. 286 Robt Greer to Thos White, 24 July 1785," https://familysearch.org/ark:/61903/3:1:3QS7-998M-FSP.

782. Robeson County, *Record of Deeds*, H:275, "Thomas White to Neill McAlphin, 26 February 1798," https://familysearch.org/ark:/61903/3:1:3QS7-998Q-789Z.

783. Lewis, *NC Patriots*, 2(2):1055; NC DAR, *Roster of Soldiers*, 49.

784. Hugh McDonald Papers, 12, https://digital.ncdcr.gov/Documents/Detail/hugh-mcdonald-papers-1776-1777/424262?item=424312.

785. Lewis, *NC Patriots*, 2(2):1055; NC DAR, *Roster of Soldiers*, 49.

786. Lewis, *NC Patriots*, 2(2):1055.

787. Second Census, "Thomas White," population schedule for Fayetteville (Cumberland), NC, 1800, NARA microfilm M32, roll 31, p. 376 (handwritten), line 15, https://familysearch.org/ark:/61903/3:1:33S7-9R8C-GX1.

788. Egan and White, "Inform the Public in General."

789. White, "Fifteen Dollars Reward."

790. White, "Notice."

791. "Thomas White."

792. Clark, "Nowlan and Vardey"; Cumberland Association Papers, https://dc.lib.unc.edu/cdm/singleitem/collection/02ddd/id/446859/rec/42.

793. "White, William (Cumberland County)."

794. Fields, *Abstracts of Minutes*, 1:274.

795. "John Hay and Co, Jan 1799," 170, line 14.

796. McBride, "Claims of British Merchants After the Revolutionary War," pt. 5, 118.

797. First Census, "John Wilson," population schedule for Cumberland (excluding Fayetteville town), NC, 1790, NARA microfilm M637, roll 7, p. 106 (handwritten), line 33, https://familysearch.org/ark:/61903/3:1:33SQ-GYY8-3W4Q; First Census, "John Wilson (Constable)," population schedule for Fayetteville, NC, 1790, NARA microfilm M637, roll 7, p. 110 (handwritten), line 24, https://familysearch.org/ark:/61903/3:1:33S7-9YY8-S214; First Census, "John Wilson," population schedule for Fayetteville, NC, 1790, NARA microfilm M637, roll 7, p. 110 (handwritten), line 27, https://familysearch.org/ark:/61903/3:1:33S7-9YY8-S214.

798. NC Land Grant Office, *Land Patent Books*, 18:179, "Cumberland Co. File No. 706, Sylvanus Wilson" and "Cumberland Co. File No. 707, Sylvanus Wilson," https://nclandgrants.com/frame/?fdr=39&frm=113.

799. Pruitt, Cumberland County, NC, Taxables, 105.

800. NC DAR, *Roster of Soldiers*, 428; "John Wilson"; "John Wilson," in Ledgers of Payments, 1818–1872, roll 8, "Volume H: Revolutionary War Pensioners Under Act of 1832," Records of the Accounting Officers of the Department of the Treasury, RG 217, National Archives, p. 360 (handwritten), line 2, https://familysearch.org/ark:/61903/3:1:3QS7-99WB-3RY1.

801. Pruitt, *Cumberland County, NC, Taxables*, 35.

802. Pruitt, *Cumberland County, NC, Taxables*, 47.

803. Pruitt, *Cumberland County, NC, Taxables*, 47.

804. "John Hay and Co, Jan 1799," 152, line 14, 150–51, header.

805. Blackstone, "Of Guardian and Ward," 463; Baird, "Legal Age."

806. "Report, [dated 1 Jly. 1800, 58–59, no. 24.

807. McBride, "Claims of British Merchants After the Revolutionary War," pt. 5, 118.

808. Cumberland County, *Record of Deeds*, 11:26, "Thomas Armstrong to John Sibley, 22 January 1790," https://familysearch.org/ark:/61903/3:1:3QS7-L9DC-6QXT.

809. Cumberland County, *Record of Deeds*, 11:506, "Mary Winslow & John Sibley Marriage Contract, 24 May 1791," https://familysearch.org/ark:/61903/3:1:3QS7-L98Q-Z74Z.

810. Pasquotank County, "Estate Records," roll 78, https://familysearch.org/ark:/61903/3:1:33S7-91QY-XNB.

811. "Feb 3. Petition of John Wilson, 1795."

812. Weaver Jr., *Barge Families*, 108–9.

CHAPTER 4

Liberty Point Ladies

The following are brief biographies of the women connected to the Liberty Point Resolves signers.

Susanna Greer Grove Rowan

ORIGINALLY SUSANNA GREER, SHE was the sister of Robert and Joseph Greer.[1] She had a son, William Barry Grove, with her first husband Richard Grove. After he died, she married Robert Rowan. The Tories fought hard to capture her husband Robert since he was their staunch foe in Cumberland. After Rowan and Theophilus had escaped their captivity, Loyalists stormed Rowan's home looking for him:

> After this Capt Rowan received a colonel commission and by his zeal and activity in the cause of liberty provoked the tories to make many efforts to get him in their power and the frequent searches made for him a company of them came to his house after searching every room in the house up stairs and in the Cuddey his wife told them that her husband did not hide in Cuddies, then their chief officer caught her by her hair with his sword drawn swore he would split head if she did not tell them where her husband was, but she dared them to injure a hair of her head and they would find out where her husband was before that time of day tomorrow. They then ordered her to prepare them their Breakfast, she shewed them the smoke house and told them if they got any they must take it, for she would not prepare it for them.[2]

Susanna outlived her husband and inherited a substantial portion of his estate before dying in 1800.[3]

Mary Walker Gee

Mary Walker was born in Wilmington, North Carolina, on March 5, 1755. She was orphaned at a young age, so her care was transferred over to Richard Lyon, who was a prominent member of Wilmington society at the time. When Mary Walker was four years old, Lyon moved to Cumberland County and made it their new residence.[4] She married James Gee around 1771 and moved to Fayetteville, where her husband built them a new family home.[5] This same dwelling would later be used as a boarding house as her husband fought in South Carolina. Aside from her exploits during the Revolutionary War in Cumberland County, she was also well-acquainted with Flora MacDonald.[6] Since the two women were on opposite sides of the political spectrum, further research may need to be done on the particulars of their relationship.

One of the first tales known about her, written in a county newspaper, took place before James Gee's deployment. A neighbor had visited Mary Gee:

> [She was] brushing the uniform, and furbishing up the old fire lock of her martial husband, while the tears ran down her cheeks. The neighbor asked her why, if it grieved her so much, she let her husband go. "Go!" she exclaimed, "he shall go. He belongs to his country, and I'd poison his coffee if he did not go!"[7]

Mary Gee experienced more adventures during the war, most often confronting the Tories and British soldiers when they were in the Cumberland area. "The Tories harried and vexed and robbed her; but, now and then, she got the best of both Tory marauder and British invader."[8] The Liberty Point signers, Theophilus Evans and John Oveler, were captured by Tories on one occasion. She supplied the Loyalists with food and drink as a payment for freeing the two men.

Although the main elements of the story are shared, there are still variations when people tell of Mary Gee's rescue of her Patriot neighbors:

> First variation: By her hospitality and furnishings the tories with meat and drink, which was scarce, she purchased the discharge of these two whigs, who ever cherished the event in grateful remembrance.[9]
> Second variation: A grandson of James Gee, one of the signers, told us his grandmother, Mary Gee, had often told him that she ransomed Theophilus Evans when a prisoner by giving his captors a bottle of

> whiskey. The old man was tied under his horse's belly and taken from his house toward Fanning's camp in Moore County when he was released on the way by Mary Gee and the bottle of whiskey.[10]
>
> Third variation: One day Mrs. Gee was raided by a band of Tories, having with them a squad of Whig prisoners, and they commanded her to prepare dinner for them. Leaving their captives in the yard, so securely bound that there was, they thought, no chance of their escaping, they all entered the house. Mrs. Gee placed an excellent dinner on the table; and, while the raiders were doing full just to it, she dashed out into the yard with a carving knife and in a [rush] cut the cords of the Whigs, who, with only time for a wave of the hand in gratitude, were out of sight in an instant.[11]
>
> Fourth variation: The Tories had captured Mr. Theophilus Evans and Mr. Jno. Oliver and tied their legs under a horse's belly, and while on their way to headquarters in the western part of this county, stopped at Mrs. Gee's house for breakfast...They asked for liquor, but she refused unless they released their prisoners. This proposition they rejected. But she finally thought she would play a trick on them to gain her wish to set the prisoners free, so she supplied them bountifully with Jamaica rum, until they became drunk. Then she went out and cut the cords that bound the prisoners and set them free. She furnished them with fresh horses and told them to flee for home as fast as they could...After the Tories had recovered from their drunken stupor they became very wrathful and threatened her, but she stood her ground and defied them.[12]

Aside from the Tories in Cumberland County, Mary Gee also dealt with the visit of the British Army during Cornwallis' march. As her husband was still fighting, Gee had to find ways to distract visiting British soldiers while also getting help.

> One morning, while the army of Cornwallis was marching through this section, Mrs. Gee was intention household cares in her kitchen, when she was startled by the entrance of an armed negroe in British uniform, who ordered her to cook breakfast for him. There was no restating the command, for she was alone in the house, and on the premises were only two or three young negroes. She set about preparing the meal, making it as elaborate as possible, in order to secure delay; and, while it was cooking, she managed to slip out, and gave this message to an intelligent negro

> boy: "Run to John Lomax, and tell him to come here just as quick as he can, and to come with his gun!" But it seemed to her that bread and meal never baked so fast before and do what she would...But just as her unwelcome guest had seated himself at the table, his musket across his knees, John Lomax strode through the door, and presented a gun at his head. Lomax kept the British negro captive till all the army of Cornwallis had passed, and then gave him up to the patrol authorities at Fayetteville.[13]

Mary Gee lived on Hay Street, where the southern direction led to a "huckleberry swamp" known as Mumford's Swamp. She later purchased and lived on a tract of land west of Fayetteville and was an active member of the Baptist denomination. She passed away at the age of eighty-eight on March 23, 1842.[14] In her younger years, she helped grow a walnut tree from a seed, which was then used as the lumber for her coffin.[15]

Ann Carver Elwell

Ann Carver was born around 1751 to Robert (Braswell) Carver.[16] She married one of the signers, John Elwell. In her father's will, she was given three enslaved persons after his death.[17] During the time of the Revolutionary War, Ann Carver Elwell helped the Patriots: "The wife of John Elwell swam the Cape Fear riding one horse and leading another to get them from the reach of the enemy."[18] She died on December 15, 1789, when she was thirty-seven or thirty-eight years old, and was buried at the John Kelly Family Catholic Cemetery.[19]

Rebecca Evans Brownlow Fletcher

Rebecca Fletcher was said to be a "courageous woman, and had great contempt for such pets as squirrels, monkeys and poodle dogs." Supposedly, "*Her* favorite pet was a she-bear, and with this pet she saved the life of a patriot friend who was pursued by the enemy. *He* was required to enter the cellar by a trap door, and bruin was stationed at the entrance, and the pursuers feared to search the cellar where their victim lay concealed."[20] Her first husband was John Brownlow, with whom she had a daughter, Mary. After he died, she married George Fletcher; he raised Rebecca's daughter, Mary Brownlow.[21]

Mary Brown

Mary Brown was formerly married to a Cumberland County millwright named John Brown, and her name appears early in 1754 through a deed between John Brown and John Nessfield. As the Browns were selling their land, Mary had to surrender her portion of the dower related to the property and signed her name on the agreement.[22] Throughout the 1740s–1760s, Mary Brown had an extensive familial and friendly network. In 1759, her granddaughter Winifer Brown was "bonded" to Mary Brown after being orphaned at the age of eight.[23] Two years later in 1761, Mary Brown petitioned the court for Winifred to be transferred instead to William Hodges.[24] Her petition most likely reflected thc instability of the household as John Brown had passed away right before. In the same court session, she is claimed to be the executrix of his will, alongside a Gilbert Clark.[25] John Brown's will also listed other family members, such as the couple's five daughters: Mary, Elizabeth, Hannah, Margaret, and Jenepha/Jemeffa Brown.[26] On August 23, 1764, Mary Brown stated in court that she was indebted to Ratchell Cliffton, whose mother had passed away. The court bonded Ratchell to Mary as an apprentice at eleven years old, and Mary Brown was meant to use £15 7s. 9d. to care for the girl.[27]

After the death of her husband, Mary Brown experienced multiple sessions in court to deal with his estate's administration or to solve financial issues. In May 1761, the court ordered her to sell the perishable estate.[28] In August 1761, Mary Brown went to court again, except for an issue involving the responsibility of payment for an individual named Gibeon Gumbo. The court ruled that Stephen Phillips would pay Mary Brown £2 17s. 8d. for Gumbo's prison fees as John's executrix.[29] Then, in November of the same year, she sued Tamer Jones.[30] The exact issue of the suit is unknown, but the November session ended with Mary requesting for another trial, as the verdict was "impertinent to the issue joined."[31] Her motion was granted, with another trial in February 1762. The verdict for the second round went to the defendant Jones, as "the intestate in his lifetime did assume," so Mary Brown had to pay damages of £8 16s. 1d. with additional costs. She was granted an appeal to the Superior Court in Wilmington.[32] In May 1763, she petitioned the court once more so that she could receive permission to sell her late husband's land to pay off his debts.[33]Mary Brown found other means to make income starting in 1764. Like many of the signers in Cumberland County, she asked for and was granted a license to keep an ordinary at her home.[34] Later the same year, the court granted her a license to keep a ferry over Lower Little River, similar to her late husband's responsibilities, except the court specifically referenced that the location of the ferry is "the place where she now lives."[35] She once again administered an estate, this time for a James Brown in 1784.[36] She delivered the account of sales for his estate in 1785.[37] This same year, she sold a portion of land to the signer Thomas Cabeen.[38] In 1788, she sold another portion of land to Edward Robeson, which Malcolm McNeill proved.[39]

Mary Brown's relationship with Thomas Cabeen expanded beyond the formal relations of business partnership, even delving into an early discussion of the influence of the state in comparison to the county justice system. The same year that she sold a deed of land to Cabeen in 1785, both she and Cabeen got into trouble with other Cumberland residents. Fellow signer James Dick and four others publicly horsewhipped the two for "many immoralities."[40] Mary Brown and Thomas Cabeen went to court against the men; they were Nathan Steadman Sr., Nathan Steadman Jr., Duncan Ockeltree, James Dick, and Anthony Rosney.[41] These men were trying to "expell" both Brown and Cabeen from Fayetteville after they were "obnoxious to the Inhabitants of Fayetteville by many immoralities repeatedly committed and continued by their lewd life and Conversation..."[42] After the assault, Mary Brown and Thomas Cabeen went to the Superior Court in Wilmington to charge the five men with assault, trespassing, and incitement to riot.[43] For Mary Brown's case, both Nathan Steadman Sr. and Nathan Steadman Jr. were judged guilty and charged, while James Dick was proclaimed not guilty.[44]

Since the accused men were charged with fines, prominent members of Cumberland County disagreed with the monetary amount and petitioned the North Carolina General Assembly for leniency. The signers argued altogether that the penalty was too harsh for actions that were supported by many members of Fayetteville's public.

> ...of the said Thomas Cabeen, and Mary Brown, persons leading disorderly lives and of lewd manners and conversation[;] and altho the Laws do not [sufficiently] vindicate the conduct of the citizens of Fayette Ville in endeavoring to expel the said Mary Brown from residing amongst them[,] yet the nature of the case may justify it[,] her house being a scene of continual Riot, and Debauchery, dangerous to the Society of the Citizens by leading into adultery the masters of families and seducing them from domestic attentions, living with them in the most open

> and shameful prostitution[,] corrupting the morals of youth, countenancing and encouraging the servants and slaves of the inhabitants of this Town in the embe[z]zlement of their owners['] property. Notwithstanding all which conduct, by reason of her artifice, the address of her friends, and the power of her money[,] she in several prosecutions escaped the punishment due to her [demerits] which induced the inhabitants to have recourse to those measures that tended to her expulsion and for which the persons before named were heavily fined.[45]

The sixty-one men from Cumberland County who signed this petition agreed that Mary Brown's house, a "scene of continual riot," disobeyed the bond rules that she agreed to, while also implicating her in charges of sexual misdemeanor.[46] Amongst the signatures, familiar names appear, such as Robert Rowan, James Gee, and Lewis Bowell.[47] In the end, the General Assembly agreed to waive the fines for the involved men.[48]

In 1788, Mary Brown passed away, leading to a written overview of her estate. For example, her inventory of the estate listed specific animals on her property, such as cattle, hogs, and a horse. She also had "three feather beds and [furniture][,] four pots and [a dutch] oven…," which may relate to her keeping an ordinary by having extra house and kitchenware.[49] On March 10, 1788, Brown's estate was for sale. Philemon Hodges, Edward Robinson, and Malcolm McNeil purchased a significant amount of goods, with particular attention to cattle, furniture, and sundries.[50] The administrator's account for Mary Brown's estate was finally returned to the court in Cumberland County on April 28, 1790.[51]

Notes

1. "Greer, Thomas 1783," in Cumberland County, "Original Wills," roll 3, https://familysearch.org/ark:/61903/3:1:3QS7-L9GW-BN8G.

2. Hugh McDonald Papers, 12, https://digital.ncdcr.gov/Documents/Detail/hugh-mcdonald-papers-1776-1777/424262?item=424312; Caruthers, *Old North State in 1776*, 174. The Merriam-Webster Dictionary defines cuddy as "1) a usually small cabin or shelter (as on a sailboat); or 2) a small room or cupboard" (https://www.merriam-webster.com/dictionary/cuddy). It was used in Colonial America as early as the 1650s (Hoadly, *Records of the Colony or Jurisdiction of New Haven*, 134–35). Perhaps the most famous colonial cuddy today is the one at Monticello ("Cuddy").

3. *Raleigh Minerva*, July 22, 1800, 3.

4. Fletcher, *The Gee Family*, 96; *Fayetteville Carolinian*, March 26, 1842.

5. Fletcher, *The Gee Family*, 98.

6. Fayetteville Carolinian, March 26, 1842.

7. "The Patriot Gee and His Brave Wife."

8. "The Patriot Gee and His Brave Wife."

9. *Fayetteville Carolinian*, March 26, 1842.

10. "Cumberland Centennial," 2.

11. "The Patriot Gee and His Brave Wife."

12. Lawrence, "Liberty Point Declaration."

13. "The Patriot Gee and His Brave Wife." John Lomax was "a free negro," described as patriotic and well-known to other White families and neighbors. The same news article mentions his son as well, although with the details that the son was a drunkard infamous at Haymount.

14. Lawrence, "Liberty Point Declaration"; *Fayetteville Carolinian*, March 26, 1842.

15. Lawrence, "Liberty Point Declaration."

16. "Carver, Robert 1766," in Cumberland County, "Original Wills," roll 2, https://familysearch.org/ark:/61903/3:1:3QS7-89GW-BYW7; "Ann *Carver* Elwell."

17. "Carver, Robert 1766," in Cumberland County, "Original Wills," roll 2.

18. "Cumberland Centennial," 1.

19. "Ann *Carver* Elwell."

20. Cumberland Centennial."

21. Johnson, *Hometown Heritage*, 1:170.

22. Bladen County, *Record of Deeds*, vol. 1738–1779, 256, "No. 179 John Brown to John Nessfield, 4 August 1754," https://familysearch.org/ark:/61903/3:1:3QS7-L98M-698C.

23. Fields, *Abstracts of Minutes*, 1:52. North Carolina General Assembly statutes made county courts responsible for assigning guardianship of orphans to households that could take care of their wellbeing. If the orphan, under the ages of twenty-one for males and eighteen for females, had a suitable estate, they would be assigned a guardian. The guardian would be responsible for the child's food, lodging, clothing, education, and financial affairs. See *CSR*, 25:319–21, 324; Watson, "Orphanage in Colonial North Carolina," 105–19; and Watson, "Public Poor Relief," 347–66.

24. Fields, *Abstracts of Minutes*, 1:78.

25. Fields, *Abstracts of Minutes*, 1:78.

26. "Brown, John 1761," in Cumberland County, "Original Wills," roll 2, https://familysearch.org/ark:/61903/3:1:3QS7-89GW-BY92.

27. Fields, *Abstracts of Minutes*, 1:160

28. Fields, *Abstracts of Minutes*, 1:85.

29. Fields, *Abstracts of Minutes*, 1:96.

30. Fields, *Abstracts of Minutes*, 1:101; Cumberland, *Minutes*, C:74v, https://familysearch.org/ark:/61903/3:1:3Q9M-CS4G-MWP6-C.

31. Cumberland, *Minutes*, C:74v, https://familysearch.org/ark:/61903/3:1:3Q9M-CS4G-MWP6-C.

32. Fields, *Abstracts of Minutes*, 1:106.

33. Fields, *Abstracts of Minutes*, 1:127.

34. Fields, *Abstracts of Minutes*, 1:143.

35. Fields, *Abstracts of Minutes*, 1:167.

36. Fields, *Abstracts of Minutes*, 2:75.

37. Fields, *Abstracts of Minutes*, 2:77.

38. Fields, *Abstracts of Minutes*, 2:76.

39. Fields, *Abstracts of Minutes*, 2:183.

40. Parker, "Revolutionary Patriot."

41. *CSR*, 18:406.

42. *CSR*, 18:406–7.

43. Criminal Docket Superior Court, 1778–1787, vol. 9, record ID SR.398.8.

44. Wilmington District Superior Court, *Minutes*, 2:11, https://digital.ncdcr.gov/Documents/Detail/wilmington-district-minutes-superior-court-1785-1788/1776820?item=1776831.

45. "Dec. 29: Resolution Acquitting Sundry Inhabitants."

46. "Dec. 29: Resolution Acquitting Sundry Inhabitants." See also, Crittenden, "Overland Travel and Transportation in North Carolina," 239–57.

47. "Dec. 29: Resolution Acquitting Sundry Inhabitants."

48. *CSR*, 18: 406–7.

49. "Brown, Mary 1788," in Cumberland County, "Estate Records," roll 4, https://familysearch.org/ark:/61903/3:2:77TD-JV9F-K.

50. "Brown, Mary 1788," in Cumberland County, "Estate Records," https://familysearch.org/ark:/61903/3:2:77TD-JV9F-K. Mary Brown had transferred a deed to Edward Robeson in 1787 for one hundred pounds, less than a year before her death. The parcel of land was originally transferred from William Roberts to John Brown, described as being on the south side of Lower Little River and at the mouth of Anderson Creek (see Cumberland County, *Record of Deeds*, 8:332, "Mary Brown to Edward Robeson, 26 May 1787," https://familysearch.org/ark:/61903/3:1:3QS7-L98J-B2KJ).

51. Fields, *Abstracts of Minutes*, 2:283.

CHAPTER 5

Cumberland County Loyalists

THE LOYALIST MOVEMENT WAS prominent in Cumberland, as seen with dozens of Cumberland Loyalists captured at the Battle of Moores Creek.[1] A sizable contingent consisted of Scottish Highlanders, with Matthew Dziennek estimating that 40 percent of eligible male Highlanders in North Carolina fought at Moores Creek, most on the Loyalist side.[2]

Many of the Highlanders who had come to Cumberland starting in the 1730s were from the Scottish island of Kintyre, which had its own town called Campbellton.[3] Their Cape Fear settlement was "called Campbeltown, in memory of the Burgh Town of that name in the Kintyre from which so many of the settlers had come."[4] The Scottish heroine Flora MacDonald joined fellow emigrants from Kintyre in Campbeltown in September 1774, before moving to what is now Harnett County.[5] By 1773, one Scottish source described Cross Creek as being filled with "mostly Highlanders, emigrants from Argyleshire, and the western isles, are settled in said county [Cumberland]," though that was an exaggeration, as while Cumberland had a substantial Highlander population, the county and Cross Creek also had a fair amount of Scottish settlers from the lowlands and other parts of Scotland.[6] There is still debate today over how many Scottish Highlanders there were in the area.

Local historian Malcolm Fowler says that the Highlanders stayed loyal to the King, because they had taken an oath after Culloden to stay loyal, and they would not go back on their word.[7] However, the former director of the Scottish Heritage Center, Bill Caudill, says that's not true, but that instead most of them were fence-sitters.[8] This can be seen too with how only around half of the Highlanders that Governor Martin had expected to join the Loyalist militias actually did so for the battle of Moores Creek.[9] If the Highlanders had truly flocked to the King's banner, more of them would have fought at Moores Creek. Many were fence-sitters, in part because they knew their property could be confiscated if they came out as supporters of the Crown.

Matthew Dziennek suggests another reason for the Highlanders support of the British was because most Highlanders in Cross Creek were not landowners but wanted to be, and supporting the British would help the Highlanders become landowners after the British decided to give numerous land patents in the preceding years. [10] The British had also promoted a conciliation program with the Scottish Highlanders during this time period, so that by the time of the Revolution, Loyalists were sometimes referred to as "the Scotch party." [11] Yet after losing at Moores Creek, enough Highlanders were captured that the Patriots then had a strong influence in Cross Creek through 1780, so when Cornwallis came through in 1780 he said that "they [the highlanders] are not equal to my expectations." [12]

The North Carolina governor, Angus McLean, confirms this in his manuscript, *Highland Scots in North Carolina*, noting that "it is...erroneous to infer that even a large majority of them [Highland Scots] were Loyalists. Indeed, from the records and documentary evidence at hand, it is more accurate to say that the majority were patriots both in word and act."[13] What can then be said about the Cumberland Loyalists? They were probably not quite as large a population of Cumberland as some have thought, and after the loss at Moores Creek, many probably hid their loyalties and waited to see how the war would turn out.[14]

One reason they hid their loyalties was because Cumberland County was enforcing loyalty oaths. Journalist Roy Parker Jr. noted that in 1778, the county court issued orders for three to four hundred citizens who were "disaffected to the American cause" to take a prescribed loyalty oath. By 1780, one-third of the taxpayers in some districts were charged penalties for refusing to do so.[15] After all, starting in 1777, the Provincial Congress had passed a law legalizing the banishment of non-jurying Loyalists and the confiscation of property of those who refused to take an oath to the Revolutionary government.[16] As a result, Col. David Smith told Governor Caswell in July 1777 that "it was evident that two-thirds of Cumberland county intend leaving this State and are already become insolent, and it is apprehended will be troublesome."[17] This is probably where Robert DeMond gets his claim that as much as two-thirds of Cumberland County were Loyalist.[18] Considering that both Rowan and Gillespie were accused of being Loyalists at some point during the war, however, it is probably accurate to say that two-thirds is an inflated number. Cumberland had a strong Loyalist population but not as high as once thought.

Cumberland's Loyalist population, while smaller than previously thought, was still substantial enough that it makes Cumberland's Association stand out. While Cumberland's Association was similar to other published associations in North Carolina, Cumberland County's population was quite unusual in comparison. Mecklenburg County, which claims to have had the Mecklenburg Declaration of Independence, was strongly Patriot and even helped enforce patriotism in the surrounding counties.[19] New Hanover County was also stalwartly Patriot and had and had the most active Committee of Safety in the colony.[20] Pitt and Tryon County had passed resolves as well, and were said to have some of the most active safety committees in the state after Wilmington.[21]

Meanwhile, Cumberland was unique as the county where previous Provincial congressmen had served as part of the growing Patriot movement before fighting against the Patriots. The 1776 Provincial Congress opened an investigation into insurgents and those captured at Moores Creek. Among those were four prisoners who had served in Congress: Farquhard Campbell, Thomas Rutherford, Alexander McKay and James Hepburn. All four of these men were from Cumberland County.[22]

These Loyalists were elite men in Cumberland society: Farquhard had served as a magistrate for at least eight years since 1761 and had served in the General Assembly before serving in the Provincial Congress.[23] James Hepburn had been a Cumberland County magistrate in 1774, and Thomas Rutherford served in both the General Assembly and had been head of the Cumberland County militia, and had previously served as a deputy secretary to Colonial Governor William Tryon.[24] The background and sheer number of Loyalists in Cumberland County makes the Cumberland Association unusual, since it was written in a county that was lukewarm at best toward Revolution. Cumberland had also been the county where the Loyalists had gathered at before heading to Moores Creek in February 1776. The strength of the Loyalist movement, particularly among elite members of the county appears to have been far stronger in Cumberland than any other county that had their own Resolves. Even with the strength of potential Loyalist peer pressure, the Cumberland Association signers stood for independence.[25]

Notes

1. See intro section. The two leading Loyalists, Thomas Rutherford and Farquhard Campbell, were both captured as well.

2. Dziennik, "Through an Imperial Prism," 338.

3. Webb, "Campbeltown in Scotland," 2–3; "Materials Not Used in Book #1," John Oates Manuscript, vertical files, Cumberland County Public Library.

4. Webb, "Campbeltown in Scotland," 6.

5. Webb, "Campbeltown in Scotland," 7.

6. Scotus Americanus, *Information Concerning the Province of North Carolina*, 18; see Maclean, *Highland Scots*, 38, and Collins, "From Clansmen to Statesmen," for more on how Cumberland was more than just Scottish Highlanders.

7. Fowler, *Valley of Scots*, 9.

8. Caudill says it's a myth that Highland Scots were mostly Loyalist during the Revolution. There were fifteen to thirty thousand Scots living in the area, but only around sixteen hundred fought as Loyalists at Moores Creek, which is less than you'd expect if they were mostly Loyalists. Instead, he argues that the majority of the Scots were fence sitters (Caudill, *The Scottish Highlander Immigration to the Sandhills*).

9. Read, "The Highlanders of Colonial North Carolina," 34.

10. Dziennik, "Through an Imperial Prism," 352–54.

11. Meyer, *Highland Scots*, 148, 150.

12. Dziennik, "Through an Imperial Prism," 356.

13. McLean, *Highland Scots*, 258.

14. Rebecca Read in her 2024 thesis, "The Highlanders of Colonial North Carolina: Loyalist Suppression 1776–1780," makes the claim that many hid their loyalties after the Battle of Moores Creek Bridge.

15. Parker, *Cumberland: Brief History*, 20–21. See also *CSR*, 24:11.

16. *CSR*, 14:11; 24:10–11.

17. *CSR*, 11: xviii.

18. DeMond, *Loyalists*, 57.

19. Syfert, The First American Declaration of Independence?, 77–81.

20. McEachern and Williams, *Safety Committee Minutes*, xix.

21. Powell, *Encyclopedia of NC*, 965–66; McEachern and Williams, *Safety Committee Minutes*, xix.

22. DeMond, *Loyalists*, 80–81; *CSR,* 10:594–95. These four individuals were the *only* representatives from Cumberland during the four Provincial Congresses, except for Alexander McAllister, at the third Provincial Congress, and David Smith, who was a member of the fourth Provincial Congress (*CSR* 9:1042, 1178, 10:165, 500, 914). Alexander McAllister himself later showed Loyalist sympathies and was ordered to leave the state because he refused to take the oath of allegiance in 1778 (Fields, *Abstracts of Minutes*, 1:307; see also Willcox, *A History of the House in the Horseshoe*, 79–80).

23. Fields, *Abstracts of Minutes*, 1:89, 103, 121, 146, 168, 202, 229, 252.

24. Fields, *Abstracts of Minutes*, 220; *CSR*, 22:413; *CSR*, 7:118.

25. The strength of peer pressure on human decisions is well-attested to. See Asch, "Opinions and Social Pressure," 31–35, among others.

CHAPTER 6

Forgotten by Fayetteville[1]

Over 150 years after the signing of the Liberty Point Resolves, in 1933, a monument to the Cumberland Association was erected in Fayetteville. This monument was a boulder featuring the names of thirty-nine of the signers of the Liberty Point Resolves; however, the remaining sixteen signers' names were absent from the boulder. Somehow, Fayetteville had forgotten sixteen signers. In 1975, the Cumberland County American Bicentennial Committee, led by chairman David Sanders Clark, set out to find the original document of the Liberty Point Resolves and discover why those signers had been forgotten.[2]

The original document had been held onto by Robert Rowan until his death in 1798. The document then passed to the hands of the executor of Rowan's will, his stepson William Barry Grove.[3] Following Grove's death, the Resolves then fell into the hands of David Hay. Hay moved out of the state and turned the document over to Maj. Thomas Jefferson Robeson.[4]

In 1825, Robeson lent the Cumberland Association Papers to James F. Conover, the editor of the weekly *Cheraw Intelligencer*, from Cheraw, South Carolina. Conover published the text of the document and named the fifty-five signers in his article.[5] but only had 54 of the 55 names, leaving out Lewis Bowell. In his article, Force included the statement, "The original manuscript is in the possession of the editor of the Cheraw Intelligencer."[6]

In 1830, Major Robeson mailed the document to Thomas G. Polk in Raleigh.[7] At the time, a fierce debate was occurring regarding the legitimacy of the Mecklenburg Declaration, as Thomas Jefferson claimed he believed the document to be spurious. The resolves were used as evidence of the Declaration's legitimacy.[8] In 1831, a pamphlet was made which included the text and signers' names from the resolves. However, some of these names were misspelled, and one name was left off entirely.[9]

Meanwhile, John Hill Wheeler published the text and names again in his *History of North Carolina* in 1851. Mr. Wheeler only listed thirty-nine names and did not mention in his book that some of the names were missing.[10]

In 1890, Col. William L. Saunders listed the names of the signers in volume ten of the *Colonial and State Records of North Carolina*. Saunders did not have access to the original document and used the list that had been published by Peter Force. Saunders also included the statement from Force's article that, "as of 1825 the original manuscript was in the possession of the editor of the *Cheraw Intelligencer*."[11]

At this point, the two lists, Wheeler's list of thirty-nine and Saunders' list of fifty-four signers, caused much confusion, and the whereabouts of the original document were now unknown. When building the monument at Liberty Point in 1933, Wheeler's list was used.[12]

In 1975, the Bicentennial Commission set out to find the original document of the Resolves. After much searching, the original document was found in the Southern Historical Collection at the University of North Carolina at Chapel Hill, filed under the heading "Thomas G. Polk Papers," along with many other correspondences. With the original document now located the Bicentennial Commission was able to confirm the actual text of the document and a list of fifty-five signers.[13]

Tradition holds that the Resolves were signed in Cumberland County on June 20, 1775. This date gained a lot of traction after the publishing of Wheeler's book which, in addition to leaving out the names of sixteen signers, also failed to include the section at the top of the document which read, "at a general meeting of the several committees of the District of Wilmington, held at the Court House in Wilmington, Tuesday, the 20th of June, 1775," and included a headline indicating the document was signed in Fayetteville on that date. David Sanders Clark, who led the Cumberland Bicentennial Committee in the 1970s, noted that this wording appearing as it does at the head of the document signed by the Cross Creek Patriots strongly suggests that the Resolves were approved in Wilmington on June 20, 1775, but not actually signed in Cross Creek until a day or so later, as with transportation methods available at the time it is unlikely they would have had time to travel the 100 miles from Wilmington to Fayetteville.[14] The actual date of the signing is still very much up to debate, as the Safety Committee minutes for Wilmington on June 20 note those in attendance, including those from other counties, but it does not list anyone in attendance from Cumberland, only that "a letter from the Committee of Cross Creek was read, and an answer was ordered to be wrote by the Chairman to the said letter."[15]

Notes

1. The Fayetteville History Museum performed a lot of similar work in tracing the chain of custody of the document for a 2008 exhibit when the original document was hosted by the museum. Their work made our job easier.

2. Clark, "Notes on the Post Revolutionary War History of the Liberty Point Resolves."

3. Clark, "Notes on the Post Revolutionary War History of the Liberty Point Resolves."

4. Clark, "Notes on the Post Revolutionary War History of the Liberty Point Resolves."

5. "From the Cheraw Intelligencer Interesting Reminiscence."

6. *CSR*, 10:29.

7. Robeson, Letter to Colonel Thos Polk.

8. Clark, "Memorandum."

9. This list included every signer except Lewis Bowell (*The Declaration of Independence by the Citizens of Mecklenburg County*, 28–30).

10. Wheeler, History of NC, 2:125.

11. *CSR*, 10:29–30.

12. Clark, "Notes on the Post Revolutionary War History of the Liberty Point Resolves."

13. Clark, "Notes on the Post Revolutionary War History of the Liberty Point Resolves."

14. Clark, "Memorandum."

15. Brunswick had twelve men in attendance, Bladen had five, and Duplin had one, but the minutes do not list anyone from Cumberland. *CSR*, 10:24.

CHAPTER 7

Are the Resolves Authentic?

NOT EVERYONE THOUGHT THE Liberty Point Resolves happened. North Carolina Historian Samuel A'Court Ashe, in a 1909 *Wilmington Morning Star* article said that the document known as the Liberty Point Resolves was "a source of pride to the people of Fayetteville," but evidence puts it "in a different light."[1] He said the following:

> By reference to Colonel Saunders' Colonial Records, Vol. X, page 25, it will be seen that on June 19th, 1775, the inhabitants of New Hanover county adopted an association paper; that the next day the committees of all the six Cape Fear counties met at Wilmington, and they adopted this same Association paper, which they directed to be printed with a recommendation that it be signed by the inhabitants of the entire district as soon as possible. Adopted by the District Committee on June 20th, it bore that date. Mr. Rowan apparently copied it, verbatim et liteartim, including the date and carried it home with him; and obtained the signatures of 39 persons to it. While other copies have not been preserved, doubtless more than a thousand people, all through the Cape Fear counties, signed the same document, about the same time, in conformity with the recommendation of the District Committee. It does not detract from the patriotic ardor of Mr. Rowan and his friends for the facts to be stated. But it would conflict somewhat with a proper understanding of the current course of events for the Liberty Point proceeding to be regarded as a step in advance of what was taking place all throughout the other counties.[2]

Ashe maintained that it was only a copy of the New Hanover statement, so there's nothing to make it unique compared to the other counties. While it is disagreeable to local sentiment to reveal this truth, he says that "isn't it better for the truth to be taught? Is one justified in perpetuating error—knowingly?"[3] He compared the Liberty Point Resolves to the Mecklenburg Declaration, which he maintains was probably a spurious document. "As disagreeable as it was to tell the truth about that, yet I had either to refrain from publishing the book or to state the facts. So likewise about this Liberty Point Affair. I correctly mentioned it."[4]

He closed his article saying:

> The inhabitants of Wilmington and New Hanover have so many glorious memories of their own, that they can enthusiastically sympathize with every other community of the State in their local demonstrations; and certainly no Wilmingtonian would ever seek to dim the glory of any patriotic action that illustrated the spirit of other communities. But ought we to refrain from putting all events in their proper light, and in their true and just relation to other contemporaneous events, because it is disagreeable to do so?[5]

Ashe had made a similar remark as far back as 1875, saying in a June 3, 1875, article that the Cumberland Association was not unique, because Lincoln and Pitt counties did similar statements in August, and that suggested "that a careful examination would reveal the fact that similar association papers were adopted in every county in the State, except in the Tory section, about the same time, and to the same effect."[6]

What are we to make of this? First off, Ashe is right that the documents are similar, and that the Resolves reflects sentiments that other counties, like New Hanover, were having at the time (not just in North Carolina, but other colonies as well). Though interestingly, as far back as 1875, Ashe did not seem so opposed to celebrating the Resolves.[7] Ashe had also just published his first volume of a history of North Carolina, where he spent a lot of time examining the Mecklenburg Declaration and Resolves but does not mention the Liberty Point Resolves.[8] He noted that the Mecklenburg Resolves did stir "the hearts of the patriot leaders [in North Carolina] and awoke enthusiasm in the breasts of their associates throughout the colony," being published in New

Bern on June 16, 1775, and in Wilmington by June 23.[9] A short time later, New Hanover had their own resolves, followed up by Cumberland. Ashe is right that Cumberland was part of a broader trend of independence in colonial North Carolina, dating back to the Mecklenburg Resolves the previous month. Yet he dismisses the Resolves' significance.

However, while Ashe dismisses the document as irrelevant, his article from 1875 reveals that the Association was actually *quite* relevant. Ashe in that article noted that "a careful examination would reveal the fact that similar association papers were adopted in every county in the State, *except in the Tory section*" (italics my own).[10] Anson County was part of the state that was largely Loyalist. However, this very region also included *Cumberland County*, which was right next to Anson County. In the same article, Ashe himself earlier said that:

> Fayetteville was the commercial centre [center] of a population much given to loyalty: the Regulators and Highlanders trading with her merchants were for the most part royalists, not only in name but in bold, determined action. The patriots of Fayetteville then by signing the Articles of Association threw themselves in direct antagonism to the bulk of the people trading in that market, and subjected themselves to the hostility of zealous leaders, who soon afterward embodied three thousand leige sons of royalty from among the newly arrived Scotch and those turbulent Regulators who so bitterly opposed the American Cause.[11]

In such a region, the fact that the Cumberland Association was publicly signed by fifty-five Cumberland residents *is* remarkable. It shows boldness on the part of these men embedded in a Loyalist County that could turn on them for signing such a statement. Ashe is too quick to dismiss the document.

The local papers did not comment on Ashe's accusation, with the closest comment being one made by the *Fayetteville Index* on June 30, 1875. The paper said the Liberty Point celebration was "the occasion of much high-class advertising for Fayetteville" through different newspapers such as the *Wilmington Star* and the *Charlotte Observer*.[12] Ashe's accusation was ignored.

Ashe was not the last skeptic. After the original copy of the Resolves was discovered in 1974, Dr. Richard W. Iobst, an archivist at Western Carolina University, said that because of how strong Cumberland County's Tory leanings were, "it would be very difficult to find much sentiment for the Revolution," and doubted that the document was authentic.[13] And yet other scholars such as Dr. Hugh Lefler believed the document to be authentic, and people who have examined the signatures on the document believe it is as well.[14] Modern scholars have concluded that the Liberty Point Resolves are authentic because the document fits its historical context, includes verifiable local figures, contains period-appropriate rhetoric, and appears in early trustworthy sources. The document shows no contradictions or anachronisms and fits into the chain of county resolves that swept North Carolina in mid-1775.

Notes

1. Ashe, "Liberty Point Resolves," 4. The *Star* ran his article, which was originally from Washington, DC, on June 23.

2. Ashe, "Liberty Point Resolves," 4.

3. Ashe, "Liberty Point Resolves," 4.

4. Ashe, "Liberty Point Resolves," 4.

5. Ashe, "Liberty Point Resolves," 4.

6. Ashe, "The Association Paper," 2, taken from the *Wilmington Journal.*

7. Ashe, "The Association Paper," 2.

8. Ashe, *History of North Carolina*, vol. 1.

9. Ashe, *History of North Carolina*, 1:457.

10. Ashe, "The Association Paper," 2.

11. Ashe, "The Association Paper," 2.

12. "Editorial Comment," p. 2, col.1.

13. Ely, "Mecklenburg Skeptic," 14b.

14. Ely, "Mecklenburg Skeptic," 14b. Our own department has found that the signatures on the document seem to match the signatures that the signers did in deeds and other documents from the time.

CHAPTER 8

Commemorations

IN 1909, FAYETTEVILLE PLANNED a commemorative celebration for the Liberty Point Resolutions. S. G. Ayer, a member of the Woman's Civic Association, was the Chairman of the Liberty Point Monument group. This association scheduled, funded, and organized the entire program, including the creation of the future Liberty Point Memorial with the names of thirty-nine signers listed upon it.[1] She was assisted by Capt. James D. McNeill, who was the Chairman of the Committee of Arrangements.[2] He features prominently in newspaper advertisements of the event to promote the actual day and discuss key issues like funding.[3]

Before the official commemoration, people wrote several articles to prepare in advance. Outside of Cumberland County, newspapers announced the June 21 celebration, encouraging veterans from other counties to participate in the event.[4] Within Cumberland County, news articles appeared a month before the 1909 commemoration event, asking for financial assistance. The Committee of Arrangements had already proposed to make that Monday the "Liberty Point Day," and included a schedule of events already planned. For example, the original program included "Thirteen Guns" at sunrise to represent the region's colonial history. A parade would lead from the Atlantic Coast Line Railroad Depot to Liberty Point, with a musical concert at the old city hall.[5] A Firemen's exhibition would be at the city hall too. At 11 a.m., the committee wanted local military and horsemen to meet visiting military personnel and veterans at the Depot. A little after, a "grand parade" would walk downtown. Floats and automobile races were planned to be a part of the downtown celebrations.[6]

Ceremonies, such as the "laying of the Corner Stone" at Liberty Point and the oration by Chief Justice Walker Clark were already scheduled in the request for financial assistance. The ladies, most likely from the Woman's Civic Association, would host a dinner for veterans and military personnel. Likewise, on Green and Gillespie streets, there would be a military drill competition for prizes. The Fayetteville Fire Department planned a water display and wanted to hold a water contest at 6 p.m. In the evening after most events, there would be fireworks at "Eccles Park." Then, the final event would be the public reception and colonial ball at Elks Temple.[7]

Aside from asking for financial assistance, the committees attempted to increase the excitement for Liberty Point Day by discussing the history of it, such as referencing the local incidents that occurred in Cumberland County during the Revolutionary War. The grandson of James Gee, G. W. Lawrence, wrote to Captain McNeill and Ayer more stories of his grandparents—especially of his grandmother, Mary Gee.[8] Maj. E. J. Hale held an incomplete lecture about "early Fayetteville and Cumberland," and the transcript was used as part of the early advertisements of the commemoration. He discussed the creation of Cumberland County during its separation from Bladen County in 1754, the county's namesake, and the town's major benefit of being an inland port for the "back Provinces" of North Carolina.[9]

Liberty Point Day on June 21, 1909, was vastly successful. The commemoration was recognized as being the 134th anniversary of the Liberty Point "Resolutions" signing, and about fifteen thousand people were in attendance. Like the planned schedule, the parades, military dinners, contests, and balls occurred throughout that Monday. Mounted marshals wore white and participated in the parade, with the Fayetteville Independent Light Infantry following right behind. The 2nd Regiment of the North Carolina National Guard also participated. Similarly, 300 Confederate veterans and 150 "members of the[ir] Junion Order" walked the parade celebration.[10] The men sitting in the first carriage included Chief Justice Walter Clark, Maj. E. J. Hale, Reverend L. W. Hughes, and "Master" James MacRae.[11] James MacRae was an eight-year-old child picked for his familial connection to Duncan K. MacRae, the six-year-old who made an introduction speech of welcome to Marquis de LaFayette in 1825. H. L. Cook and George W. Lawrence rode together on the carriage that LaFayette sat in when entering Fayetteville; these two men were the descendants of James Gee.[12]

The parade also involved a float competition. Several organizations participated in the float designs, such as: State Normal and Industrial College, Daughters of the Confederacy, municipal utilities, the "Highlanders," Elks, and the firemen in Fayetteville. Margaret Ayer played the Goddess of Liberty on the Liberty Point float. Other floats illustrated animal visuals as well, such as a butterfly float and "Red Birds."[13] Aside from the floats, visitors could also participate in the contests. A baseball game was held, and the fire department conducted the watermelon contests and water fights. Inside the city hall, incandescent lamps provided an electrical display; the display included "four great arch lights." Earlier in the day, Capt. J. D. McNeill acted as the Master of Ceremonies, while Mayor Bullard conducted the address of welcome. H. L. Cook performed the Liberty Point Resolutions reading as they held the corner-stone-laying event. The eight-year-old, James MacRae, presented the event's orator, Chief Justice Walter Clark.[14]

Later in the day, the Ladies Liberty Point Monument Association served military veterans' dinner at the city hall: "a bountiful dinner, prepared by the ladies, was served to the Veterans." Liberty Point Day reached the end of the event with fireworks. The fireworks display was shot from Liberty Point.[15] The final event itself was the public reception and colonial ball at night; these programs took place at the new building for the Elks. In the previous days before the event, Fayetteville residents voted to crown Annie Theresa McMillan queen of the ball that night.[16] Altogether, Liberty Point Day was seen as a grand success, with all the compliments directed to S. G. Ayer and Capt. James D. McNeill, who assisted her.[17]

The discussion of Liberty Point Day continued after Monday. Judge Walter Clark and Maj. E. J. Hale both went down the Cape Fear on the "new government boat Mercur" for a tour of the waterways. *Mercur* had originally traveled from its home in Wilmington to Fayetteville, captained by Earl L. Brown; it was preceded by an Apex government tugboat. From Fayetteville to Wilmington, the tour would check on the construction status and maintenance of the Cape Fear River.[18] The committees involved with Liberty Point Day's planning requested further funding help in the *Fayetteville Observer*: "Thousands enjoyed the day—only 118 have helped to pay the expenses... Checks have been drawn for all except the last two."[19] The article contains the entire bill list of the event, with the total cost being $425.95, which would be worth about $14,969.05 in 2025.[20]

In 1933, the Liberty Point Monument Association, headed by President Sewberry, planned for another celebration to mark the creation of a "boulder" memorial with thirty-nine of the signers' names.[21] To prepare for the funding of the granite memorial, the ladies of the association held several programs. In one event, each household decorated their house as a representation of a country and allowed visitors inside as part of a "Trip Around the World." Aside from donating their own money for funding, they also sold photographs of Liberty Point.[22] For one photograph, they drew by hand an image of a woman with the word "Liberty" inscribed below, layering it over the background photo of Liberty Point.[23] On a Monday afternoon during the first week of July, the granite monument was unveiled at the corner of Bow and Person streets. The monument itself was helped in its creation by "several small boys and girls, all lineal descendants of the Cumberland county" signers.[24] Judge N. A. Sinclair introduced Judge George W. Connor, who spoke the address of dedication for the commemoration.[25]

In 1973, the point between Bow and Person streets (known as Liberty Point after the Cumberland Association was signed there) became part of the National Register of Historic Places as part of Liberty Row, which covers the buildings on that side of Person street from the Market House to Liberty Point.[26] As America prepared for the Bicentennial in 1976, Cumberland County celebrated the Liberty Point Resolves again in 1975, hosting receptions, performances, and lectures. The Liberty Point Chapter of the Daughters of the American Revolution planned two events on the anniversary of the June 20 signing. The first event in the afternoon involved "exercises" by the Colonel Robert Rowan Chapter, and the evening event consisted of a "special ceremony" at Liberty Point.[27] Two days later, on June 22, Cumberland County hosted several events. In the morning, churches around the county participated in the celebration. At 2 p.m., the Bicentennial flag was presented during the "Official Bicentennial Designation Ceremony," with another dedication at Heritage Square within the same hour. A public reception was also held at Heritage Square right after the dedication. Another dedication ceremony started at the Arsenal House about 4:30 p.m.–5 p.m. At 8 p.m. at the Market House on Person Street, Harlan Duenow directed "200 voices" as part of the celebration using Revolutionary and patriotic songs before the presentations. The presentations themselves included the Liberty Point Resolutions, the historical significance of the Resolves, the recognition of special guests, a seal and flag contest, and a presentation by Pine Forest High School on the "History of Cumberland County." The day ended with the dramatic reenactment of the Liberty Point Resolves adoption at Liberty Point by the Fayetteville Little Theatre.[28]

In 2008, Fayetteville received the original Cumberland Association document and held it at the Fayetteville Area Transportation Museum (now the Fayetteville History Museum). The loan from Wilson Library was possible with the assistance of State Representative Margaret Dickson.[29] Commemorations had dropped off, but they once more revived again in 2021. The Sons of the American Revolution president, Roderick Mullen, advised the local chapter (Le Marquis de Lafayette Chapter of the North Carolina Society of the Sons of the American Revolution [NCSSAR]) to revive commemorations for the signing of the Liberty Point Resolves. David Mann procured permission from First Presbyterian Church to hold the ceremonies, and the event has been annually celebrated since 2021. These events are also coordinated with local lineage societies, such as the Liberty Point Chapter NCSDAR, Colonel Robert Rowan Chapter NCSDAR, the Isham Blake Society NC Society Children of the American Revolution, and The Lafayette Society.[30]

In 2025, participants gathered for the 250th Anniversary Commemoration for the Liberty Point Resolves. Multiple, familiar groups cosponsored this gathering, including: Le Marquis de Lafayette NCSSAR, Liberty Point NSDAR, Colonel Robert Rowan NSDAR, Isham Blake Society of the Isham Blake Society of the NCSCAR, and the Lafayette Society. The First Presbyterian Church spatially hosted the event, and multiple other groups in Fayetteville, like the Arts Council and Fayetteville History Museum, provided materials and programs for the rest of the celebration.[31]

The 250th Anniversary Commemoration started with the "Presentation of Colors" by the Le Marquis de Lafayette NCSSAR color guard, with bagpipes playing in the background as the members carried out a multitude of flags, such as the American flag, NC Sons of the American Revolution flag, and the North Carolina state flag. Cumberland County Commissioners Kirk deViere and Glenn Adams, along with Mayor Pro Tempore Katherine Jenson of Fayetteville, conducted proclamations for the commemoration. After short "greetings," two presentations on the historic importance of the Liberty Point Resolves were performed, with one from Major Bruce J. Daws and another from America 250 Ranger Steven Roberts. Members of the NC Sons and Daughters of the American Revolution read aloud the Liberty Point Resolves itself and the names of each signer. Afterward, the "ringing of the bell" was conducted, with final programs involving the honoring of the wreaths, SAR recessional, benediction, and the retirement of colors. The chairman of the entire commemoration was David W. Dowless Jr.[32] The overall commemoration reached state news when Governor Stein signed a proclamation recognizing the Resolves.[33]

Two months later, on August 16, 2025, the 250th Celebration continued with the commemoration of the Liberty Tree in downtown Fayetteville. Sponsored by the America 250 NC Grant, Airborne & Special Operations Museum (ASOM) Foundation, and the Sons of the American Revolution, the commemoration was hosted near the large Virginia Oak that sat by the city's railroad station. Like the other event, the program was started with the presentation of the colors and proclamations by North Carolina Representative Diane Wheatley; Cumberland County Commissioner, Kirk deViere; the Executive Director of the ASOM Foundation, Renee Lane; and Dan Brosz, the America 250 NC Project Coordinator. The final presenter was Charles Broadwell, a former editor and publisher of the *Fayetteville Observer*, who regaled tales of the Liberty Tree.[34] Author Beth Hutson quoted the event's release for the *Fayetteville Observer*, describing the importance of the tree, "Local tradition says the signers nailed the resolution to the Liberty Tree in an act of defiance against British rule."[35] There is currently no historical evidence that proves this local legend however. Finally, the presentations led up to the most important part of the commemoration—the unveiling of a new, permanent historical marker for the Liberty Tree itself.[36]

Notes

1. "An Enormous Crowd"; "Historic Fayetteville," 3.

2. "Liberty Point Day."

3. McNeill, "Liberty Point Day: Programme for June 21st"; McNeill, "Committees Liberty Point Celebration"; McNeill, "Expense Fund 'Liberty Point Day.'"

4. "The Exchange," 3.

5. McNeill, "Liberty Point Day: Programme for June 21st." In the 1909–1910 Fayetteville City Directory, the old city hall sat at 117 Gillespie St., which is currently the site for a downtown parking lot close to the Cumberland County Courthouse in 2025 (46).

6. McNeill, "Liberty Point Day: Programme for June 21st."

7. McNeill, "Liberty Point Day: Programme for June 21st."

8. Lawrence, "Liberty Point Declaration."

9. "Early Fayetteville and Cumberland."

10. "An Enormous Crowd." The Junior Order included a younger demographic of participants following the Confederate veterans.

11. "An Enormous Crowd." The usage of the term "master" for James MacRae was both a polite social term and a reference to his role in the ceremonies. As a

young boy, MacRae would be called "master" until he reached adulthood, in which the term would switch to the well-recognized "mister" term ("Master vs. Mister."). Secondly, since he introduced the speakers and events, he became the master-of-ceremonies as well.

12. "An Enormous Crowd."

13. "An Enormous Crowd."

14. "An Enormous Crowd."

15. "Liberty Point Day."

16. "An Enormous Crowd."

17. "Liberty Point Day"; "An Enormous Crowd."

18. "Judge Clark and Maj. Hale Go Down the Cape Fear."

19. Cooper and McNeill, "Receipts and Expenses."

20. Cooper and McNeill, "Receipts and Expenses"; Webster, "$425.95 in 1909 Is Worth $14,969.05 Today."

21. "Unveil Liberty Point Boulder About July 1"; *Independent* (Elizabeth City), 2.

22. "Unveil Liberty Point Boulder." Originally, the Liberty Point Monument Association was a "society formed by a few patriotic men of our city," with the women's group as part of the association's auxiliary. The men were also responsible for raising funds for the Liberty Point monument, but the men's group gave up their association to the women's group later. The Liberty Point Monument Association then joined the Civic Association of Fayetteville.

23. Parker, *Fayetteville, North Carolina*, 110.

24. *Independent* (Elizabeth City), 3.

25. "Marker Honors Patriots," 8.

26. "Liberty Row"; "Fayetteville Historic Districts Official Map – September, 2014."

27. "Liberty Point Commemoration," 1.

28. Cumberland County Bicentennial Commission, "Bicentennial News"; "Bicentennial Chorus," 4.

29. Worthington, "'Liberty' Document Comes Home." The museum later hosted the document again in 2014.

30. David Mann, email message to author, November 18, 2025.

31. *Cumberland Association: Liberty Point Resolves*, 1–5; Hutson, "Ceremony to Commemorate Signing of Liberty Point Resolves."

32. Cumberland Association: Liberty Point Resolves, 5–6.

33. "Governor Stein Proclaims Recognition of the 250th Anniversary of the Liberty Point Resolves."

34. *Liberty Tree.*

35. Hutson, "Weekend Event."

36. *Liberty Tree.*

CHAPTER 9

The Resolves Today

As America approaches the 250th anniversary of the Declaration of Independence, Cumberland has just passed the 250th anniversary of their Resolves for freedom made in 1775. This study has filled a gap in the literature on the Liberty Point Resolves, allowing the Resolves to take their place as a significant document in the American Revolution in North Carolina.

In popular memory, the Liberty Point Resolves does not stand out because it was not a declaration of independence, unlike the Mecklenburg Declaration of Mecklenburg County. The Mecklenburg Declaration was a declaration of independence and predated the national Declaration of Independence by over a year, which is why it made it onto the North Carolina state flag.[1] However, there is no original document for the Mecklenburg Declaration, and it remains disputed till this day. Yet the Liberty Point Resolves differentiates from the Mecklenburg Declaration because there *is* an original document of the Resolves, which currently resides at the University of North Carolina's Wilson Library in Chapel Hill.[2] The document proves that the event happened, a stark contrast to the Mecklenburg Declaration.

Cumberland was not the only county to make Resolves; they were joining onto the Wilmington Association, and Wilmington had bigger names state-wide in the Patriot cause, such as Cornelius Harnett. Perhaps Wilmington's preeminence in the independence movement in North Carolina is one reason why the Liberty Point Resolves was overlooked—the Resolves was not breaking new ground, and no one from Cumberland may have had the political influence across the state the way some other counties did. Even in Fayetteville, residents forgot sixteen signers, which is directly influenced by John Wheeler's 1851 publication that dropped off sixteen names.[3] As for why it was overlooked on a state level, it is probably because it was seen as being insignificant because it was a restatement of the New Hanover Association, as historian Samuel Ashe claimed.[4]

However, as seen in this study, Cumberland County had a stronger Loyalist population than the other counties that made similar Resolves, even if it was not as staunchly Loyalist as some have previously claimed. The Loyalist strength was demonstrated by the Provincial Congress's examination of the insurgents captured at Moores Creek at Halifax in April 1776. Of the 101 men listed, the most are from Cumberland County (19), followed by Anson County (11), and New Hanover County (1).[5] Cumberland even has the notoriety of being the one county in North Carolina that had multiple individuals captured as Loyalists who had previously *served* in the Provincial Congress.[6] The number of Cumberland politicians in the Loyalist movement makes the signing of the Resolves more significant due to the courage needed to sign the document in hostile territory.[7] This study has shown how a minority of Cumberland County residents fought for independence from Great Britian in the runup to the American Revolution.

This study has also dispelled multiple myths relating to the Liberty Point Resolves. For instance, one common myth was that Robert Rowan wrote the Liberty Point Resolves.[8] That is not true; the Association was based on the Wilmington Association and was a copy of it, besides the replacement of Wilmington with Cumberland. Another commonly told myth is that the Liberty Point Resolves was a 'Declaration of Independence.'[9] The Resolves did *not* declare independence from Great Britain, unlike the disputed Mecklenburg Declaration and the more famous American Declaration of Independence, which declared that "these United Colonies are, and of Right ought to be Free and Independent States; that they are Absolved from all Allegiance to the British Crown."[10] The Cumberland Association never declared independence, the group of men united themselves:

> under every tie of religion and honour, and associate as a band in her defence against every foe, hereby solemnly engaging that whenever our continental or Provincial Councils shall decree it necessary, we will go forth and be ready to sacrifice our lives and fortunes to secure her freedom and safety: *This obligation to continue in full force until a reconciliation shall take place between Great Britain and America, upon constitutional principles: an event we most ardently desire* [italics mine].[11]

The signers were not severing their bonds *from* Great Britain, only promising to defend colonial North Carolina against foes, which at the time included Great Britain—who they wanted reconciliation with. That is not a Declaration of Independence, which this study should make clear.

One issue this study encountered was the lack of records from the time period. There was little information found on some of the signers, such as Daniel Doyle, Thomas Rea and Charles Stevens. On a broader level, even though Cumberland had their own Committee of Safety, no records of those minutes were discovered. Further research would need to be done to see if there are any records available that just have not been discovered yet.

The fifty-five men who signed the Liberty Point Resolves, while from a diverse group of backgrounds, were united (besides two exceptions) in the fight for independence. They demonstrated courage in signing their lives to the "death warrant," knowing they would die if the British caught them.[12] Their signing demonstrated that even though Cumberland County had the greatest number of Loyalist claims after the Revolution, it also had its own independence spark.[13] As the Revolution ended, the community decided to carry on the legacy of independence by renaming Cross Creek as 'Fayetteville,' after the Marquis de Lafayette, leaving a legacy of independence that stretches to today.[14]

Notes

1. Faulkner and Agan, "Mecklenburg Declaration of Independence."

2. There are original documents for the Cumberland and Wilmington-New Hanover Associations. For Wilmington's, see New Hanover Association, *Wilmington, North Carolina-New Hanover County Committees of Safety.*

3. The Cumberland Association was mentioned much more frequently in the local newspapers before the Civil War than afterward.

4. Ashe, "Liberty Point Resolves," 4.

5. *CSR,* 10: 594–603; Anson and Cumberland were two of the most Loyalist counties in the state according to Robert Demond (*Loyalists*, 59).

6. *CSR,* 10:595.

7. Westendorf, "The Association of Cumberland County."

8. See "The 20th of June, 1775," 2; "Traditions of Cross Creek and Reminiscences of Fayetteville," 2.

9. For just one example, Woolverton, "This Weekend, Celebrate the 250th Anniversary of Cumberland County's Declaration of Revolution." He says that it was a "mini-declaration of independence."

10. "Declaration of Independence: A Transcription."

11. Force, *American Archives*, vol. 2, "Association Adopted and Signed by the Committees of the District of Wilmington, in North-Carolina," doc. ID S4-V2-P01-sp32-D0392, *Northern Illinois University Digital Library*, https://digital.lib.niu.edu/islandora/object/niu-amarch%3A80845.

12. "American Independence."

13. Westendorf, "The Association of Cumberland County."

14. Bill to Change the Name of Campbellton to Fayetteville, May 12, 1783, 1989, [1783].

APPENDIX 1: THE SIGNERS IN COMPOSITE[1]

The signers came from a variety of backgrounds. They differed in their occupations and government roles from local government officials to planters and blacksmiths, along with many signers whose occupation remains unknown.

Occupations of the Signers:

01 Occupations of the Signers Table

Signer	Occupation
Robert Rowan	Local government official
Lewis Barge	Planter, Hatter, also owned a tavern
John Jones	Planter
Philip Herin	Planter
Samuel Hollingsworth	Planter, Turpentine
Thomas White	Planter
John Carraway	Planter, Cooper
William Gillespie	Cooper
William Herin	Blacksmith
Peter Messer	Blacksmith
James Gee	Bricklayer, Tavern-owner
Martin Leonard	Tavern-owner
George Fletcher	Tavern-owner
John Oveler	Tavern-owner
David Shepherd	Tavern-owner
James Dick	Carpenter
Thomas Cabeen	Tanner
John Stevenson	Tailor
William Bathgate	Watchmaker
Aaron Vardy	Tavern-owner
William Carver	Miller
Maurice Nowlan	Merchant
Joshua Hadley	Merchant
Lewis Bowell	Baker, Tavern-owner

Twenty-three of the signers were confirmed enslavers: Lewis Barge, William Bathgate, Thomas Cabeen, John Carraway, Robert Carver, William Carver, Benjamin Elwell, John Elwell, James Emmet, David Evans, Theophilus Evans, George Fletcher, James Gee, Joshua Hadley, Samuel Hollingsworth, Peter Messer, Thomas Moody, Maurice Nowlan, John Oveler, Robert Rowan, Charles Stevens, Aaron Vardy, and Thomas White.

Signers in Local and State Government:

02 Signers in Local Government Table

Signer	Government role
Robert Rowan	Deputy Court Clerk for Johnston County (1763), Cumberland County Sheriff: 1770-71, 1774, Cumberland County Judge: 1772, 1774-75, 1778, 1780, 1782, 1784-88, 1790 Colonial and State Assembly: 1773-1775, 1778-79, 1785 Colonial Provincial Congress: 1775-76 Fayetteville Town Commissioner: 1783 State Tobacco Commissioner for Fayetteville: 1786-87 Federal Commissioner of Loans for North Carolina (1798)
Lewis Barge	Commissioner of Upper and Lower Campbellton (1778), Fayetteville Town Commissioner (1783)
George Fletcher	Commissioner of Upper and Lower Campbellton (1778)
Walter Murray	Justice of the Peace 1776-77, Cumberland County Judge: 1778-1782, Cumberland County Coroner 1778
James Emmet	Fayette County Sheriff (1784), Cumberland County Sheriff (end of 1784-1786), representative for Fayette County in the General Assembly (1784)
James Dick	Commissioner for laying out Fayetteville (1783), representative for Fayetteville in the General Assembly (1797)

Thirty-One signers fought on the Patriot side during the Revolution:

03 Signers Who Fought on the Patriot Side Table

Robert Rowan	Lewis Bowell	Martin Leonard	George Fletcher	Walter Murray
David Evans	John Elwell	Robert Greer	Robert Carver	Theophilus Evans
Thomas Moody	Arthur Council	Robert Varner	Simon Banday	John Jones
Robert Council	Samuel Carver	David Shepherd	Micajah Terrell	James Emmet
Philip Herin	James Gee	Joshua Hadley	William Carver	James Dick
James Pearl	Thomas Cabeen	John Clendenin	James Giles	Thomas White
James Edmunds				

Note

1. Look at the preceding sections for information and sources on a particular signer.

Front

1. Rob.[t] Rowan
2. Lewis Barge
3. Maurice Nowlan
4. Lewis Bowell
5. Martin Lennard
6. Theophilous Evans
7. Thos Moody
8. Joseph De Lespine
9. Arthur Council
10. John Oveler
11. David Shepherd
12. Micajah Terrell
13. Peter Messer
14. John Wilson

Back

15. Thomas Cabeen
16. Tho.[s] Rea
17. Dan'll Doyle
18. James Emmet
19. James Dick
20. Aaron Vardey
21. John Stevenson
22. One.[rs] West
23. W[m] Bathgate
24. George Fletcher
25. Cha[s] Stevens
26. James Pearl
27. John Parker
28. Walter Murray
29. John Caraway
30. Wm Gillespy

31. William Herin
32. Philip Herin
33. David Evans
34. Robert Varner
35. James Gee
36. John Elwell
37. Benjamin Elwell
38. David Dunn
39. Willm White
40. Simon Banday
41. Joseph Greer
42. Robt Greer
43. Thos White
44. Joshua Hadly
45. John Jones
46. Wm Blocker
47. Robt Council
48. Saml. Hollingsworth
49. James Giles
50. John Clendenin
51. Robt Carver
52. Samuel Carver
53. Wm Carver
54. George Barns
55. James ^{his} X ^{mark} Edmunds

APPENDIX 3: THE LIBERTY POINT MONUMENT AND THE FORGOTTEN SIGNERS

When the Liberty Point Association erected the monument in August 1933 to commemorate the signers of the Resolves, they utilized Wheeler's list of thirty-nine names so sixteen names were originally left off.[1] The names of these "forgotten signers" were added to the back of the monument in February 1976 by the Colonel Robert Rowan Chapter of the National Society of the Daughters of the American Revolution after David Sanders Clark tracked down the original document.[2] They are as follows:

James Dick
James Pearl
Daniel Douse [*sic*]
George Barns
Thomas Cabeen
John Clendenin
John Stevenson
William Bathgate
Thomas Pea
James Giles
Peter Messer
Thomas White
James Edmunds
John Carraway
William Gillespy
Onesiphorus West

Notes

1. Anderson, "Will Commemorate Early Independence Declaration."
2. Johnson, "Sixteen Names Added to Liberty Point Boulder."

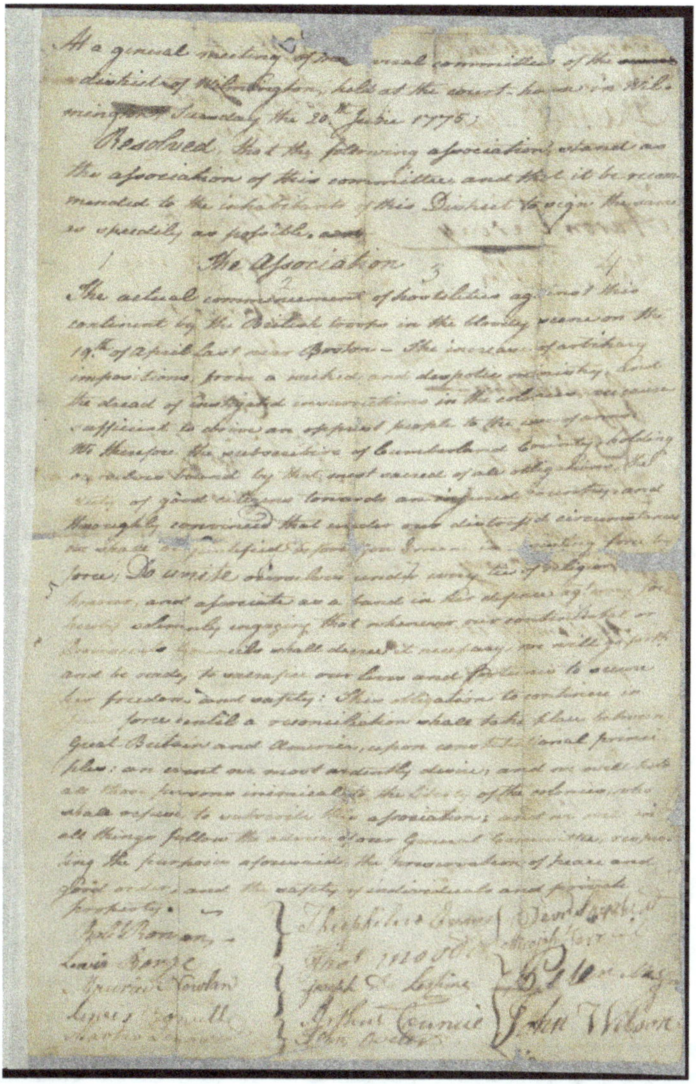

At a general meeting of the [illegible] committees of the [illegible] district of Wilmington, held at the court-house in Wilmington [illegible] Tuesday the 20th June 1775:

Resolved, that the following association stand as the association of this committee and that it be recommended to the inhabitants of this District to sign the same as speedily as possible.

The Association

The actual commencement of hostilities against this continent by the British troops in the bloody scene on the 19th of April last near Boston – the increase of arbitrary impositions from a wicked and despotic ministry, and the dread of instigated insurrections in the colonies, are causes sufficient to drive an oppressed people to the use of arms. We therefore the subscribers of Cumberland County, holding ourselves bound by that most sacred of all obligations, the duty of good citizens towards an injured country, and thoroughly convinced that under our distressed circumstances we shall be justified [illegible] in resisting force by force; do unite ourselves under every tie of religion and honour, and associate as a band in her defence [illegible] solemnly engaging that whenever our continental or provincial councils shall decree it necessary, we will go forth and be ready to sacrifice our lives and fortunes to secure her freedom and safety: This obligation to continue in force until a reconciliation shall take place between Great Britain and America, upon constitutional principles: an event we most ardently desire; and we will hold all those persons inimical to the liberty of the colonies, who shall refuse to subscribe this association; and we will in all things follow the advice of our General Committee, respecting the purposes aforesaid, the preservation of peace and good order, and the safety of individuals and private property.

[illegible signatures] ... John Wilson

The original copy of the Liberty Point Resolves is held by UNC's Wilson Library. The first page consists of the Association and lists the beginning signers. Photo Credit: Cumberland Association Papers, scan 8, Cumberland Association Papers, Wilson Special Collections Library, UNC-Chapel Hill.

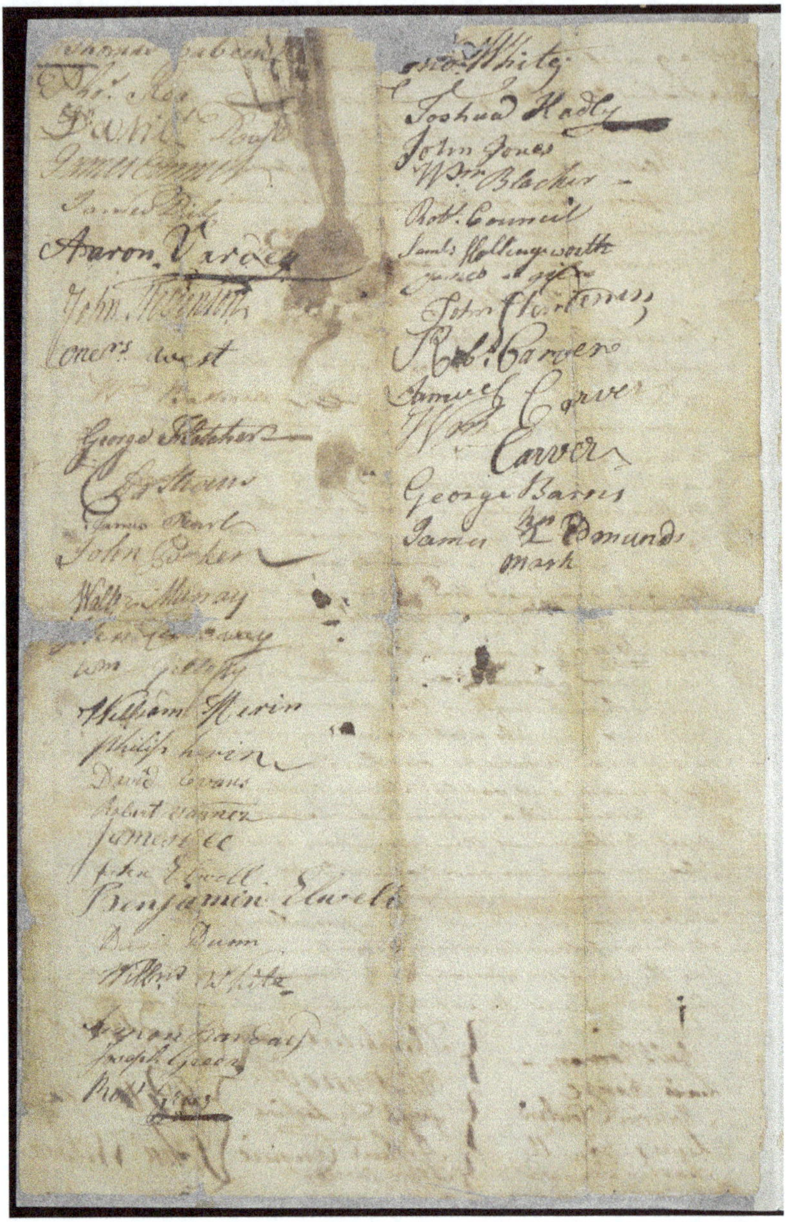

More of the signers are displayed on the 2nd page. Of note is Daniel Doyle's name on the left-handed side, which has been interpreted as 'Daniel Douse' in the past. Photo Credit: Cumberland Association Papers, scan 9, Cumberland Association Papers, Wilson Special Collections Library, UNC-Chapel Hill.

Prior to the Battle of Moore's Creek, General Moore and his Patriot forces-including many Liberty Point Resolves Signers-camped on what is now PWC property near Highway 87 in Fayetteville.
Photo by Joseph Westendorf

Cornwallis passed through Cross Creek after the Battle of Guilford Courthouse, where his forces pillaged residents' homes when passing through. This historic marker is on Green Street in what is now Fayetteville. Photo by Joseph Westendorf.

This marker commemorating the Resolves is on the side of the Liberty Point Building on Person Street. It was placed before 1909, but it is unclear the exact date. Photo taken by Joseph Westendorf.

This marker was placed during the 1909 commemoration at Liberty Point. Photo by Joseph Westendorf

This monument was erected in 1933 on Person Street and listed only 39 signers. The other 16 had been forgotten about. Photo taken by Joseph Westendorf.

The backside of the Liberty Point Monument had the 16 forgotten signers' names added to it in Feb 1976, after the document was re-discovered. Photo by Joseph Westendorf

Cumberland County Chairman of the Board of Commissioners Kirk deViere speaks at the 250th commemoration ceremony of the Liberty Point Resolves on June 21, 2025, at First Presbyterian in downtown Fayetteville. Photo by Kaitlyn Santos-Porter.

Cumberland County Commissioner Glenn Adams speaks at the 250th anniversary commemoration of the Liberty Point Resolves on June 21, 2025. Photo by Kaitlyn Santos-Porter.

"Abbot, Mrs. Josiah to Dean, Samuel." FamilySearch. https://familysearch.org/ark:/61903/3:1:33SQ-GPF9-BKB.

Adams County, Mississippi. *Orphans Court Minutes*. Vols. 1–7. Microfilm. 4 rolls. FamilySearch. https://www.familysearch.org/en/search/catalog/239785.

Adams County, Mississippi. *Will Records*. Vols. 1–7. Microfilm. 6 rolls. FamilySearch. https://www.familysearch.org/en/search/catalog/236732.

"American Independence." *National Intelligencer*, August 6, 1816. Nineteenth Century U.S. Newspapers. https://link.gale.com/apps/doc/GT3017476570/NCNP?u=txshrpub100185&sid=bookmark-NCNP&xid=96bd2932.

American Loyalist Claims Papers. Record ID 21.111. State Archives of North Carolina. Raleigh, NC.

Americanus, Scotus. *Information Concerning the Province of North Carolina Addressed to Emigrants from the Highlands and Western Isles of Scotland*. Glasgow, 1773.

Amount of the Tax of Cumberland County for 1783. "List of Taxables 1777–1783." Record ID CR.029.701.001. Cumberland County. State Archives of North Carolina. Raleigh, NC. FamilySearch. https://familysearch.org/ark:/61903/3:1:3QSQ-G98M-Z99F.

"An Anniversary." *Fayetteville* (NC) *Observer*, March 25, 1909.

"An Enormous Crowd Celebrate Fayetteville's Declaration of Independence." *Fayetteville Observer*, June 24, 1909.

Anderson, Mrs. John H. "Will Commemorate Early Independence Declaration: Fayetteville Will Dedicate Memorial to Liberty Point Patriots." *News and Observer* (Raleigh, NC), August 27, 1933. Newspapers.com. https://newspapers.com/article/the-news-and-observer-will-commemorate-e/185204128/.

"Ann *Carver* Elwell." Find a Grave. https://findagrave.com/memorial/153497198/ann-elwell.

Anson County, North Carolina. *Minutes, Court of Pleas and Quarter Sessions*. Vol. 1771–1776. FamilySearch. https://familysearch.org/ark:/61903/3:1:3Q9M-CSLV-P9ML-B

Anson County, North Carolina. *Record of Deeds*. Vols. K–M. FamilySearch. https://familysearch.org/en/search/catalog/330384.

Apr. 29: Report on Petition of Robert Rowan and Others (Rejected), 1784. Record ID 66.8.32.1.6. General Assembly Session Records. State Archives of North Carolina. Raleigh, NC.

"Arthur Council (1739–1777)." Find a Grave. https://findagrave.com/memorial/118807630/arthur-councilhttps://findagrave.com/memorial/118807630/arthur-council.

Asch, Solomon. "Opinions and Social Pressure." *Scientific American* 193, no. 5 (1955): 31–35

Ashe, Samuel A'Court. *History of North Carolina*. Vol. 1, *From 1584 to 1783*. Charles L. Van Noppen, 1908.

Ashe, Samuel A'Court. "Liberty Point Resolves." *Wilmington* (NC) *Morning Star*, June 27, 1909.

Ashe, Samuel, A'Court. "The Association Paper of the Cape Fear Region." *North Carolina Gazette* (Fayetteville), June 3, 1875.

"At a Late Meeting of the Inhabitants of This Town." *Fayetteville* (NC) *Gazette*, March 3, 1793. Microfilm.

Baird, Robert W. "Legal Age." *Bob's Genealogy Filing Cabinet*. https://genfiles.com/articles/legal-age/.

Baird, Robert W. "Wills, Intestates, & Probate." *Bob's Genealogy Filing Cabinet*. https://genfiles.com/articles/wills-intestates-probate/.

Barnes, George. "Three Pounds Reward." *Cape Fear* (NC) *Mercury*, September 22, 1773. Newspapers.com. https://newspapers.com/article/north-carolina-gazette-and-wilmington-w/188527091/.

Barnhill, Celeste Jane Terrell. *Richmond, William, and Timothy Terrell: Colonial Virginians*. Mitchell, 1934. HathiTrust. https://catalog.hathitrust.org/Record/005769500.

Bathgate, William. "The Subscriber Intends to Leave Petersburg." *Virginia Gazette* (Williamsburg), August 18, 1774.

"Battle of Elizabethtown Culminated at the Tory Hole." *Historical Marker Database* (blog), August 27, 2016. North Carolina Department of Natural and Cultural Resources. https://www.dncr.nc.gov/blog/2016/08/27/battle-elizabethtown-culminated-tory-hole.

Berenson, Laura Lee, Johanna Schuster Jones, Emily Johanna Perkins, and Mary Pauline Schuster. "Francisca de Paula Petronita Fontanet; Joseph Delespine; Frances Jane Delespine; Christian Jacob Bernhard Boye." In *Florida Pioneer Biographies*. Florida State Genealogical Society, March 10, 2023. https://fsgs.org/florida-pioneer-biographies/francisca-de-paula-petronita-fontanet-joseph-delespine-frances-jane-delespine-christian-jacob-bernhard-boye/.

"Bicentennial Chorus." *Bicentennial News* (Arts Council of Fayetteville, Inc.) 1, no. 1 (March 1975): 4.

Blackstone, William, Sir. "Of Guardian and Ward." In *Book the First: The Rights of Persons* Vol. 1 of *Commentaries on the Laws of England*, 4th ed. Dublin, 1771. Internet Archive. https://archive.org/details/commentariesonla711blac/page/460/mode/2up.

Blackstone, William, Sir. "Of Title by Descent." In *Book the Second: Of the Rights of Things*. Vol. 2 of *Commentaries on the Laws of England*, 3rd ed. Oxford, 1768. Internet Archive. https://archive.org/details/commentariesonla021768blac/page/200/mode/2up.

"Bladen Co. File No. 4372, Benjamin Elwell." North Carolina Land Grants and Data. https://nclandgrants.com/grant/?mars=12.14.33.4370&qid=1233159&rn=1.

"Bladen Co. File No.783, Samuel Carver." North Carolina Land Grants and Data. https://nclandgrants.com/grant/?mars=12.14.33.787&qid=1232025&rn=2.

Bladen County, North Carolina. *Record of Deeds*. 37 vols. FamilySearch. https://familysearch.org/en/search/catalog/330546.

Bladen County, North Carolina. *Wills: 1766–1961*. 5 vols. FamilySearch. https://familysearch.org/en/search/catalog/352524.

Bill to Add Part of Bladen County to Cumberland (with Petition). November 9, 1789. Record ID 66.8.54.54. General Assembly Session Records. State Archives of North Carolina. Raleigh, NC.

Bill to Change the Name of Campbellton to Fayetteville, May 12, 1783, 1989, [1783]. Record ID N.89.5.18-19. General Assembly Session Records. State Archives of North Carolina. Raleigh, NC. https://appx.archives.ncdcr.gov/solrDetailPages/series/NCA/Series_detail.html?fq=seriesRid:243181.

Bill to Divide Anson County. January 30, 1779. Record ID 66.8.16.28. General Assembly Session Records. State Archives of North Carolina. Raleigh, NC.

"The Boating Business." *Fayetteville* (NC) *Observer*, September 12, 1895.

Boddie, William Willis. *Marion's Men: A List of Twenty-Five Hundred*. Heisser Printing, 1938.

Bowell, Lewis. "Strayed or Stolen." *The Encyclopedian Instructor* (Edenton, NC), November 27, 1792.

Bristol County, Massachusetts. *Minutes of Inferior Court of Common Pleas*. Vol. 4. FamilySearch. https://familysearch.org/ark:/61903/3:1:3Q9M-CS41-Y93L-N.

Bristol, Massachusetts. *Probate Records*. Vol. 25, *1777–1779*. FamilySearch. https://familysearch.org/ark:/61903/3:1:3Q9M-C9YR-X7ML.

Buck, William J. "Washington's Encampment on the Neshaminy." *The Pennsylvania Magazine of History and Biography* 1, no. 3 (1877): 275–84. https://www.jstor.org/stable/20084292.

Cain, Robert J. "James Hepburn: A Loyalist Odyssey." *North Carolina Historical Review* 102, no. 1 (2025): 1–35.

Camin, Betty J. "Revolutionary War Pension Applications at the NC Archives." Pt. 3. *North Carolina Genealogical Society Journal* 11, no. 1 (1985): 16–24.

Campbell, Wanda Suggs. *Bladen County, North Carolina, Abstracts of Deeds*. 2 vols. Published by the author, 1977 and 1980.

Cane Creek Monthly Meeting. Vol. 1, *1751–1796*. Quaker Archives, Hege Library, Guilford College.

"Capt Joshua Hadley." Find a Grave. https://findagrave.com/memorial/71865471/joshua-hadley.

Caruthers, Eli W. *The Old North State in 1776: Volumes I and II with Index*. Guilford County Genealogical Society, 1985. Originally published as *Revolutionary Incidents: and Sketches of Character, Chiefly in the "Old North State"* in 1854 (vol. 1) and 1856 (vol. 2) in Philadelphia.

Cates, Larry W. "Legislative Petitions, 1778." *North Carolina Genealogical Society Journal* 38, no. 1 (2012): 47–48.

Cates, Larry W. "Legislative Petitions, 1779." *North Carolina Genealogical Society Journal* 38, no. 2 (2012): 136–49.

Cates, Larry W. "Legislative Petitions, 1780–1781." *North Carolina Genealogical Society Journal* 39, no. 1 (2013): 35–44.

Caudill, Bill. *The Scottish Highlander Immigration to the Sandhills*. Lecture. Cumberland County Public Library. June 19, 2025.

Cemeteries: Kelly Steps. Vertical files. Cumberland County Public Library. Fayetteville, NC.

Civil Engineer Corps Officers Naval School. *Mess Night Manual*. Department of the Navy, 1986.

Charleston County, South Carolina. *Miscellaneous Records*. Vol. 1774–1779. FamilySearch. https://familysearch.org/en/search/catalog/288737.

Charleston County, South Carolina. *Record of Deeds*. Vols. D4–E4. FamilySearch. https://familysearch.org/en/search/catalog/361547.

Chatham County, North Carolina. "Deeds, Bills of Sale, Inventories of Estates & Wills." Microfilm. 3 rolls. FamilySearch. https://familysearch.org/en/search/catalog/511757.

Chatham County, North Carolina. *Record of Deeds*. Vols. A–DM. FamilySearch. https://familysearch.org/en/search/catalog/403727.

Cheney, John L., Jr., ed. *North Carolina Government 1585–1979: A Narrative and Statistical History*. North Carolina Department of the Secretary of State, 1981.

Chowan County, North Carolina. "Estate Records." Genealogical Society of Utah, 1991. Microfilm. 67 rolls. FamilySearch. https://familysearch.org/en/search/catalog/456853.

Chowan County, North Carolina. "Original Wills." Genealogical Society of Utah, 1988. Microfilm. 4 rolls. FamilySearch. https://familysearch.org/en/search/catalog/456853.

Chowan County, North Carolina. "Suits Dismissed and Miscellaneous Court Papers, 1687–1783." Genealogical Society of Utah, 1941. Microfilm. 26 rolls. FamilySearch. https://familysearch.org/en/search/catalog/360059.

"[Claim of] John Hay and Company. 22 Jan., 1799." Record ID 21.111.23.5. State Archives of North Carolina. Raleigh, NC.

Clark, David Sanders. "Memorandum for Members of the Committee for Development of Historical Material, Cumberland County Bicentennial Commission." August 25, 1975. In LMJ Collection, folder 83, Cumberland County Public Library.

Clark, David Sanders. "Notes on the Post Revolutionary War History of the Liberty Point Resolves." In Cumberland Association Papers, SHC Z box 106, folder 2, scans 18–23. https://dc.lib.unc.edu/cdm/search/collection/02ddd/searchterm/folder_2!02075-z/field/all!all/mode/exact!exact/conn/and!and/order/relatid.

Clark, D. S. "Nowlan and Vardey: Resolves Signers Fought with Loyalists." *Fayetteville* (NC) *Observer*, February 15, 1976.

Clark, D. S. "Resolves Signers Fought with Loyalists." *Fayetteville* (NC) *Observer and Fayetteville Times*, February 15, 1976.

Clark, Murtie June. *Colonial Soldiers of the South, 1732–1774*. Genealogical Publishing Company, 1983.

Clark, Murtie June. *Official Rolls of Loyalists Recruited from North and South Carolina, Georgia, Florida, Mississippi, and Louisiana*. Vol. 1 of *Loyalists in the Southern Campaign of the Revolutionary War*. Genealogical Publishing Company, 1981.

"Col. J. G. Hollingsworth Dead." *Fayetteville* (NC) *Observer*, September 7, 1910.

"Col Robert Rowan." Find a Grave. https://findagrave.com/memorial/59402288/robert-rowan.

Coldham, Peter Wilson. *American Migrations 1765–1799*. Genealogical Publishing Company, 2000.

"Colonel Alexander McAllister: Patriot and Revolutionary Hero." *Historical Markers Database*. https://www.hmdb.org/m.asp?m=31594.

"Committees of Wilmington District, North-Carolina." In Vol. 2 of *American Archives: Fourth Series*, 1030. Washington, DC, 1839. https://dn790008.ca.archive.org/0/items/americanarchives42forc/americanarchives42forc.pdf.

Compiled Service Records of Soldiers Who Served in the American Army During the Revolutionary War, 1894–ca. 1912. NAID 570910. War Department Collection of Revolutionary War Records, RG 93. National Archives, Washington, DC.

"Continental Association, 20 October 1774." *Founders Online*. National Archives, https://founders.archives.gov/documents/Jefferson/01-01-02-0094.

Continental Congress. *Journals of the Continental Congress, 1774–1789*. 34 vols. Edited by Worthington C. Ford et al. Washington, DC, 1905–1937.

Cooper, C. J., and Jas. D. McNeill. "Receipts and Expenses Liberty Point Celebration." *Fayetteville* (NC) *Observer*, July 8, 1909.

Coquillon, Naomi. "Practicing Measurement with Historic Surveying." *Minerva's Kaleidoscope* (blog), July 16, 2021. Library of Congress. https://blogs.loc.gov/families/2021/07/practicing-measurement-with-historic-surveying/.

Cornell Law School. "Assumption of Risk." *Legal Information Institute*. https://www.law.cornell.edu/wex/assumption_of_risk.

"Council of War, 21 August 1777." *Founders Online*. National Archives. https://founders.archives.gov/documents/Washington/03-11-02-0021.

Councill, Judson. *Hodges Councill of Virginia and Descendants*. J. H. Furst, 1941.

Crane, Jack. "FILI to Pay Tribute to 'The Old Fifer.'" *Fayetteville* (NC) *Observer*, May 3, 1964, 1d.

Crane, Jack. "The Signing of the Liberty Point Resolves." *Fayetteville* (NC) *Observer*, June 22, 1975, 1b.

Craven County, North Carolina. *Record of Deeds*. Vols. 1–11. FamilySearch. https://familysearch.org/en/search/catalog/321810.

Craven County, North Carolina. *Wills, Deeds, and Inventories: 1749–1766*. FamilySearch. https://familysearch.org/en/search/catalog/359019.

Criminal Docket Superior Court, 1778–1787. Vol. 9. Record ID SR.398.8. State Archives of North Carolina. Raleigh, NC.

Crittenden, Charles Christopher. "Overland Travel and Transportation in North Carolina, 1763–1789." *NCHR* 8, no. 3 (July 1931): 239–57.

"Cuddy." The Jefferson Monticello. https://www.monticello.org/research-education/thomas-jefferson-encyclopedia/cuddy/.

Cumberland Association: Liberty Point Resolves. Le Marquis de Lafayette NCSSAR, 2025.

Cumberland Association Papers. Collection ID 2075-z. Southern Historical Collection, Wilson Special Collections Library, University of North Carolina at Chapel Hill. http://finding-aids.lib.unc.edu/02075.

Cumberland County Bicentennial Commission. *Bicentennial News* 1, no. 2 (June 1975): 1–4.

"Cumberland Centennial." *Weekly Sentinel* (Raleigh, NC), June 29, 1875.

Cumberland County, North Carolina. *Trial Docket Fayetteville District Superior Court*. Vol. 1, *1788–1795*. Record ID CRX.010. State Archives of North Carolina. Raleigh, NC.

Cumberland County, North Carolina. "Estate Records." Genealogical Society of Utah, 1992. Microfilm. 36 rolls. FamilySearch. https://familysearch.org/en/search/catalog/456876.

Cumberland County, North Carolina. "Original Wills." Genealogical Society of Utah, 1988. Microfilm. 8 rolls. FamilySearch. https://familysearch.org/en/search/catalog/456876.

Cumberland County, North Carolina. *Minutes, Court of Pleas & Quarter Sessions.* Vols. A–D and 1784–1835. FamilySearch. https://familysearch.org/en/search/catalog/354464.

Cumberland County, North Carolina. *Record of Deeds.* 35 vols. *FamilySearch.* https://familysearch.org/en/search/catalog/330732.

Cumberland County Genealogical Society. *Bible Records Book: Collected in Cumberland County, N. C.* Published by the author, 1996.

Dartmouth, Massachusetts. *Dartmouth Records 1667–1844: Births, Intentions of Marriage, Forbidden Bans, Marriages, Deaths.* FamilySearch. https://familysearch.org/ark:/61903/3:1:3QS7-L979-CWCV.

Dartmouth, Massachusetts. *Records of Town of Dart'th: Marriages 1667–1787, Deaths 1687–1781.* FamilySearch. https://familysearch.org/ark:/61903/3:1:3QS7-L97M-R5L4.

Daughters of the American Revolution (DAR). "Historic Site: Moland House." https://www.dar.org/national-society/historic-sites-and-properties/moland-house.

"Death of Mrs. Lucy Carver." *Fayetteville* (NC) *Observer,* June 27, 1895.

"Dec. 29: Resolution Acquitting Sundry Inhabitants of Fayetteville from Payment of Fines (Petition and Committee Report Only), 1786." Record ID: 66.8.43.8.12. General Assembly Session Records. State Archives of North Carolina. Raleigh, NC.

Decisions, Examinations, Army and Navy, 1789. American Loyalist Claims, Series 1. Record ID AO12/73. National Archives of the UK. Kew, Surrey, England.

"Declaration of Independence: A Transcription." National Archives. https://www.archives.gov/founding-docs/declaration-transcript.

The Declaration of Independence by the Citizens of Mecklenburg County. Raleigh, NC, 1831. https://archive.org/details/declarationofindoonort/page/28/mode/2up.

"Definitive Treaty of Peace Between the United States and Great Britain, 3 September 1783." *Founders Online.* National Archives.

DeLancey Evans Papers. Wilson Special Collections Library, University of North Carolina at Chapel Hill. https://dc.lib.unc.edu/cdm/ref/collection/02ddd/id/486469.

Delmar Transcripts: Transcriptions of Petitions to the General Assembly of North Carolina Relating to the Revolutionary War. North Carolina Genealogical Society, 2017.

DeMond, Robert O. *The Loyalists in North Carolina during the Revolution.* Archon Books, 1964.

Dicken, Emma. *Terrell Genealogy.* Naylor Company, n.d. Internet Archive. https://archive.org/details/l-013-dicken-with-new-index-s.

"Died." *Fayetteville* (NC) *Observer*, January 21, 1834.

"DIED, at Fayetteville, on the 1st Inst Lewis Barge, Sen." *North-Carolina Star* (Raleigh), February 16, 1809. Newspapers.com. https://newspapers.com/article/the-north-carolina-star-died-at-fayette/172220738/.

"DIED, in Child Bed, on the 10th Instant." *Raleigh* (NC) *Minerva*, February 16, 1809. Newspapers.com. https://newspapers.com/article/the-raleigh-minerva-lewis-barge-obit-feb/63737743/.

"DIED—On the 1st Inst. in the Vicinity of Fayetteville." *Raleigh* (NC) *Minerva*, November 12, 1807. Newspapers.com. https://newspapers.com/article/the-raleigh-minerva-obitscarboroughliz/37907951/.

Dunn, David. "2092C." In *Accounts Audited of Claims Growing Out of the Revolution*, series S108092, South Carolina Department of Archives and History. https://www.archivesindex.sc.gov/ArchivesImages/S108092/S108092003800279000/images/2092C_DUNN,%20DAVID.pdf.

Dziennik, Matthew P. "Through an Imperial Prism: Land, Liberty, and Highland Loyalism in the War of American Independence." *Journal of British Studies* 50, no. 2 (2011): 332–58. https://jstor.org/stable/23265315.

Great Britain Audit Office. *American Loyalists: Transcripts of the Manuscript Books and Papers of the Commission of Enquiry into the Losses and Services of American Loyalists*. Vol. 47, 1783–1790, transcribed 1900.

"Early Fayetteville and Cumberland." *Fayetteville* (NC) *Observer*, June 17, 1909.

Edgecombe County, North Carolina. "Estate Records." Genealogical Society of Utah, 1997. Microfilm. 38 rolls. FamilySearch. https://familysearch.org/en/search/catalog/456901.

Edgecombe County, North Carolina. "Marriage Bonds, ca.1741–ca.1868." North Carolina Department of Archives and History, 1962. Microfilm. 3 rolls. FamilySearch. https://familysearch.org/en/search/catalog/345644.

Edgefield County, South Carolina. Probate Records. 90 boxes. FamilySearch. https://familysearch.org/en/search/catalog/363944.

"Editorial Comment." *Fayetteville* (NC) *Index*, June 30, 1909.

Egan, John, and Thomas White. "Inform the Public in General." *North-Carolina Minerva & Fayetteville Advisor*, January 21, 1797.

"Elwell Ferry (I-84)." *Historical Marker Database* (blog). NC Department of Natural and Cultural Resources, January 2, 2024. https://www.dncr.nc.gov/blog/2024/01/02/elwell-ferry-i-84.

Ely, Robert. "Dramatic Resolves Reenactment Raises Question: 'What's The Point?.'" *Fayetteville* (NC) *Observer*, June 22, 1975.

Ely, Robert. "Mecklenburg Skeptic Questions Resolves," *Fayetteville* (NC) *Times*, October 4, 1975.

Ervin, Sara Sullivan. *South Carolinians in the Revolution with Service Records and Miscellaneous Data*. Southern Historical Press, 2023.

Evidence, North Carolina, 1785–1786. American Loyalist Claims, Series 1. Record ID AO12/34. National Archives of the UK. Kew, Surrey, England.

"The Exchange." *Laurinburg* (NC) *Exchange*, June 10, 1909.

Faulkner, Ronnie W., and Kelly Agan. "Mecklenburg Declaration of Independence." NCpedia, December 2021. State Library of North Carolina. https://www.ncpedia.org/mecklenburg-declaration.

Fayetteville (NC) *Carolinian*. March 26, 1842.

Fayetteville, N.C. Directory: 1909–1910. Hill Directory Co., 1909.

"Fayetteville Historic Districts Official Map – September 2014." https://www.fayettevillenc.gov/files/sharedassets/main/v/1/development-services/documents/historic-properties/historic-districts-map.pdf.

Fayetteville (NC) *Observer*, April 7, 1836.

"Fayetteville—On Saturday Last." *Fayetteville* (NC) *Gazette*, January 1, 1791. Microfilm.

"Feb 3. Petition of John Wilson, 1795." Record ID 66.8.75.17.15. General Assembly Session Records. State Archives of North Carolina. Raleigh, NC.

Fields, William C., ed. *Abstracts of Deeds of Cumberland County, North Carolina*. 2 vols. Cumberland County Genealogical Society, 1994.

Fields, William C., ed. *Abstracts of Minutes of the Court of Pleas and Quarter Sessions of Cumberland County*. 2 vols. Cumberland County Bicentennial Commission, 1978.

Fifth Census of the United States, 1830. NARA microfilm M19. 201 rolls. Records of the Bureau of the Census, RG 29. National Archives. Washington, DC. https://www.archives.gov/research/census/microfilm-catalog/1790-1890/part-02#1830.

First Census of the United States, 1790. NARA microfilm M637. 12 rolls. Records of the Bureau of the Census, RG 29. National Archives. Washington, DC. https://www.archives.gov/research/census/microfilm-catalog/1790-1890/part-02#1790.

First Presbyterian Church, Fayetteville, North Carolina. "Minutes, Church Records, and Sermons, 1792–1957." Microfilm. 3 rolls.

Fletcher, W. J. "The Gees of Cumberland County, North Carolina." In *The Gee Family: Descendants of Charles Gee (d. 1709) and Hannah Gee (d. 1728) of Virginia*. Tuttle Publishing, 1937.

Force, Peter, comp. *American Archives: Documents of the American Revolutionary Period, 1774–1776*. https://onlinebooks.library.upenn.edu/webbin/book/lookupid?key=olbp70176.

Fourth Census of the United States, 1820. NARA microfilm M33. 142 rolls. Records of the Bureau of the Census, RG 29. National Archives, Washington, DC. https://www.archives.gov/research/census/microfilm-catalog/1790-1890/part-02#1820.

"The Fourth of July at Fayetteville." *Weekly Raleigh* (NC) *Register*, July 29, 1805. Newspapers.com. https://newspapers.com/article/weekly-raleigh-register-the-fourth-of-ju/168214116/.

"Forty-Seven Republicans Met at the House of William Dick." *Weekly Raleigh* (NC) *Register*, March 21, 1803. Newspapers.com. https://newspapers.com/article/weekly-raleigh-register-fayetteville-cel/172049807/.

Fowler, Malcolm. *They Passed This Way: A Personal Narrative of Harnett County History*. Friends of the Harnett County Library, 1992.

Fowler, Malcolm. *Valley of the Scots: A History of the First Scottish Settlers in North Carolina*. Wynona Fowler, 1986.

"From the Cheraw Intelligencer Interesting Reminiscence." *Fayetteville* (NC) *Observer*, August 11, 1825.

"From John Adams to United States Senate, 12 February 1798." *Founders Online*. National Archives. https://founders.archives.gov/documents/Adams/99-02-02-2336.

"From John Ramsey, 21 August 1781." In Governors' Papers: Thomas Burke, Correspondence, August 1781. Record ID SR.311.1. State Archives of North Carolina. Raleigh, NC. https://digital.ncdcr.gov/Documents/Detail/governors-papers-thomas-burke-correspondence-august-1781/997775?item=997981.

"Further Report on Claim of John Hay and Co. To Debts Due in North Carolina [n.d.], [1800]." Record ID 21.111.39.22. In American Loyalist Claims, State Archives of North Carolina. Raleigh, NC.

Garvin, Maj. Wilford A. "Conduct of the Mess: Role of Tradition in Unit Social Gatherings." *ARMOR* 135, no. 2 (2021). https://www.benning.army.mil/Armor/eARMOR/content/issues/2021/Spring/2Garvin21.pdf.

"Gen. James Robertson and the Corps of Invincibles." *Wilmington* (NC) *Gazette*, March 3, 1807.

"Genealogical and Biographical Research Part 2: Genealogical and Biographical Research: A Select Catalog of National Archives Microfilm Publications (Part 2)." National Archives. Washington, DC. https://www.archives.gov/publications/microfilm-catalogs/biographical/part-02.html.

"General Orders, 1 October 1779." *Founders Online*. National Archives. https://founders.archives.gov/documents/Washington/03-22-02-0481.

"General Orders, 31 August 1779." *Founders Online*. National Archives. https://founders.archives.gov/documents/Washington/03-22-02-0239.

"George Cooper & Wife to William Farmer, 25 October 1768." FamilySearch. https://familysearch.org/ark:/61903/3:1:3QSQ-G9DC-ZSYR.

George Washington Papers. Library of Congress. Washington, DC. https://www.loc.gov/collections/george-washington-papers/.

Georgia Society DAR. *Thronateeska Chapter, Albany, Cemetery & Family Records.* Vol. 1. FamilySearch. https://familysearch.org/ark:/61903/3:1:3QHK-Q35R-G89.

Gibbons, Carolyn. "Cumberland County Deed Book 13 (1794–98)." Pt. 1. *NCGS Journal* 47, no. 4 (2021): 343.

"Glossary of Genealogical Terms." Ancestry. https://support.ancestry.com/s/article/Glossary-of-genealogical-terms?language=en_US#L.

"Governor Arthur Dobbs: Bond of Rowan, July 19, 1763. Record ID 308.7. State Archives of North Carolina. Raleigh, NC.

"Governor Stein Proclaims Recognition of the 250th Anniversary of the Liberty Point Resolves." North Carolina Office of Governor, June 20, 2025. https://governor.nc.gov/governor-stein-proclaims-recognition-250th-anniversary-liberty-point-resolves.

Great Britain Audit Office (GBAO). *American Loyalists: Transcripts of the Manuscript Books and Papers of the Commission of Enquiry into the Losses and Services of American Loyalists.* Vol. 47., 1783–1790, transcribed 1900.

"Guide to the Military Dining-In." West Point Association of Graduates. https://www.westpointaog.org/wp-content/uploads/2023/01/Great-Hall-Military-Dining-Guide.pdf.

Hadley, Chalmers. *Notes on the Quaker Family of Hadley.* Denver, 1916. Internet Archive. https://archive.org/details/notesonquakerfam00hadl/page/38/mode/2up.

Hadley, John. "Captain Joshua Hadley 1753–1830." RootsWeb. https://freepages.rootsweb.com/~hadleysociety/genealogy/index201.html. Accessed May 23, 2025.

Hagist, Don N. "Untangling British Army Ranks." *Journal of the American Revolution*, May 19, 2016. https://allthingsliberty.com/2016/05/untangling-british-army-ranks/.

Hairr, John. *Colonel David Fanning: The Adventures of a Carolina Loyalist.* Averasboro Press, 2000.

Hall, Virginius Cornick, comp. "Marriages and Obituaries, 1736–1820, Abstracted Mainly from Virginia Newspapers." Genealogical Society of Utah, 1987. Microfilm. 4 rolls. FamilySearch. https://familysearch.org/en/search/catalog/474907.

Hamburger, Philip. *Law and Judicial Duty.* Harvard University Press, 2008.

Harris, Maurine, and Glen Harris. *Ancestry's Concise Genealogical Dictionary.* Ancestry, 1989.

Hartmann, Walter. "Munro's Doctrines: A Forgotten Pioneer in Holism and Hypnosis." *Proceedings of the Indiana Academy of Science* 94 (1984): 475–82.

Hatch, Charles E., Jr. *The Battle of Moores Creek Bridge.* Office of History and Historic Architecture, 1969.

Haun, Weynette Parks, comp. and ed. *North Carolina Revolutionary Army Accounts: Secretary of State, Treasurer's & Comptroller's Papers.* Pts. 1–7. Published by the author, 1989–95.

Hay, Gertrude Sloan, and Harriett Reed Whitaker, eds. *Rosters of Soldiers from North Carolina in the American Revolution.* Genealogical Publishing Company, 1967.

Heads of Families at the First Census of the United States Taken in the Year 1790: North Carolina. Genealogical Publishing Company, 1966.

Healton, Curtis. *A Hadley Genealogy: Ancestry of Simon Hadley, the Immigrant and Some of His Descendants.* Hadley Genealogical Society of Southern California, 1974.

Heitman, Francis B. *Historical Register of Officers of the Continental Army During the War of the Revolution, April 1775 to December 1783.* Rare Book Shop Publishing Company, 1967.

Hill, Michael. "Confederate Women's Home." In *Encyclopedia of NC.* NCpedia, https://www.ncpedia.org/confederate-womens-home.

Hilldrup, R. L. "The Salt Supply of North Carolina During the American Revolution." *North Carolina Historical Review* 22, no. 4 (1945): 393–417.

Hillsborough District Superior Court. "Estate Records." Microfilm. 6 rolls. FamilySearch. https://familysearch.org/en/search/catalog/689402.

"Historic Fayetteville." *Union Republican* (Winston-Salem, NC). June 24, 1909.

"History of Sheriffs." Cumberland County Sheriff's Office. https://ccsonc.org/history-of-sheriffs/. Accessed July 30, 2025.

Holcomb, Brent Howard. *Greer and Related Families: Sanders, Sims, Glenn, Christmas, Smith, Ferris and Carver of the Carolinas and Virginia.* Published by the author, 1987.

Hollingsworth, Randall. "General History." *The Descendants of Valentine Hollingsworth, Sr. Society.* https://dvhss.org/index.php?option=com_content&view=article&id=7&Itemid=124.

House Bills (April 21): Bill for Regulating Campbellton and Erecting Public Buildings (with Petition). Record ID 66.8.13.21. General Assembly Session Records. State Archives of North Carolina. Raleigh, NC.

House Bills (May 21): Bill to Change the Name of Campbellton to Fayetteville, May 12, 1783, 1989, [1783]. Record ID N.89.5.18-19. General Assembly Session Records. State Archives of North Carolina. Raleigh, NC. https://appx.archives.ncdcr.gov/solrDetailPages/series/NCA/Series_detail.html?fq=seriesRid:243181.

House Resolution for Appointing Field Officers of Cumberland County. Record ID 66.8.23.15.5. General Assembly Session Records. State Archives of North Carolina. Raleigh, NC.

Hugh McDonald Papers. Record ID PC.1178. State Archives of North Carolina. Raleigh, NC. https://digital.ncdcr.gov/Documents/Detail/hugh-mcdonald-papers-1776-1777/424262.

Hutson, Beth. "Ceremony to Commemorate Signing of Liberty Point Resolves." *Fayetteville* (NC) *Observer*, June 20, 2025.

Hutson, Beth. "Weekend Event to Celebrate National Airborne Day, Liberty Tree and ASOM in Fayetteville." *Fayetteville* (NC) *Observer*, August 15, 2025.

"IN RE Estate of Thomas Cabeen." File 9, package 136, in archive no. 000012/.L 12021-000004. South Carolina Department of Archives and History. Microfilm. FamilySearch. https://familysearch.org/ark:/61903/3:1:939L-FN5G-1.

Independent (Elizabeth City, NC). September 1, 1933.

"It Gives Us Pleasure to Lay the Following Before Our Readers." *Fayetteville* (NC) *Observer*, August 11, 1825. Nineteenth Century U.S. Newspapers. https://link.gale.com/apps/doc/GT3017368229/GDCS?u=txshrpub100185&sid=bookmark-GDCS&xid=734c04df.

Jack Crane Collection. Vertical files. Cumberland County Public Library. Fayetteville, NC.

Jacobs, Chick. "5 Days of Destruction in Fayetteville: Union Gen. William T. Sherman's Occupation of 'Offensively Rebellious' City." *Fayetteville* (NC) *Observer*, March 7, 2015. https://www.fayobserver.com/story/news/military/2015/03/08/5-days-destruction-in-fayetteville/22264148007/.

"James Gee." Find a Grave. https://findagrave.com/memorial/66666718/james-gee.

John Oates Manuscript. Vertical files. Cumberland County Public Library. Fayetteville, NC.

"John Elwell." Find a Grave. https://findagrave.com/memorial/153413063/john-elwell.

"John Hay and Co, Jan 1799." Record ID 21.111.23.5. State Archives of North Carolina. Raleigh, NC.

John Locke Foundation. *North Carolina History Project*. https://northcarolinahistory.org/.

Johnson, Lucile Miller. *Hometown Heritage*. Graphic Press, 1978.

Johnson, Lucille [*sic*]. "Sixteen Names Added to Liberty Point Boulder." *Fayetteville* (NC) *Observer*, February 17, 1976. In Cumberland Association Papers, SHC Z box 106, folder 2: 1975, scan 7. Wilson Special Collections Library, University of North Carolina at Chapel Hill. https://dc.lib.unc.edu/cdm/ref/collection/02ddd/id/446814.

Joint Select Committees: Committee for Examinations of the State Prisoners, Dec. 11–18. Record ID 66.8.42.5. General Assembly Session Records. State Archives North Carolina. https://digital.ncdcr.gov/Documents/Detail/joint

-select-committees-committee-for-examinations-of-the-state-prisoners -dec.-11-18/835735?item=835736.

Joint Standing Committees: Committee on Finance – Subcommittee No. 4 on Application of L 100,000 Emitted (Fraud) (Nov. 21–Dec. 27). Record ID 66.8.41.14. General Assembly Session Records. State Archives of North Carolina. Raleigh, NC. https://digital.ncdcr.gov/Documents/Detail/joint-standing-committees -committee-on-finance-subcommittee-no.-4-on-application-of-l-100000 -emitted-fraud-nov.-21-dec.-27/828307?item=828342.

Joint Standing Committees: Committee on Finance – Subcommittee No. 2 on the Treasury, Nov. 21–Jan. 5. Record ID 66.8.41.12. General Assembly Session Records. State Archives of North Carolina. Raleigh, NC. https://digital.ncdcr .gov/Documents/Detail/joint-standing-committees-committee-on-finance -subcommittee-no.-2-on-the-treasury-nov.-21-jan.-5/837887?item=837888.

Jones, H. G. *North Carolina History: An Annotated Bibliography*. Greenwood Press, 1995.

"Joseph De L'espine." *South-Carolina Gazette* (Charleston), October 11, 1770. Newspapers.com. https://newspapers.com/article/the-south-carolina-gazette -joseph-de-le/160908960/.

"Judge Clark and Maj. Hale Go Down the Cape Fear." *Fayetteville Observer*, June 24, 1909.

"July 4: Petition of Thomas Cabeen, 1781." Record ID 66.8.25.7.4. General Assembly Session Records. State Archives of North Carolina. Raleigh, NC.

"Last Will of Lewis Barge Senr." In *Boyd to Brooks*, "Wills 1757–1967." Record ID CR.029.801.005. Cumberland County. State Archives of North Carolina. Raleigh, NC.

Lawrence, G. W. "The Liberty Point Declaration." *Fayetteville* (NC) *Observer*, June 3, 1909.

Ledgers of Payments, 1818–1872, to U.S. Pensioners Under Acts of 1818 Through 1858 from Records of the Office of the Third Auditor of the Treasury. NARA microfilm T718. 23 rolls. Records of the Accounting Officers of the Department of the Treasury, RG 217. National Archives. Washington, DC.

Lefler, Hugh T. *History of North Carolina*. Vol. 1. Lewis Historical Publishing, 1956.

Lepine, Kate James, and Anna Sherman. *Will Abstracts Cumberland County, North Carolina 1754–1863*. Katana, 1984.

"Lewis Barge." Find a Grave. https://findagrave.com/memorial/58222014/lewis -barge.

Lewis, J. D. "Brunswick County Regiment of Militia." Carolana. n.d. https://www.carolana.com/NC/Revolution/nc_brunswick_county_regiment .html.

Lewis, J. D. "Capt. Arthur Council." Carolana, 2013. https://carolana.com/NC/Revolution/patriots_nc_capt_arthur_council.html.

Lewis., J. D. "1st NC Regiment." Carolana. n.d. https://carolana.com/NC/Revolution/revolution_nc_first_regiment.html.

Lewis, J. D. "Lieutenants." Carolana. n.d. https://www.carolana.com/NC/Revolution/nc_patriot_military_lieutenants.html.

Lewis, J. D. *NC Patriots 1775–1783: Their Own Words*. 2 vols. Published by the author, 2012.

"Liberty Point Commemoration." *Bicentennial News* 1, no. 2 (June 1975): 1.

"Liberty Point Day." *Fayetteville* (NC) *Index*, June 23, 1909.

"Liberty Row." National Register of Historic Places. National Park Service, August 8, 1973. https://npgallery.nps.gov/AssetDetail/096e4fb6-c016-4b6d-8601-bf3135e71af5.

Liberty Tree: 250TH Celebration. Fayetteville, NC, 2025.

Linn, Jo White. "Revolutionary War Claims: Abstracts from the Delamar Transcripts." Pt. 3. *North Carolina Genealogical Society Journal* 3, no. 3 (1977): 160–65

Linn, Jo White. "Revolutionary War Claims: Abstracts from the Delamar Transcripts." Pt. 4. *North Carolina Genealogical Society Journal* 3, no. 4 (1977): 22-28.

Linn, Jo White. "Revolutionary War Claims: Abstracts from the Delamar Transcripts." Pt. 7. *North Carolina Genealogical Society Journal* 5, no. 1 (1979): 24–30.

Linn, Jo White, and B. R. McBride. "Private Petitions in the NC Legislative Papers: Revolutionary War Service-Related Benefits; Abstracts of the Delamar Transcripts." Pt. 1. *North Carolina Genealogical Society Journal* 1, no. 3 (1975): 141–68.

Linn, Jo White, and B. R. McBride. "Private Petitions in the NC Legislative Papers: Revolutionary War Service-Related Benefits; Abstracts of the Delamar Transcripts." Pt. 3. *North Carolina Genealogical Society Journal* 2, no. 2 (1976): 108–16.

Lucile Miller Johnson (LMJ) Collection. Vertical files. Cumberland County Public Library. Fayetteville, NC.

Lynch, Louise Gillespie. *Our Valiant Men: Soldiers and Patriots of the Revolutionary War Who Lived in Williamson County, Tennessee*. Published by the author, 1976.

MacKethan, E. R. "Turning the Pages." *Fayetteville* (NC) *Observer*, February 12, 1962.

MacMillan, Dan. *Fayetteville About 1770 (After Sauthier)*. 2014. Maps, Cumberland County Public Library. Fayetteville, NC.

"Marker Honors Patriots." *Robesonian* (Lumberton, NC), August 31, 1933.

Mann, Bruce H. *Republic of Debtors: Bankruptcy in the Age of American Independence*. Harvard University Press, 2002.

Marsh, G. Franklin, and Cathrine Marsh Cashwell. *The History of the Cape Fear Baptist Church*. Southern Baptist Association, 1991.

Marshall, Michael L. "A Norfolk, Virginia, Clock Signed 'John Jones.'" *Decorative Arts: Furniture*, May 16, 2014. Edenton Historical Commission. https://ehcnc.org/decorative-arts/furniture/john-jones-clock/.

Massengale, James. "Edward I Munro 1732 Inverness, Scotland." Genealogy.com, September 30, 2006. https://www.genealogy.com/forum/surnames/topics/munro/1678/.

"Master vs. Mister." Grammar.com. https://www.grammar.com/master_vs._mister.

Mathews, Barbara Allen. "Forgive Us Our Debts": Bankruptcy and Insolvency in America 1763–1841." PhD diss., Brown University, 1994.

"May 3: Remitting the Tax on Houses of Lewis Barge, Campbellton (with Petition and Certificate), 1780." Record ID 66.8.20.17.4. General Assembly Session Records. State Archives of North Carolina. Raleigh, NC.

McBride, Ransom. "Claims of British Merchants After the Revolutionary War." Pt. 4. *North Carolina Genealogical Society Journal* 6, no. 1 (1980): 17–26.

McBride, Ransom. "Claims of British Merchants After the Revolutionary War." Pt. 5. *North Carolina Genealogical Society Journal* 6, no. 2 (1980): 110–18.

McBride, Ransom. "Claims of British Merchants After the Revolutionary War." Pt. 6. *North Carolina Genealogical Society Journal* 6, no. 3 (1980): 195–200.

McBride, Ransom. "Claims of British Merchants After the Revolutionary War." Pt. 11. *North Carolina Genealogical Society Journal* 11, no. 4 (1985): 243–51.

McBride, Ransom. "Revolutionary War Service Records and Settlements." *North Carolina Genealogical Society Journal* 8, no. 4 (1982): 209–24.

McEachern, Leora H., and Isabel W. Williams. *Wilmington-New Hanover Safety Committee Minutes 1774–1776*. American Revolution Bi-Centennial Association, 1974.

McLean, Angus W. *Highland Scots in North Carolina*. North Carolina Scottish Heritage Society, 1993.

McNeill (Chairman). "Committees Liberty Point Celebration." *Fayetteville* (NC) *Observer*, June 10, 1909.

McNeill (Chairman). "Expense Fund 'Liberty Point Day.'" *Fayetteville* (NC) *Observer*, June 10, 1909.

McNeill, Jas. D. (Chairman of Committee of Arrangements). "Liberty Point Day: Programme for June 21st." *Fayetteville* (NC) *Observer*, May 27, 1909.

"Mercantile Reports." *Fayetteville* (NC) *Observer*, December 2, 1824.

Mesa, AZ, Genealogical Library Records: Newspaper Clippings, vol. Caverly–Devinney. FamilySearch. https://familysearch.org/ark:/61903/3:1:3Q9M-CSLG-N8H4.

Meyer, Duane. *The Highland Scots of North Carolina 1732–1776*. University of North Carolina Press, 1961.

Miller, Julie. "Colonial Currency." Library of Congress, May 2020. https://crowd-media.loc.gov/cm-uploads/resources/colonial_currency.pdf.

"Moores Creek Bridge." American Battlefield Trust. https://www.battlefields.org/learn/revolutionary-war/battles/moores-creek-bridge.

Morgan, Jim. "Cross Creek: A Fifer and Constitution." *AmRevNC*. Accessed August 15, 2024. https://amrevnc.com/cross-creek/.

Morgan, Jim. "North Carolina Loyalists: Many Reasons for Loyalty," *AmRevNC*. https://amrevnc.com/north-carolina-loyalists/#_edn8. Accessed October 21, 2024.

Moss, Bobby Gilmer. *Roster of the Loyalists in the Battle of Moores Creek Bridge*. Scotia-Hibernia Press, 1992.

Moss, Bobby Gilmer. *Roster of the Patriots in the Battle of Moores Creek Bridge*. Scotia-Hibernia Press, 1992.

Moss, Bobby. *Roster of South Carolina Patriots in the American Revolution*. Vol. 1. Genealogical Publishing Co. Inc., 1983.

"Mr. Jefferson and North Carolina." *Raleigh* (NC) *Register*, September 23, 1830. Nineteenth Century U.S. Newspapers. https://link.gale.com/apps/doc/GT3016243988/NCNP?u=txshrpub100185&sid=bookmark-NCNP&pg=4&xid=23a57480.

"Multiple Classified Advertisements." *Fayetteville* (NC) *Observer*, November 1, 1826. Nineteenth Century U.S. Newspapers. https://link.gale.com/apps/doc/GT3016263958/GDCS?u=txshrpub100185&sid=bookmark-GDCS&xid=a52dce1b.

National Park Service. "Revolutionary War Pension Files: Tips and a Guide for the Curious." https://nps.gov/articles/000/what-might-you-find-in-the-revolutionary-war-pension-files.htm.

New Hanover Association, June 19, 1775. *Wilmington, North Carolina-New Hanover County Committees of Safety*. Record ID SR12.13.3.002. State Archives of North Carolina. Raleigh, NC. https://digital.ncdcr.gov/documents/detail/430201?item=430352.

Newman, Donna. "Cases Heard Before Wilmington District Superior Court, Summary Information." Pt. 5, "1781–1782." *North Carolina Genealogical Society Journal* 41, no. 2 (2015): 147–52.

Norfolk (Independent City), Virginia. *Record of Deeds*. 41 vols. FamilySearch. https://familysearch.org/en/search/catalog/370384.

Norfolk (Independent City), Virginia. *Will Books*. Vol. 1, *1784–1800*. Microfilm. FamilySearch. https://familysearch.org/ark:/61903/3:1:3QS7-L9PX-X9YM.

North Carolina Daughters of the American Revolution (DAR). *Roster of Soldiers from North Carolina in the American Revolution*. Genealogical Publishing Company, 1967.

North Carolina General Assembly. *The Colonial and State Records of North Carolina (CSR)*. Edited by William L. Saunders and Walter Clark. 26 vols. Various publishers, 1886–1907. *Documenting the American South*. https://docsouth.unc.edu/csr/.

North Carolina Land Grant Office. *Land Patent Books*. 198 vols. NC Land Grant Images and Data. https://nclandgrants.com/books/.

North Carolina Land Grant Office. "Warrants, Surveys, and Related Documents – Bladen County." Microfilm. 35 rolls.

North Carolina Land Grant Office. "Warrants, Surveys, and Related Documents – Chatham County." Microfilm. 8 rolls.

North Carolina Land Grant Office. "Warrants, Surveys, and Related Documents – Cumberland County." Microfilm. 24 rolls.

North Carolina Land Grant Office. "Warrants, Surveys, and Related Documents – Davidson County, Tennessee." Microfilm. 12 rolls.

North Carolina Land Grant Office. "Warrants, Surveys, and Related Documents – Washington County." Microfilm. 6 rolls.

"North Carolina, Revolutionary Pay Vouchers, 1779–1782." Database with images. FamilySearch. https://familysearch.org/en/search/catalog/4092049.

North Carolina Secretary of State, comp. "Secretary of State Original Wills." Genealogical Society of Utah, 1989. Microfilm. 7 rolls. FamilySearch. https://familysearch.org/en/search/catalog/457752.

Oates, John A. *The Story of Fayetteville*. Dowd Press, 1950.

"Obituary. Mrs. Harriet DeLespine Munro." *Southern Christian Advocate* (Macon, GA), July 3, 1872. Georgia Historic Newspapers. https://gahistoricnewspapers.galileo.usg.edu/lccn/sn91099152/1872-07-03/ed-1/seq-4/.

O'Kelley, Patrick. *Nothing but Blood and Slaughter: The Revolutionary War in the Carolinas*. Vol. 1, *1771–1779*. Booklocker, 2004.

O'Kelley, Patrick. *"Unwaried Patience & Fortitude": Francis Marion's Orderly Book*. Infinity Publishing, 2006.

Olds, Fred. "Fayette County Existed Brief Period 4 Months; Fred Olds Recalls Past." *Fayetteville* (NC) *Observer*, June 24, 1920.

Orange County, North Carolina. "Estate Records 1754–1944." Genealogical Society of Utah, 1996–1997. Microfilm. 62 rolls. *FamilySearch*. https://familysearch.org/en/search/ catalog/543585.

Parker, Hershel. "The Tryon County Patriots of 1775 and Their "Association." *Journal of the American Revolution*, August 11, 2014. https://allthingsliberty.com/2014/08/the-tryon-county-patriots-of-1775-and-their-association/.

Parker, Josephus Derward. *The Parker Family*. Times Virginia Print, 1984?.

Parker, Roy, Jr. "City Owes Its Existence to Revolutionary Patriots." *Fayetteville* (NC) *Observer*, March 6, 2003.

Parker, Roy, Jr. *Cumberland County: A Brief History*. North Carolina Department of Cultural Resources, 1990.

Parker, Roy, Jr. "Revolutionary Patriot." *Fayetteville* (NC) *Observer*, October 5, 2000.

Parker, Weeks. *Fayetteville, North Carolina: A Pictorial History*. The Donning Company/Publishers, 1984.

Pasquotank County, North Carolina. "Estate Records." Genealogical Society of Utah, 1995. Microfilm. 75 rolls. FamilySearch. https://familysearch.org/en/search/catalog/457102.

Pasquotank County, North Carolina. "Original Wills." Genealogical Society of Utah, 1988. Microfilm. 4 rolls. FamilySearch. https://familysearch.org/en/search/catalog/457102.

"The Patriot Gee and His Brave Wife." *Wilmington* (NC) *Messenger*, February 10, 1905.

"Patriotism." *Weekly Raleigh* (NC) *Register*, August 6, 1807. Newspapers.com. https://newspapers.com/article/weekly-raleigh-register-patriotism-cont/172083303/.

Peele, W. J. *Lives of Distinguished North Carolinians with Illustrations and Speeches*. Raleigh, 1898.

Perquimans County, North Carolina. "Estate Records." Genealogical Society of Utah, 1995. Microfilm. 61 rolls. FamilySearch. https://familysearch.org/en/search/catalog/457109.

Perquimans County, North Carolina. "Original Wills." Genealogical Society of Utah, 1988. Microfilm. 4 rolls. FamilySearch. https://familysearch.org/en/search/catalog/457109.

"Petitions: Revolutionary War, 28 December 1791." Record ID 66.8.62.6. General Assembly Session Records. State Archives of North Carolina. Raleigh, NC. https://digital.ncdcr.gov/ Documents/Detail/petitions-revolutionary-war/797284?item=797438.

Phoenix Lodge No. 8. "The Cumberland Association." https://www.phoenixlodge8.com/history/the-cumberland-association-or-liberty-point-resolves/.

Potts, Jessee. *A Map of Campbelton: Early Lot Owners 1762–1800*. 1795. Maps, Cumberland County Public Library.

Powell, William S., ed. *Dictionary of North Carolina Biography*. 6 vols. University of North Carolina Press, 1979–1996.

Powell, William S., ed. *The Encyclopedia of North Carolina*. University of North Carolina Press, 2006.

Pringle, Elizabeth W. Allston, comp. *The Register Book for the Parish, Prince Frederick, Winyaw*. Baltimore, 1916. Internet Archive. https://archive.org/details/registerbookforpooprin.

"Proud Descendants of Revolutionary War Hero Gather in Williamson County." *Williamson Herald* (TN), May 25, 2015. https://williamsonherald.com/communities/bethesda/proud-descendants-of-revolutionary-war-hero-gather-in-williamson-county/article_f22bbc68-0323-11e5-a5a2-df0fc6c64fe1.html.

Pruitt, A. B. *Abstracts of Land Entrys – Bladen County, North Carolina: 1778–1781*. Published by the author, 1989.

Pruitt, A. B. *Abstracts of Land Entrys – Cumberland County, North Carolina: 1778–1795*. Published by the author, 1988.

Pruitt, A. B. *Cumberland County, NC, Taxables 1777–1783, 1815, and 1767*. Published by the author, 2015.

Raleigh (NC) *Minerva*, July 22, 1800.

"Ran Away." *Wilmington* (NC) *Gazette*, January 27, 1807. Newspapers.com. https://newspapers.com/article/the-wilmington-gazette/167447940/.

Rankin, Hugh F. *The Moores Creek Bridge Campaign, 1776*. Eastern National Park and Monument Association, 1996.

Rayburn, Richard H. "Infallible Power: The 'Musquetoe,' the Wilmington-New Hanover County Safety Committee, and the Coming of Revolution in the Lower Cape Fear, 1774–1776." *North Carolina Historical Review*, 92, no. 4 (2015): 387–425.

Read, Rebecca C. "The Highlanders of Colonial North Carolina: Loyalist Suppression 1776–1780." Master's thesis, University of Texas, 2024. https://repositories.lib.utexas.edu/items/9f4d11f8-6dc7-454d-a606-427dbed95086.

Ready, Milton. *The Tar Heel State: A New History of North Carolina*. University of South Carolina Press, 2020.

"Rebecca *Evans* Brownlow Fletcher." Find a Grave. https://findagrave.com/memorial/71404079/rebecca-brownlow_fletcher.

Registers of Enlistments in the United States Army, 1798–1914. 170 vols. Records of the Adjutant General's Office, 1780's–1917, RG 94. National Archives. Washington, DC. FamilySearch. https://familysearch.org/en/search/catalog/1880762.

"Reminiscences of Fayetteville in the Olden Times." *North Carolina Gazette* (Fayetteville), October 22, 1874.

"Report, [dated 1 Jly. 1800], Accounts, and Letter (Henry Urquhart, Wilmington, 14 Aug. _____ to John Hay) and Schedule of Debts (1770–1784), 1 Jly., [1800]." Record ID 21.111.39.21. State Archives of North Carolina. Raleigh, NC.

"Residences of the First Settlers of Watauga." *Loudon* (TN) *Free Press*, April 2, 1853. FamilySearch. https://familysearch.org/ark:/61903/3:1:3QHV-B3T3-NXXX.

"Returns of the Election for Members of the Next General Assembly of North Carolina." *Hall's Wilmington* (NC) *Gazette*, September 7, 1797. Newspapers.com. https://newspapers.com/article/north-carolina-gazette-and-wilmington-w/172042278/.

Revolutionary War Pension and Bounty Land Warrant Application Files. NAID 300022. Records of the Department of Veterans Affairs, RG 15. National Archives. Washington, DC.

Revolutionary War Rolls. NAID 602384. War Department Collection of Revolutionary War Records, RG 93. National Archives. Washington, DC.

Richards, Leonard L. "John Adams and the Moderate Federalists: The Cape Fear Valley as a Test Case." *North Carolina Historical Review* 43, no.1 (1966): 14–30.

Richmond County, North Carolina. *Minutes, Court of Pleas & Quarter Sessions [transcribed]*. 5 vols. FamilySearch. https://familysearch.org/en/search/catalog/163832.

Richmond County, North Carolina. *Record of Deeds*. Vols. A–C. FamilySearch. https://familysearch.org/en/search/catalog/165708.

"Robert Rowan (circa 1738–1798)." *Fayetteville* (NC) *Observer*, March 25, 2004.

Robertson, James. "To Major General Andrew Jackson." *Wilmington* (NC) *Gazette*, March 3, 1807. Newspaper Archive. https://www.newspaperarchive.com/other-articles-clipping-mar-03-1807-5201584/.

Robeson, James. Letter to Colonel Thos Polk. December 24, 1830. https://dc.lib.unc.edu/cdm/singleitem/collection/02ddd/id/446806/rec/14.

Robeson County, North Carolina. *Record of Deeds*. Vols. A–V. FamilySearch. https://familysearch.org/en/search/catalog/167161.

Robeson County, North Carolina. *Wills: 1783–1851*. 4 vols. FamilySearch. https://familysearch.org/en/search/catalog/271376.

Rockwell, Paul A. "Council, Arthur." In *NC Biography*. NCpedia. https://ncpedia.org/biography/council-arthur.

Roebuck, Haywood. "Cape Fear River Basin Debtors, 1752." *North Carolina Genealogical Society Journal* 1, no. 2 (1975): 97–101.

Rose, Hon. Charles, III. "The Signing of the Liberty Point Resolves." U.S. Congress, *House of Representatives Extensions of Remarks*, June 25, 1975, 20927. https://www.congress.gov/94/crecb/1975/06/25/GPO-CRECB-1975-pt16-4-3.pdf.

Salemson, Daniel J. "Slave Patrols." In *Encyclopedia of NC*. NCpedia. https://www.ncpedia.org/slave-patrols.

Salley, A. S., Jr., ed. *Stub Entries to Indents Issued in Payment of Claims Against South Carolina Growing Out of the Revolution*. Vol. 4, *Books U–W*. South Carolina Department of Archives and History, 1918. FamilySearch. https://familysearch.org/ark:/61903/3:1:3Q9M-CSFF-L5LV.

"Samuel Hollingsworth." In Comptroller's Office Accounts, War of the Revolution, Book B, 1776–1780, 1785. Record ID SR.204.28.007. Microfilm. Treasurer's and Comptroller's Papers, State Archives of North Carolina. Raleigh, NC.

"Samuel Hollingsworth Senr. & Saml. Carver." In Cumberland County Marriage Bonds, H, 1803–1868, 25 Dec. 1804. FamilySearch. https://familysearch.org/ark:/61903/3:1:S3HY-66R7-XB8.

Scarborough, Quincy. "Resolves Lost." *Bicentennial News* (Arts Council of Fayetteville, Inc.) 1, no. 1 (1975): 1–4.

Second Census of the United States, 1800. NARA microfilm M32. 52 rolls. Records of the Bureau of the Census, RG 29. National Archives. Washington, DC. https://www.archives.gov/research/census/microfilm-catalog/1790-1890/part-02#1800.

Sheperd, Henry E. "Gen. D. H. Hill: A Character Study." *Confederate Veteran* 25, no. 8 (1917): 366. Internet Archive. https://archive.org/details/confederateveter25conf/page/366/mode/2up.

"Sheriff Sales." *Weekly Raleigh* (NC) *Register*, November 10, 1808.

"A Short History of the Founding of Phoenix Lodge No. 8." Phoenix Lodge No.8. https://www.phoenixlodge8.com/history/a-short-history-of-phoenix-lodge-no-8/.

South Carolina Department of Archives and History. "Combined Alphabetical Index." South Carolina Department of Archives & History, 1992. Microfilm. 19 rolls. FamilySearch. https://familysearch.org/en/search/catalog/485140.

South Carolina Gazette, July 5, 1770.

South Carolina Secretary of State. *Columbia, South Carolina, Mortgages*. Vols. CCC–DDD. FamilySearch. https://familysearch.org/en/search/catalog/362980.

Spencer, Renee. "There Is No Cape Fear, NC on My Map. Where Exactly Is It?" *Wilmington* (NC) *Star News*, August 12, 2024. https://www.starnewsonline.com/story/news/local/2024/08/12/what-area-is-designated-as-cape-fear-nc/74549224007/.

Staff Report. "Ceremony Marks 248th Anniversary of Liberty Point Resolves." *CityView*, July 10, 2023, updated April 22, 2024. https://www.cityviewnc.com/stories/ceremony-marks-248th-anniversary-of-liberty-point-resolves/.

"Steamboat Henrietta for Sale 6 June 1827." *Fayetteville* (NC) *Observer*, June 7, 1827.

Stewart, Joseph. *Descendants of Valentine Hollingsworth, Sr.* John P. Morton, 1925.

Studebaker, Robert B. *History of Eagle Lodge*. Orange Printshop, 1937.

Suffolk County, Massachusetts. *Minutes of Superior Court*. Vol. *October 1740*, action 164. FamilySearch. https://familysearch.org/ark:/61903/3:1:3Q9M-CSZV-H9VV-D.

Sumner County, Tennessee. *Minutes of the Court of Pleas and Quarter Sessions*, vol. Sept.1805–Dec. 1808. FamilySearch. https://familysearch.org/ark:/61903/3:1:3QHV-D3CD-B3X9.

Sumner County, Tennessee. *Record of Deeds*. Vols. 1–11. FamilySearch. https://www.familysearch.org/en/search/catalog/291679.

"Surveyor's Chain." Smithsonian National Museum of American History. https://americanhistory.si.edu/collections/object/nmah_761634.

Syfert, Scott. *The First American Declaration of Independence?: The Disputed History of the Mecklenburg Declaration of May 20, 1775*. McFarland, 2014.

Syrett, Harold C., ed. *The Papers of Alexander Hamilton*. Vol. 13, *November 1792–February 1793*. Columbia University Press, 1967.

Tax Lists, Cumberland County, NC, 1767. Record ID SR.204.11, box 3. State Archives of North Carolina. Raleigh, NC. https://digital.ncdcr.gov/Documents/Detail/tax-lists-cumberland-county-1767/355294.

T. D. McDowell Papers. Wilson Special Collections Library, University of North Carolina at Chapel Hill.

"Tench Coxe to Alexander Hamilton, 13 December 1792." *Founders Online*. National Archives. https://founders.archives.gov/documents/Hamilton/01-13-02-0148.

"Theophilus Evans." Find a Grave. https://findagrave.com/memorial/269024464/theophilus-evans.

Third Census of the United States, 1810. NARA microfilm M252. 71 rolls. Records of the Bureau of the Census, RG 29. National Archives. Washington, DC. https://www.archives.gov/research/census/microfilm-catalog/1790-1890/part-02#1810.

"Thomas White." Find a Grave. https://findagrave.com/memorial/12790847/thomas-white.

Tidwell, Ettie [Mrs. Howard McCall]. *Roster of Revolutionary Soldiers in Georgia and Other States, Volume II*. Clearfield, 2010.

"To John Adams from Joshua Winslow, 27 October 1798." *Founders Online*. National Archives. https://founders.archives.gov/documents/Adams/99-02-02-3165.

"To John Adams from Robert Rowan, 13 March 1798." *Founders Online*. National Archives. https://founders.archives.gov/documents/Adams/99-02-02-2374.

"Town of Fayetteville." *The American* (Fayetteville, NC), July 23, 1818. Newspapers.com. https://newspapers.com/article/the-american-town-of-fayetteville-supe/160733546/.

"Traditions of Cross Creek and Reminiscences of Fayetteville." *Fayetteville* (NC) *Weekly Observer*, September 28, 1893.

"The Tragic Death of a Patriot of '76." *Wilson* (NC) *Advance*, October 24, 1889. Newspapers.com. https://newspapers.com/article/the-wilson-advance-the-tragic-death-of-a/174426087/.

"The Tryon County Patriots of 1775 and Their "'Association.'" *Journal of the American Revolution*, August 11, 2014. https://allthingsliberty.com/2014/08/the-tryon-county-patriots-of-1775-and-their-association/.

Turner, Grace W. "A Bill to Bring Traitors to Trial, 1782." *North Carolina Genealogical Society Journal* 28, no. 4 (2002): 420–27.

"The 20th of June 1775." *North Carolina Gazette* (Fayetteville), May 20, 1875. Newspapers.com. https://newspapers.com/article/north-carolina-gazette-the-20th-of-june/185198743/.

"Unveil Liberty Point Boulder About July 1." *Fayetteville* (NC) *Observer*, June 20, 1933.

"USS *Chesapeake*– HMS *Leopard* Affair." Naval History and Heritage Command. https://www.history.navy.mil/our-collections/art/exhibits/conflicts-and-operations/the-war-of-1812/uss-chesapeake--hms-leopard-affair.html.

Virginia Historical Society. "The Bank of the United States: Petitions of Virginia Cities and Towns for the Establishment of Branches, 1791." *The Virginia Magazine of History and Biography* 8, no. 3 (1901): 287–95. https://www.jstor.org/stable/4242358.

Walker, Alexander M. *New Hanover County NC Court Minutes.* 4 vols. Published by the author, 1959.

Washington, George. "General Orders, 15 May 1778." *Founders Online.* National Archives. https://founders.archives.gov/documents/Washington/03-15-02-0117.

Washington, George. "Orders for March from Valley Forge, 17 June 1778." *Founders Online.* National Archives. https://founders.archives.gov/documents/Washington/03-15-02-0443.

"Washington Co. File No. 283, Simon Bunday." North Carolina Land Grant Images and Data. https://nclandgrants.com/grant/?mars=12.14.20.283&qid=1145441&rn=1.

Washington County, North Carolina, and Washington County, Tennessee. "Court Records, 1779–1806." Microfilm. 1 roll. FamilySearch. https://familysearch.org/en/search/catalog/134476.

Watson, Alan D. "The Committees of Safety and the Coming of the American Revolution in North Carolina, 1774–1776." *North Carolina Historical Review* 73, no. 2 (1996): 131–55.

Watson, Alan D. "Orphanage in Colonial North Carolina: Edgecombe County as a Case Study." *North Carolina Historical Review* 55, no. 2 (April 1975): 105–19.

Watson, Alan D. "Public Poor Relief in Colonial North Carolina." *North Carolina Historical Review* 54, no. 4 (October 1977): 347–66.

Watterson, John S., III. "The Ordeal of Governor Burke." *North Carolina Historical Review* 46, no. 2 (1971): 95–117.

Weaver, Oliver C., Jr. *Barge Families of Philadelphia, Pennsylvania, Cumberland County, North Carolina, and Butler and Wilcox Counties, Alabama: This Being the Story of Lewis Barge (1741–1809) of Fayetteville, North Carolina, His Ancestors and Descendants and Barge Families of Philadelphia, Pennsylvania 1696–1800 A.D. (Revised).* Published by the author, 1999. FamilySearch. https://familysearch.org/library/books/viewer/212222/.

Webster, Ian. "$425.95 in 1909 Is Worth $14,969.05 Today." *CPI Inflation Calculator*, June 1, 2025. Official Data Foundation. https://in2013dollars.com/us/inflation/1909?amount=425.95.

Weis, Frederick Lewis. *The Colonial Clergy of Virginia, North Carolina and South Carolina.* Genealogical Publishing Company, 1976.

"West, Zilpha, 1773." In Bristol, Massachusetts, "Probate Records," *microfilm*, roll 348. FamilySearch. https://familysearch.org/ark:/61903/3:1:3Q9M-C9YR-PGSS.

Westendorf, Joseph. "The Association of Cumberland County, North Carolina." *Journal of the American Revolution*, January 8, 2026. https://allthingsliberty.com/2026/01/the-association-of-cumberland-county-north-carolina/.

Wheeler, John Hill. *History of North Carolina: Historical Sketches of North Carolina, From 1584 to 1851.* 2 vols. Philadelphia, 1851.

Whisker, James Biser. *Virginia Clockmakers and Watchmakers, c. 1660–1860.* Edwin Mellen Press, 1999.

White, Isabella. "Fifteen Dollars Reward." *Raleigh* (NC) *Minerva*, December 28, 1802.

White, Isabella. "Notice." *Raleigh* (NC) *Minerva*, March 28, 1803.

"White, William (Cumberland County)." Record ID 12.96.27.40. 1774. Secretary of State of North Carolina. State Archives of North Carolina. Raleigh, NC.

Willcox, George W. *A History of the House in the Horseshoe: Her People and Her Deep River Neighbors.* George W. Willcox, 1993.

Wilmington District Superior Court. *Minutes.* Record ID SR 398.8. State Archives of North Carolina. Raleigh, NC. https://digital.ncdcr.gov/Documents/Detail/wilmington-district-minutes-superior-court-1785-1788/1776820?item=1776831.

Wood, Bradford J. *This Remote Part of the World: Regional Formation in Lower Cape Fear, North Carolina, 1725–1775.* University of South Carolina Press, 2004.

Wood, Mark F. "Crises of Authority: Honor Violence in Nineteenth-Century American Literature." PhD diss., University of Kentucky, 2006.

Woolverton, Paul. "This Weekend, Celebrate the 250th Anniversary of Cumberland County's Declaration of Revolution." *CityView*, June 16, 2025. https://www.cityviewnc.com/stories/this-weekend-celebrate-the-250th-anniversary-of-cumberland-countys-declaration-of-revolution/.

Worthington, Don. "'Liberty' Document Comes Home." *Fayetteville* (NC) *Observer.* July 23, 2008. https://infoweb.newsbank.com/apps/news/document-view?p=AWNB&docref=news/1221FE8ECF9EBFB0&f=basic.

Wyche, Kathleen. "North Carolina Militia Paroled by Lord Cornwallis in 1781." *North Carolina Genealogical Society Journal* 4, no. 3 (1978): 147–51.

York County, South Carolina. *Minutes of the Court.* Microfilm. FamilySearch. https://familysearch.org/ark:/61903/3:1:3Q9M-CSLK-V1JG.

CONTRIBUTORS

Authors of Sections

The fifty-five signers were split up between the four Local & State History Department Staff: Joseph Westendorf, Anthony Dykhouse, Kaitlyn Santos-Porter, and Matthew Morgan respectively. While the editing of this publication was a group effort, individual staff members took the main responsibility for the following sections:

JOSEPH WESTENDORF: Introduction, Context, Loyalists, Resolves Authenticity, Thomas Cabeen, John Carraway William Carver, Daniel Douse, James Edmunds, George Fletcher, Rebecca Fletcher, Samuel Hollingsworth, Peter Messer, Walter Murray, Maurice Nowlan, Thomas Rea, Robert Rowan, Susanna Rowan, John Stevenson, Aaron Vardy.

ANTHONY DYKHOUSE/JOSEPH WESTENDORF: Forgotten by Fayetteville, William Blocker, Robert Carver, Joseph De Lespine, David Dunn, James Emmet, David Evans, Theophilus Evans, Joshua Hadley, William Herin, Thomas Moody, John Oveler, Charles Stevens, Robert Varner.[1]

KAITLYN SANTOS-PORTER: Commemorations, Liberty Point Ladies, George Barnes, William Bathgate, Lewis Bowell, Mary Brown, Samuel Carver, John Clendenin, Benjamin Elwell, John Elwell, Ann Carver Elwell, James Gee, Mary Gee, James Giles, William Gillespie, Martin Leonard, James Pearl, Onesiphorous West, Thomas White.

MATTHEW MORGAN: Simon Banday, Lewis Barge, Arthur Council, Robert Council, James Dick, Joseph Greer, Robert Greer, Philip Herin, John Jones, John Parker, David Shepherd, Micajah Terrell, William White, John Wilson.

Note

1. Anthony Dykehouse started on this section before moving on elsewhere, and Joseph Westendorf finished it up.

ABOUT THE AUTHORS

JOSEPH WESTENDORF is the manager of the Cumberland County Public Library's Local & State History Department. He holds a Master's degree in Library Science and a B.A. in History, with highest honors and a concentration in Public History from Rutgers University. He has been a local history librarian for Cumberland County since 2021.

ANTHONY DYKHOUSE served as a librarian in the Local & State History Department for the Cumberland County Public Library. He earned his Master's degree in Library and Information Science at the University of North Carolina Greensboro. He has several years of experience programming as well as producing a history podcast with the Carteret County Public Library.

KAITLYN SANTOS-PORTER is a Local & State History Department Library Associate at the Cumberland County Public Library. She holds a B.A. in Anthropology and Religious Studies from the University of North Carolina at Chapel Hill and a M.A. in Social Sciences from the University of Chicago. She has been a member of the North Carolina Archaeological Society since 2022.

MATTHEW MORGAN is a Local & State History Department Library Associate at the Cumberland County Public Library. As a life-long genealogy enthusiast, Matt works at his dream job at the Cumberland County Public Library, where he focuses on genealogical research. Previously, Matt served in the United States Army as a SOF Governance Officer. Matt is a member of the National Genealogical Society, and is working towards becoming a Certified Genealogist.

www.ingramcontent.com/pod-product-compliance
Lightning Source LLC
Chambersburg PA
CBHW071831170626
46849CB00021B/261
* 9 7 8 1 4 6 9 6 9 8 8 0 9 *